# Debating Cosm

V

# Debating Cosmopolitics

### Edited by
## DANIELE ARCHIBUGI

*with contributions by*

Mathias Koenig-Archibugi, Robin Blackburn,
Timothy Brennan, Craig Calhoun, David Chandler,
Richard Falk, Peter Gowan, Geoffrey Hawthorn,
David Held, Andrew Strauss, Mario Pianta,
Thomas Pogge and Nadia Urbinati

**VERSO**
London • New York

First published by Verso 2003
© in the collection Verso 2003
© in individual contributions the contributors 2003
All rights reserved

**Verso**
UK: 6 Meard Street, London W1F 0EG
USA: 180 Varick Street, New York, NY 10014–4606
www.versobooks.com

Verso is the imprint of New Left Books

ISBN 1–85984–505–3
ISBN 1–85984–437–5 (pbk)

**British Library Cataloguing in Publication Data**
Debating cosmopolitics
1. Representative government and representation 2. World
politics – 1989–
I. Archibugi, Daniele
321.8

ISBN 1859844375 (PB)
ISBN 1859845053 (HB)

**Library of Congress Cataloging-in-Publication Data**
A catalog record for this book is available from the Library of Congress

Typeset in 10/12.5pt Baskerville by SetSystems Ltd, Saffron Walden, Essex
Printed in the UK by Bath Press

# Contents

# Preface

We are currently experiencing a period of history when events are happening at a faster rate than historians can record them. Just twenty years ago, nuclear missiles were being deployed in Europe and a generation was growing up with the nightmare of the risk of an atomic war between the United States and the Soviet Union. Unexpectedly, the situation has changed: the Soviet Empire has fallen apart at the seams and, with it, so has the 'bipolarity' between the USA and the USSR. We have now progressed from 'bipolarity' to hegemony, and the United States has become an undisputed imperial power. Those who feared an 'American crisis' and those who hoped it would happen have had to think again and acknowledge that the hegemony of the United States is now more solid than ever. The fact is that there is no single player in world politics who can oppose it.

Any hegemonic power – not only America's – should be viewed with some suspicion, and apprehension. Economic theory teaches us that anyone who becomes a monopolist raises his or her prices. Likewise, anyone who rules the world easily misuses its power. Many thinkers argue that the internal constitution of a state should be a guarantee against the abuse of power, but the last decade confirms that this is not the case. It is undoubtedly worrying that, following the collapse of the Soviet Union, Western countries have been involved in numerous military conflicts. In the majority of cases these conflicts have not even led to peace and prosperity; Iraq, Somalia, Kosovo, Afghanistan have been stricken and subsequently left with their historical problems unresolved. It is revealing too that, in the last decade, the concern of the West for the Third World has diminished: even economic aid has been cut by one third.

But only a part of the world's problems are associated with the hegemonic ambitions of Western countries. Other and equally serious problems are endemic to the Third World, where many countries are still run by bloody dictatorships, human rights are violated every day and internal income inequalities are again increasing. Even the nuclear threat, fast receding at the global level, is appearing in local conflicts, most notably the India-Pakistan one.

How can political choices on decisive issues such as resource distribution, environmental protection, the defence of human rights and the control of military threats be made compatible with the general interest? Many thinkers and politicians argue that a balance of power is the best alternative to any hegemonic design. But since it gives considerable autonomy to individual states, a balance of power is able neither to help individual countries to foster democratic participation, nor to take decisions on global issues in a more shared way. There is a glimmer of hope in world politics; namely that the political systems inside hegemonic countries are liberal democracies. Though Western political systems are unsatisfactory in terms of any ideal vision of democracy, if we compare them with others elsewhere we can't fail to notice that they at least involve an elected government, periodic elections, an independent judiciary, and parliamentary institutions to control the executive. In other words, those who are citizens of today's hegemonic bloc are governed, and are reasonably happy to be governed, democratically.

Many of these values and principles have, alas, not been reflected in the international policies of these hegemonic democracies. States which, internally, regulate even the use of words by the concept of what is and what is not 'politically correct', protect citizens from tobacco smoke and defend animal rights, behave cynically and brutally when they have dealings with other communities. Whenever it's deemed useful, people residing in the 'evil' countries are treated to indiscriminate bombing.

The essays published in this volume discuss the cosmopolitan democracy project, whose aim is to extend some of the principles and values of democracies that have been asserted in a growing number of countries to the sphere of international relations.

Cosmopolitan democracy is based on the assumption that democracy inside states does not necessarily lead to global democracy.
Something more – namely a deliberate decision by states to accept
some of the principles of the rule of law and of democracy at the
international level – is needed.

The 1990s offered the possibility to test this assumption: while
many Western pundits were, certainly with good reasons, applaud-
ing the collapse of the Soviet bloc, others noted that it was naïve
to assume that this would lead automatically to a more satisfactory
world order. We urged the winners – Western democracies – to
be consistent and to use that historical occasion to reform the
United Nations, to reduce military weapons' acquisition, to give
more power to international judicial institutions and to increase
aid to developing countries. None of these ideas has been taken
seriously. It is therefore not surprising that some critics of the
cosmopolitan democracy project have asked to what extent the
project relates to contemporary international politics, still marked
as they are by the iron logic of power and prepared as ever to
resort to the indiscriminate use of violence. Other critics have
pointed out that the USA and its closest allies have been particularly careful not to apply democratic principles or the rule of law
outside their own borders. Others still question to what extent a
political project of this kind can be effectively compatible with
democracy as we know it today. The debate was originally hosted
in the *New Left Review*, which published six of the essays in this
volume (see Acknowledgements for further details).

The essays collected here have one common denominator:
total dissatisfaction with the way in which international relations
are regulated today. To prevent violence from becoming the
routine way of solving controversies, it is essential that stakehold-
ers are given a political voice in issues that concern every one of
us. 'Cosmopolitics' already exists, but it is still confined to too
narrow a group of institutions, as the protests of new mass
movements continually remind us. A poster shown by a street
demonstrator during an intergovernmental summit said 'You G8,
we six billion'. Is it possible to make 'cosmopolitics' accessible to
all? This is the question that this book tries to answer.

# Cosmopolitical Democracy

## Daniele Archibugi

If we pause to ask ourselves, at the dawn of the twenty-first century, which political institutions constitute the world's major depositories of power, we would have to reply: states. It is the same answer that any seasoned observer would have given in 1815. In the course of the last two centuries, state structures have only increased in the scale and scope of their dominion – a fact strikingly illustrated by a glance at the political map. With the exception of Antarctica, the entire land-surface of the planet is now divided into the bright, bold blocks of colour that denote states' territory. If the United States is green, Canada is red; while inside states' borders, the colours are homogeneous. The cartographical convention testifies to a certain political reality: however mixed the human experience – social, religious, ethnic – within its borders, unitary state power predominates overall. It is states that have armed forces; control police; mint currency; permit or refuse entrance to their lands; states that recognize citizens' rights and impose their duties. Since states began, there has also been a slow, complex interaction between those who hold power and those who are subject to it. In part of the world – fortunately, a growing one – the arbitrary use of government force is now subject to the checks and balances of a wider political community. The state has evolved, under the pressure of citizens, to become not only a tool of dominion but also an instrument of service. Never in the history of the human race has there been such a successful structure, one which has, *de facto*, become of crucial importance to all the inhabitants of the planet. No single religion – not even all the religions put together – has ever held as much power as the world's states possess today.

Since their inception, states have had to come to terms with their own internal heterogeneity: their populations are made up of people who speak different languages, have different traditions, profess different religions and belong to different races. Some states may be more homogeneous than others, but none can consider itself totally uniform. In the course of centuries, states have used a variety of means to pursue a greater degree of homogeneity: some have sought to found their own national identity on religion, others on language, blood or race; the concept of the nation – not to be found in nature – has served precisely for this purpose. States have tried to impose homogeneity on their populations through treaties and negotiations, wars and revolutions; by altering their borders, provoking exoduses or incorporating new territory. Populations have been forcibly converted to the dominant religion and vernacular languages rooted out; where this proved impossible, the die-hards have been deported, repressed or even slaughtered. States have attempted to drum up support by fomenting nationalist or patriotic sentiment against a foreign menace or internal threat; they have tried to strengthen themselves internally through the creation of a unified cultural identity, drawing on the flag, national achievements, even sports teams and television programmes. Other states, more enlightened, have looked for institutional devices to regulate, rather than homogenize, diversity; they have legislated for religious tolerance and, for over two hundred years, have developed forms of consensual government endorsed in constitutional charters.

States have always faced constraints, of course, both at home and abroad. International power politics imposes limitations on sovereignty: only a few states have been fully independent and not had to account for their choices to other, more powerful rivals, whether under threat of open military intervention or through lower grades of pressure. Internal adversaries have posed a different sort of threat. Neither nature nor civil society are great respecters of a state's frontiers. Men and women love travelling and describing what they see, imitating what their neighbours do, allowing themselves to be convinced and even converted. Trade –

the movement of goods and people – has flowed across state boundaries.

Only the most obtuse and despotic regimes, however, have attempted to prevent their subjects from travelling abroad and seeing what life is like elsewhere. Most states have merely sought to regulate international exchange through passports, customs authorities and financial rules. Until a short time ago, state authorization was even needed to translate books, or profess religious beliefs different from the established creed. The apparatus of norms and permits imposed by the state was a sign of its attitude towards the individual: You are mine, the state authority seemed to warn, but I benevolently allow you to travel. Going further, states have set up transnational arrangements, bilateral agreements and multilateral institutions to regulate events outside their own borders.[1] An impressive array of sophisticated juridical constructions now exists, including international law, diplomacy and numerous intergovernmental organizations whose services states can draw upon to regulate relations among themselves.

## Globalization and the state

Recently, however, the state system has been showing signs of pressure. The new fissures have not appeared overnight and there is no reason to believe that it will collapse like the Roman Empire; many critics probably exaggerate the size of the cracks. But irrespective of the depth of the present crisis, it is evident that many of the problems of the political organization of contemporary society go beyond the scope of the nation-state. Firstly, a significant number of the problems that states have to address lie outside their autonomous jurisdiction. The planet is experiencing a process of growing interdependence: the US Federal Reserve's decision to raise the interest rate may provoke a substantial rise in unemployment in Mexico; the explosion of a nuclear power station in the Ukraine can trigger environmental disasters throughout Europe; the lack of prompt information about the diffusion of AIDS in Nigeria may cause epidemics throughout the world.[2] Here, state sovereignty is not called into question by armies, missiles and armoured cars, but by elements which spontaneously escape national government control. This process has for some decades now been known as globalization.[3] States have naturally sought to react to it, though the traditional response of creating intergovernmental institutions to manage or mediate specific systems – trade, industrial property, nuclear energy or epidemics – has met with only partial success.

Secondly, in the course of the eighties and nineties the state has been challenged by a new critique from within. I am not referring here to the classic process of revolution, whose fundamental aim is to replace one government (or form of government) with another, but to the belief of growing numbers of people that their existing state is too centralized for their needs. Political forces bent on greater local autonomy, or even secession, have gained in strength – witness the myriad smaller states that have sprung up since the dissolution of Yugoslavia, Czechoslovakia and the USSR. In Canada, Spain, Great Britain and Italy, separatist forces have consolidated their role. We have also seen the painful phenomenon of peoples left stateless, or oppressed by the alien state to which they belong. The interstate system has so far failed, for example, to provide an adequate political community for Palestinians or for Kurds.

Globalization has also brought the problem of mass migration in its wake. In Western cities whole immigrant communities with a language and culture of their own have taken root. Turks in Berlin, Chinese in Los Angeles, Arabs in Paris, Bangladeshis in London, Vietnamese in Montreal, all pose new challenges for consolidated political unity. These are minorities who do not aim at the creation of independent states but do want their cultural identity to be respected and protected.[4] Such enclaves within existing political communities will grow in importance in the course of the next century. Will the state system be capable of meeting their needs?

Taken together, the external threats to the state from the process of globalization and the internal demands for greater autonomy give new force to the old aphorism that the state is too large for small issues, too small for bigger ones. It is here that pressures arise for a new form of world governance, more potent than anything that exists – an ideal evoked so often after the fall of the Berlin Wall. But what form should this take?

States have best met the needs of their populations where they have involved the people in running public affairs, and it must be said that one of the great successes of the state system over the

last two centuries has been the quantitative extension of democracy. Despite all the uncertainties and ambiguities of the process
in neophyte countries, and the persisting contradictions of low
turnout and high candidacy costs in the developed nations,
parliamentary democracy is increasingly emerging as a legitimate
– and legitimizing – form of government.[5] The last decade of the
twentieth century will be remembered for the interminable
queues of men and women in the East and South, waiting
patiently outside polling stations to participate in the sacred rite
of democracy – free elections – in countries where it had previously been prohibited.

## Internal democracy and international system

To what extent has the new wave of democratization washed over
into the international system? International political choices have
never been dictated by anarchy alone. From the Congress of
Vienna to the end of the Cold War, threats, wars, accords and
diplomacy have regulated affairs between states; but this process
has never been inspired by the principles of democracy. In place
of transparency of action, there have been summits held behind
closed doors; cunning diplomats and secret agents have usurped
the functions of elected representatives, and judicial power has
been overshadowed by intimidation or reprisal. In the final analysis, it is force – political, economic or, ultimately, military – that
has regulated conflict. International institutions – the League of
Nations, the UN – founded on such democratic principles as
constitutional charters, transparency of action and independent
judicial authority, have been hamstrung in carrying out the noble
tasks that their statutes envisaged. Democracy has achieved real
gains within states, but very meagre ones in the wider sphere,
both in terms of relations between states and on global issues.

What explains this paradox? One argument advanced is that it
is impossible to deal in a democratic fashion with undemocratic
governments, and that the opportunistic conduct of democracies
in foreign policy is actually caused by the existence of autocratic
regimes. This thesis has been used to justify the Cold War policies
of the liberal democracies: troops sent to Vietnam to check the
advance of Soviet communism; apartheid in South Africa justified
as a means of keeping out the 'red menace'; the elected govern-

ment in Chile overthrown to avoid a 'second Cuba'. We might, then, have expected a radical change in the foreign policy of liberal states after the fall of the Berlin Wall: this has conspicuously not been the case.

A further contention is that democracies do not fight each other. New statistical evidence has recently been adduced in support of this thesis, which proposes that if all states were democratic, the problems of war, self-determination and human rights would automatically be solved; global democracy itself would result through the simple adjustment of national systems.[6] As an argument this is gravely flawed. Firstly, it is not clear which countries deserve the licence of 'democratic', or who would be authorized to issue it in the first place. The attitudes of other states – friends or foes – will clearly be distorted by prevailing interests. To cite a few glaring examples: are we really convinced that Indonesia is more democratic than Iraq, Guatemala than Cuba, or Turkey than Serbia? If, as suggested by scholars who have tried to measure the actual levels of democracy within different countries, it emerged that in *all* these states democratic participation was either non-existent or merely formal, how do we justify the difference in attitude towards Turkey – a full member of the military community of Western democracies (NATO) – and Serbia, whom they bombed?

Secondly, the huge social and cultural variations that exist in the world inevitably entail a corresponding unevenness in political practice. The long march towards democracy has to be made by countries that walk at different speeds: the institutional system has to accept diversity. Finally, there is no historical or theoretical proof that the more democratic states really are more respectful of international legality than other powers. The United States, Great Britain and France – industrial powers who vaunt their long-established liberal-democratic traditions – do not hide the fact that they defend their own interests in the international sphere. The foreign interventions of democratic states are not always inspired by the principles of their own constitutions: the non-democratic peoples of Indochina had to conquer their independence by fighting first against the troops of democratic France and then against those of liberal-democratic America. The history of democracies is sadly scarred by aggression against communities which, if not democratically constituted, certainly had the sacrosanct right to their own independence. The history of colonialism shows that Britain, France and the United States – the last two famous for their declarations of human rights – while they may have respected these principles with increasing rigour regarding their own citizens, have not given a second thought to trampling over the rights of Indians, North Africans or Native Americans. To be democratic with your 'own' people does not necessarily entail being democratic with others as well.

In short, something more than internal democracy is called for if we are to attempt to solve the social, political and environmental problems facing the world. What is needed is the democratization of the international community, a process joining together states with different traditions, at varying stages of development. This has been defined as the cosmopolitical democracy project.

## Cosmopolitical democracy

Cosmopolitical democracy is based on the assumption that important objectives – control of the use of force, respect for human rights, self-determination – will be obtained only through the extension and development of democracy.[7] It differs from the general approach to cosmopolitanism in that it does not merely call for global responsibility but actually attempts to apply the principles of democracy internationally. For such problems as the protection of the environment, the regulation of migration and the use of natural resources to be subjected to necessary democratic control, democracy must transcend the borders of single states and assert itself on a global level.

Many projects have envisaged a universal republic or world government founded on consensus and legality.[8] There are real conceptual and political difficulties, however, in importing the democratic model conceived and developed at the state level on to a meta-state dimension. It is clearly not enough simply to project the process of internal development that states have undergone over the last two centuries on to a world scale. Fundamental aspects of that experience – the majority principle, the formulation of norms and the use of coercive power – will have to be reformulated, if they are to be applied globally.

Cosmopolitical democracy does not argue – as the federalist tradition does – that existing states must be dissolved to create a world state. Certain political and administrative functions can only be performed by states; but neither can the problems that states currently face be solved simply by increasing their size. The global extension of democracy thus involves both a new form of organization, which does not seek to merely reproduce the state model on a world scale, and a revision of the powers and functions of states at an international level, which will deprive them of the oligarchic power they now enjoy.

Above all, what distinguishes cosmopolitical democracy from other such projects is its attempt to create institutions which enable the voice of individuals to be heard in global affairs, irrespective of their resonance at home. Democracy as a form of global governance thus needs to be realized on three different, interconnected levels: within states, between states and at a world level.

Within states themselves, the aim must be to encourage the wave of popular participation that has swept the planet for the last decade, above all within countries – half the world's states – that still have autocratic regimes. We should caution, however, against democratic fundamentalism; paraphrasing Robespierre, we cannot make people democratic against their will. There is a widespread attitude among some supporters of democracy (more accurately: some Western politicians) which may be summed up as: 'I, democratic state, teach you what you have to do – by fair means or foul.' Ineffective in practice – and intolerably paternalistic – this approach is itself the very negation of democracy, which presupposes the existence of a dialogue between speakers of equal dignity. The community of democratic states may make an important contribution to the development of democracy in autocratic countries, but such support will be all the more effective if it anchors itself within civil society and works to further existing claims, in compliance with international rules.

Between states, the existing network of intergovernmental bodies – the United Nations and its various agencies – clearly needs to be strengthened. Numerous proposals have been made for the democratic reform of the UN, the General Assembly, the Security Council, the Court of International Justice and so on: all too often it has been the Western democracies that have shot them down – another example of how loth the West can be to accept democratic procedures that conflict with its own interests.[9]

## Global democracy

Further problems arise on issues such as environmental protection and the defence of human rights where a democratic state contains no representatives of the communities that suffer the – direct or indirect – consequences of the policies it employs. It can be argued that it is consistent with the interests of French people for a democratic French government to carry out nuclear experiments in the Pacific Ocean, if all the advantages go to France and the radioactive waste only harms people in another hemisphere.[10] No 'national interest' is involved for Italy, France or Great Britain if Iraq, Iran or Turkey commit genocide against the Kurdish population; and even if these states decide to intervene outside their borders, how can it be decided whether their actions are motivated by self-interest or ethical responsibility? A parallel series of democratic institutions needs to be developed on a global level, in order to involve the world's citizens in decision-making in areas such as these, irrespective of the political role they are allowed to play within their own states.

Why is international democratic practice so backward and so slow? Given the dramatic growth and efficiency of multinational enterprises and military force (think of NATO), it seems astonishing that political parties should still be confined almost exclusively to the national level.[11] The Socialist and Christian Democrat Internationals are devoid of effective power, while the Communist International, founded on the idea of the unity of the world proletariat, ceased to have an independent role long before Stalin suppressed it. Europe now has a single market, a single currency and a parliament elected by universal suffrage; yet European parties operate essentially on a national basis, the most evident demonstration that political representation has remained locked inside state borders in an era in which civil and economic society has become internationalized. This is the true deficit of democracy: the existence of organized transnational interests far removed from any popular mandate.[12] Simultaneously, new social and political subjects are appearing in international life. Movements for peace, human rights and environmental protection are playing a growing role which, while it should not be overestimated, nevertheless demands appropriate institutional channels if all the world's citizens are to participate.[13]

What form should these institutions take? A world parliament on the model of the European parliament is one proposal, and the Italian Peace Association has organized world assemblies, taking care to invite representatives of peoples rather than states. As far as individual duties are concerned, the statute of the International Criminal Court has now been approved; if it is effectively instituted, it will at last allow due procedure against the perpetrators of crimes against humanity. Progress is unbearably slow, but political institutions must adjust eventually to the boom of globalization. Why shouldn't the process of democracy – which has already had to overcome a thousand obstacles within individual states – assert itself beyond national borders, when every other aspect of human life today, from economy to culture, from sport to social life, has a global dimension?

## Humanitarian intervention

The model of cosmopolitical democracy summed up here has immediate policy implications. In what circumstances is the international community entitled to interfere in the domestic affairs of other states? How should it react to instances of ethnic cleansing, repression and the violation of human rights? It should be clear by now that the cosmopolitical project does not base itself upon the stubborn defence of state sovereignty.[14] Immanuel Kant noted over two centuries ago that people had already reached such a degree of association that 'a violation of rights in *one* part of the world is felt *everywhere*'.[15] Yet international human rights protection devices can only respond to a few of the thousands of abuses committed or consented to by governments every year; in such a situation, humanitarian intervention is too precious a concept to be decided on the hoof or, worse still, invoked to mask special interests or designs on power.

During the NATO air raids on Serbia, Tony Blair (the shrillest of the supporters of 'humanitarian' war) claimed: 'It's right for the international community to use military force to prevent genocide and protect human rights, even if it entails a violation of national sovereignty.' Yet his argument – clearly paving the way for future military adventures in the post-Cold War era – says nothing about *which* authority may use force to violate state sovereignty, *who* such force should be used against or *which* human rights have to be protected. Studying the statements of politicians and commentators in support of military intervention to defend human rights, it becomes clear that a coherent philosophy to guide the international community (inevitably spearheaded by the liberal democracies on such occasions) simply does not exist. While the accuracy of military technology has increased so much that 'smart' missiles now have a margin of error of mere metres, there is a total short-sightedness about the social objectives to be achieved by war.[16] A decade after the fall of the Berlin Wall, the seventeenth-century notion of state sovereignty is threatened by something older still: the law of the jungle.

In contrast to this, the cosmopolitical perspective on humanitarian intervention is informed by three principles: tolerance, legitimacy and effectiveness. Tolerance serves to set the violations of law within the appropriate political and anthropological framework. The history of the human race is marked by amazement at the customs of others. Europeans have been at once leaders in studying the habits of other populations, developing the whole field of anthropology, and ferocious oppressors of customs different from their own. The disease of violence and the saving antibody of toleration have cohabited here. The Spanish Conquistadors justified their genocide of the pre-Colombian peoples on the grounds of the Aztec practice of human sacrifice, during the very years in which the plazas of Spain blazed with the bonfires on which heretics and witches were put to death – while the outraged cries of observers such as Bartolomé de Las Casas set another standard, opposing violent repression with appeals to tolerance. Nothing could be further from the principle of global responsibility than a policy of religious or racial prejudice. Far from demonizing 'otherness', cosmopolitical democracy would seek to understand the underlying reasons behind human rights conflicts and apply positive pressures to solve them.

Secondly, it is important to establish a clear gradation of methods to be used when the international community does decide to intervene within a given state. Economic or cultural sanctions (as used against the system of apartheid in South Africa) are quite a different thing to air raids. 'Humanitarian intervention' at present is an umbrella term comprising an array of practices which differ widely in their juridical and political impact. Military force should only be used as an extreme measure, and then only on the basis of recognized international legitimization. By this I mean, first and foremost, the application of existing procedures, as envisaged in Chapter VII of the United Nations Charter. These procedures are by no means perfect and may require alteration; what would be unjustifiable would be to rewrite them unilaterally, for the convenience of major states. Where these norms have proved themselves to be totally inadequate is in regulating intervention in cases of rights being violated inside a sovereign state – as so frequently in the last ten years. Here it is necessary for intervention to be legitimated by new, meta-state institutions, to prevent the slogan 'humanitarian intervention' being used as a cover for narrow geopolitical interests.

There is undoubtedly a contradiction here: the cosmopolitical project would delegate to structures devoid of coercive powers (international judicial bodies, institutions of the world's citizens) the job of establishing when force should be used, while asking states, who monopolize the means of military might, to acquiesce in their decisions. But if the governments that defined themselves as 'enlightened' during the Gulf and Kosovo wars intend to perform their democratic mandate effectively, they should consult global civil society and international judicial authorities before flexing their muscles. Once humanitarian intervention in another state has been legitimated, a rigorous separation must be made between the responsibilities of the rulers and those of the ruled, especially where force is involved. It is intolerable to apply sanctions indiscriminately to all members of a community. If humanitarian interference is justified as an operation of 'international policing', the principle of protecting individuals and minimizing so-called 'collateral damage' must be fully espoused. A democratic order is founded on the premise that sanctions should affect only those who have violated the law.

'If a government commits any offence against a neighbouring sovereign or subject, and its own people continue to support and protect it . . . they thereby become accessory and liable to punishment along with it . . . In a like manner a nation must either allow itself to be liable for the damages, or give up the government altogether,' wrote Adam Smith.[17] On this basis, the international community has felt authorized to repress the Iraqi and Serbian people for the actions of Saddam Hussein and Slobodan Milošević.

In the cosmopolitical perspective, on the contrary, the citizens of an autocratic country whose government performs unlawful actions would be treated as hostages in a kidnapping: force should be used precisely to guarantee the security of the citizens of the enemy country. What is striking about the interventions in Iraq in 1991 and Serbia in 1999 is the total lack of correspondence between the culprits of the crimes and the individuals who suffered the sanctions. Saddam Hussein and Slobodan Milošević are more firmly in power than ever, while fresh waves of suffering have been inflicted on their people. 'Humanitarian intervention' may be judged effective if it saves victims and brings presumed criminals to justice, and it is this criterion of effectiveness that should be borne in mind in planning an operation.

These principles are clearly different from the ones which inspired the Gulf War and the 'humanitarian' intervention in Kosovo. In both cases, the international alliance, guided by the democratic states, resorted to the use of military force long before other means, such as diplomacy and sanctions, had been exhausted. The cosmopolitical deontology proposed here would have envisaged a very different course, basing itself on the civilian populations, the first victims of war. It would have offered a prospect of development founded on social and economic integration, depriving the warmongers of mercenary arms and support. It would have asked the peoples in question to turn against dictators who spoke of ethnic cleansing or the annexing of other states. It would have risked sending in huge numbers of 'blue helmets' on the ground, accompanied by numerous representatives of civil society and peace workers.

Would this have proved effective in restoring sovereignty to Kuwait or ending the attacks on Albanians in Kosovo? It is hard to say. But one only has to see the results of interventionism based solely on bombing to realize that the international community's cure was much worse than the sickness. Almost a decade after the Gulf War, Saddam Hussein is still in power in a country crippled by his dictatorship and the West's embargo. Milošević rules virtually unchallenged in Serbia while, in Kosovo, ethnic cleansing continues, the only difference being the identity of the people on the receiving end and the direction in which the refugees are walking. This is not the cosmopolitical responsibility we are fighting for.

# Notes

1. See the vivid account in J. Rosenau, *Along the Domestic-Foreign Frontier. Exploring Governance in a Turbulent World*, Cambridge 1997.

2. The impact of globalization on national political communities is emphasized by David Held, *Democracy and the Global Order*, Cambridge 1995, pp. 99–135.

3. See, for example, David Held, A. McGrew, D. Goldblatt and J. Perraton, *Global Transformations. Politics, Economics and Culture*, Cambridge 1999.

4. See W. Kymlicka, *Multicultural Citizenship*, Oxford 1995, pp. 121–3; J. Tully, *Strange Multiplicity. Constitutionalism in an Age of Diversity*, Cambridge 1995, pp. 183–7.

5. The problems of democratic consolidation are discussed in a growing literature. See J. Linz and A. Stepan, *Problems of Democratic Transition and Consolidation: Southern Europe, South America, and Post-Communist Europe*, Baltimore 1996.

6. An articulated exposition of this thesis can be found in B. Russett, *Grasping the Democratic Peace*, Princeton 1993. Some of the most significant contributions to this debate are now collected in M.E. Brown, S.M. Jones and S.E. Miller, eds, *Debating the Democratic Peace*, Cambridge, MA 1996.

7. See, among others previously cited, Daniele Archibugi and David Held, eds, *Cosmopolitan Democracy. An Agenda for a New World Order*, Cambridge 1995; R. Falk, *On Humane Governance: Toward a New Global Politics*, University Park, PA 1995; Daniele Archibugi and M. Köhler, eds, 'Global Democracy', *Peace Review* Special Issue IX 1998, pp. 309–98; A. Linklater, *The Transformation of Political Community*, Cambridge 1998; D. Archibugi, D. Held and M. Köhler, eds, *Re-imagining Political Community. Studies in Cosmopolitan Democracy*, Cambridge 1998; B. Holden, ed., *Global Democracy*, London 2000. Contrary to previous work, I have been convinced that the term 'cosmopolitical' should be preferred to 'cosmopolitan'. See T. Chataway, *The Relationship between International Law and Democracy*, Melbourne 1999.

8. For a review, see D. Heater, *World Citizenship and Government. The Cosmopolitan Idea in the History of Western Thought*, London 1996.

9. Ambitious proposals to reform the world order have been formulated by the Commission on Global Governance: *Our Common Neighbourhood*, Oxford 1995. On the issue of democratization, the former Secretary-General of the UN, Boutros-Ghali, has released a specific Agenda (*Agenda for Democratization*, New York 1996) which, unfortunately, received much less attention than his previous *Agenda for Peace*, New York 1992.

10. B. Gleeson and N. Low, eds, *Government for the Environment*, London and Basingstoke 2000.

11. U. Beck, 'Democracy beyond the Nation-State', *Dissent* XLV 1999, pp. 53–5.

12. See *Democracy and the Global Order*, pp. 16–17.

13. See *On a Humane Governance*, p. 17.

14. On humanitarian intervention in the new international context, see R. Falk, *Law in an Emerging Global Village*, New York 1998.

15. I. Kant, 'Perpetual Peace. A Philosophical Sketch', in *Political Writings*, H. Reiss, ed., Cambridge 1991, pp. 107–108.

16. M. Kaldor, *New and Old Wars. Organized Violence in a Global Era*, Cambridge 1998.

17. A. Smith, 'The Law of Nations', in *Lectures on Jurisprudence*, R.L. Meek, D.D. Raphael and P.G. Stein, eds, Oxford 1978, p. 547.

# 2

# Running the World
# through Windows

*Geoffrey Hawthorn*

Even those who embrace 'globalization' are nervous of its contradictions and what exists to control them. Its critics have no doubts. They wish to counter both. Fredric Jameson looks forward to transnational solidarities of opposition, Daniele Archibugi to a transnational democracy.[1] Jameson is confessedly utopian, Archibugi more practical. He sees that a new politics will have to be constructed out of the old.

It may not matter that the problems he detects in the new 'globalization' are not new. None of those he mentions has been caused by that lifting of controls on currency and capital markets and of restrictions on international trade, of that ease of communication and explosion of information and disinformation, even of that dissolution of clear and separate local tastes, which most clearly mark the recent past. Some states, as he says, do face more demands than they once did. Some even face secession. Many create problems for which they are disinclined to take or even admit responsibility. Many have to take decisions, about terms of trade with other states, for instance, or drugs, or immigration, that they cannot act on alone. And there are certainly transnational interests that are 'far from any popular mandate'. But people have been protesting against the powers of rule since rule began. The crystallization, in Europe, in the seventeenth century, of the idea of state sovereignty, and its extension to the rest of the world, have served merely to give such protests a sharper shape. For five hundred years, Europe's imperialisms created crises of subsistence, disease and toleration far worse than any in the past forty. Large famines are now rare; genocides are a shadow of those perpetrated in the past; the great migrations are over; and transnational powers responsible to no one, from the Roman Church to finance capital, are not recent.

Yet there is a new enthusiasm for what liberals used to call 'world government'. As before, it has followed war. It flared in Washington's self-serving talk, in the early nineties, of a 'New World Order' and the 'dividends' of peace, and sputters on. The demand itself, however, is old. Archibugi mentions Kant's *Perpetual Peace*. His assumptions are similar, his politics different. 'Cosmopolitical democracy is based on the assumption that important objectives – control of the use of force, respect for human rights, self-determination – will be obtained only through the extension and development of democracy.' He is unpersuasive, and in distinguished company. Kant is unpersuasive also.

## Liberals and democrats

Archibugi does not brush states aside. They are the ultimate powers, and can coerce. But Kant would not have been alone in 1795, and would not be alone now, in upbraiding him for suggesting that their authority has come to be 'subject to the checks and balances of a wider political community' of citizens. There is a difference between the 'checks and balances' of a constitutional kind and those which citizens can impose in their intermittent vote. Constitutionalists have not always been leery of state power. The illiberal, in France and Japan and elsewhere in the nineteenth century, in much of Latin America and Asia in the twentieth, and a few already in the twenty-first, have wanted to concentrate it. ('The state will eventually collapse', remarked one of the architects of the Meiji constitution in the 1880s, 'if politics is entrusted to the reckless discussions of the people.') The more liberal have wanted to disperse it, even if the constitutions by which they stand have often stood idle. Democrats, by contrast, as some of Kant's republican contemporaries, like Madison, clearly saw, may not always speak of power, but are sure that they should have it all. The state should be the instrument of the people. Archibugi is a democrat, morally liberal, but not constitutionally so. To him, checks and balances lie in that 'pressure of citizens' which turns a 'tool of dominion' into 'an instrument of service'.

One may disagree. The important point is that the politics of modern liberal democratic states, and of those states in which liberal democrats fight those of different persuasions, has been and remains a battle between those who have power, those who wish to limit that power, and those who want power for themselves. The important difference, Archibugi would insist, is between states in which the people, as the saying is, are 'sovereign', and those in which they are not. But it does not follow, as he suggests, that all that is good about modern states comes from the 'wider political community' of citizens, and that the best state is one in which this community rules. Kant's own argument against democracy in 1795, it is true, owed more to fear and prejudice than to reason, and was transparently bad. (It is telling testimony to the power of piety over intelligence that so many have for so long thought *Perpetual Peace* an impressive work.) A democracy, Kant claimed, is necessarily despotic 'because it establishes an executive power through which all the citizens may make decisions about (and indeed against) the single individual without his consent, so that decisions are made by all the people and yet not by all the people; and this means that the general will is in contradiction with itself, and thus also with freedom'.[2] He was convinced that there was a general will, but recoiled at the thought of an executive of the people deciding what this was. Most would now accept that no executive should have unrestrained power. Only those who are certain, as Kant was in theory, but not in fact, that 'the people' are fundamentally of one right mind could disagree.

## Global parties?

What distinguishes 'cosmopolitical democracy' from other projects for world government, Archibugi claims, including that federation of republics to which Kant himself looked forward and which Archibugi here misdescribes (Kant did not, as he says, intend this to be an international state under another name, but its opposite), 'is its attempt to create institutions that enable the voice of individuals to be heard in global affairs, irrespective of their resonance at home'. Those who represent 'the people' in the nominally representative governments of existing republics are not merely not part of the solution. Addicted as they are to duplicity, secret agents, and conferring behind closed doors, they are a large part of the problem. Archibugi's solution is 'a parallel series' – parallel, he says at the start of a shifting argument, not superordinate – 'of democratic institutions [that] needs to be developed on a global level in order to involve the world's citizens in decision-making' on matters of international importance, 'irrespective of the political role [that they] are allowed to play within their own states'.

Put so, his proposal differs little from others that have been made since the end of the Cold War. In 1995, the Commission on Global Governance, a descendant of former Swedish Prime Minister Palme's Independent Commission on Disarmament and Security, former Norwegian Prime Minister Brundtland's World Commission on Environment and Development, and former Tanzanian President Nyerere's South Commission, went so far as to commend a 'people's assembly' to complement the General Assembly of the United Nations. In the beginning, this would be an assembly of parliamentarians from the national assemblies of the UN's member states. Eventually, it might be directly elected by 'the people' in these states. In the meantime, the Commission suggested, there could be 'a forum of civil society', an assembly of the representatives of several hundred of the more important non-governmental organizations with an interest in 'global' matters. Archibugi is less hesitant. He wants an assembly of representatives whom the people will elect through international parties. With Ulrich Beck, he finds it 'astonishing' that political parties 'should still be confined almost exclusively to the national level'.

What seems really astonishing is that he should take the modern political party as a model for a politics in which the 'voices of individuals' might be heard. Parties are organizations for power. They are the machines with which professional politicians in representative democracies control admission to their number, compete for votes, and get support for their side. These machines cannot do what they have to do without discipline, and the discipline they impose, as disillusioned observers of the German SPD a hundred years ago were but the first to remark, serves all but completely to subvert their representative purpose. No one can now sensibly hope that it is through parties of professional politicians, and in the assemblies in which such parties face each other, that the 'voices of individuals' could possibly be heard.

## Asking and acquiescing

What more decisively distinguishes Archibugi's proposal, however, is his view of who might listen to these voices and why. The Commission on Global Governance did not propose that any of the bodies it described should actually have power. They would merely deliberate on the agenda of what the Commission hoped might be a 'revitalized' General Assembly of the UN, and pass on their views. Archibugi wants to go much further. He seems, indeed, to want to go all the way. He wants his assembly to be able to 'delegate to structures devoid of coercive powers (international judicial bodies, institutions of world citizens) the job of establishing when force should be used, while asking states, who monopolize the means of military might, to acquiesce in their decisions'. Plainly, everything here depends on the 'asking'. Anyone may ask. But if they may only ask, none need listen. If Archibugi's assembly is to be more than a seat of discursive virtue, it would have to be able to order and to enforce what it orders. It would have to be armed, to be able convincingly to threaten and, effectively, defeat those who refused it. This, given the difficulty, a difficulty which Archibugi does not touch upon, of financing itself – governments are not going gracefully to subscribe to their supersession – would mean that it would probably have to have nuclear powers. Only then would 'fundamental aspects' of our experience of national parliaments, in Archibugi's words, 'the majority principle, the formulation of norms, and the use of coercive power', that's to say the very sovereignty of states, actually 'have', as he wishes, 'to be reformulated'.

If by some extraordinary transformation, the nature of which Archibugi wisely leaves undescribed, these reformulations were to be enacted, and we were to find ourselves with such an authority, the result would be what to Kant the liberal, let alone to us in a now nuclear world, would be the ultimate nightmare: a legislature and executive rolled into one, run by factions of professionalized politicians for the purposes of their own power, directing what would, in all but name, be a world state against which there would even in principle be no countervailing authority. If a state of this kind were to embody the 'tolerance, legitimacy and effectiveness' which, like all men of simple virtue, Archibugi hopes for, these qualities could depend only on the vain hope of Kant the philosopher of right who, in the tortured course of *Perpetual Peace*, lost the battle with Kant the practical politician: that the parties in the assembly should consist of wholly virtuous cosmopolitan politicians ventriloquizing wholly virtuous 'peoples'. The picture, were it not so absurd, would be appalling. We had better think of something else.

## Uneven statehood

What is truly new about the present is that we see and hear about much more of what is going on about us than before, and that that 'about us' is a foreshortened place. What is also new, as Archibugi acknowledges, is the expanded roster of international associations to which states belong, and the far larger number of associations of individuals which are pressing an increasing array of particular interests on such bodies. The first have increased more than ten-fold in the past thirty years, the second even more dramatically. Here, there is indeed something more 'global' than before. Issues in international politics are more widely known and have come to be pressed in new ways, both by states and by those who wish to influence them. Yet the issues themselves are not so very different from those that have presented themselves since the end of the First World War, and to the three most fundamental, the authority of states, the regulation of relations between them, and the ways in which their governments might be driven to do more (and less) than they do, 'democracy', as Archibugi thinks of it, has virtually nothing to say. Indeed, in his criticism of those who believe in 'the democratic peace', he all but concedes as much.

States continue to run the world. 'Never in the history of the human race', Archibugi declares, 'has there been such a successful structure.' Perhaps. But the successes of modern states are very varied. Many are not even able to exercise control over their territory and ensure the elementary security of the citizens within it. Some indeed, most noticeably in sub-Saharan Africa, have never managed to do so. (This may not always be cause for regret.

States' presences have often been capricious, greedy, and violent. Relieved of their exactions, their bereaved citizens can believe themselves to be safer and more prosperous without them.) Some states, in parts of the former Soviet Union, for example, and in Central and South America, have lost the authority they used to have. In a few, Colombia is an instance, the condition of statehood has come almost entirely unspun. In many, the state continues to fight for what it takes to be its right. It battles with groups of armed bandits and death squads from its own former ranks, groups which may claim a civil interest but whose actions are devastating for those in their crossfire, and more enduringly destructive. States or their agents have acted in these ways in recent decades in Sudan, Rwanda, the Congo, Liberia, Sierra Leone and Zimbabwe; in Guatemala, Nicaragua and El Salvador; in Russia, the Caucasus, Central Asia and Afghanistan; in Pakistan, India, Sri Lanka and Burma; from Northern Ireland to Croatia to Turkey. In some of these places, they still do.

One does not have to be a 'humanitarian' to suggest that the absence of statehood, and its violent and rapacious presences, are the most fundamental of political issues. To be a humanitarian, indeed, can lead to error. Humanitarians, as Carl Schmitt observed at the end of the twenties, tend to be liberals, and liberals will avoid talk of power. They speak instead of ethics and economics, a polarity from which 'they attempt to annihilate the political as a realm of conquering power and repression'. They turn the state 'into society: on the ethical-intellectual side into an ideological humanitarian conception of humanity, and on the other into an economic-technical system of production and traffic'. From this, they argue that what any country needs is a modicum of liberal democracy and liberal markets, forgetting that peaceful political competition and regulated exchange can only flourish, indeed can only work at all, where the authority of the state and the security this provides is present. From this in turn, they claim in the name of 'humanity' the right forcibly to impose such authority in ways that subvert both that name and the liberalism that informs it. Thus Haiti, Somalia, Iraq and, most evidently, in the brazen transparency with which it was done, Kosovo.[3]

It is easy to say and, close though he is in other ways to Schmitt's picture of the liberal, Archibugi does, that states cannot

be repaired by interventions of this kind. It is much more difficult
to say how they might be. Even if one sets aside the *Realpolitik* that
tends to drive such intervention; even if one ignores the insouci-
ance with which power, glossed with morality, is used to override
juridical sovereignty and what there is of international law; and
asks how states can be made and remade, there is no sure answer.
Outsiders may issue ultimata, send in troops, drop bombs, point
smart weapons, impose sanctions, even try patiently – as, in 1993,
the United Nations Transitional Authority in Cambodia tried – to
persuade the warring parties to share power. But everything seems
to fail. The forces of intervention must depart, and when they do,
the disputes resume. Even Archibugi cannot convince himself
that a people's world state, offering 'the prospect of development
founded on social and economic integration, depriving the warmongers of mercenary arms and support', politely asking people
to turn against dictators who speak 'of ethnic cleansing or the
annexing of other states', all with the help of 'huge numbers of
"blue helmets" on the ground, accompanied by numerous representatives of civil society and peace workers', could actually do
what it might want to do. Effective and morally acceptable 'governance', leached of the distasteful impurities of 'government', has
been the desire of most of the well disposed in the past decade
but, since the end of empire, no one has known how to secure its
most basic condition in someone else's country. All properly
political thinkers since Thucydides have known that this condition
is power, and that until this obtains, nothing else can.

### New actors

None of this is to say that we must leave things as they are. There
are many issues in the world, including the authority of particular
states, that are of concern to all. For these, it is worth continuing
to construct what, in the euphemistic parlance of what is itself the
euphemism of 'the international community', are called 'multilateral institutions', places in which governments can talk instead
of go to war, and to pursue international law. Power being what it
is, of course, the more powerful states will always have more say
in the institutions than others. They will insist on the ends and,
when it suits them, be selective about the means. But no state,
not even the United States, without the risk of bringing things

down around its ears, can now so easily realize (quite) as much as it would wish to do on its own. Each needs to persuade others that they have an interest in acting with it. The international courts, Archibugi does not make clear, are not even open, at least overtly, to political negotiation, and are certainly not institutions for democracy. But they can do what the more overtly political associations of states cannot, which is to rule on the powers of states as states. Some of their rulings, like that of the International Court of Justice for Nicaragua against the United States in the eighties, will die in the wind. But if courts can produce the kind of judgement that the Law Lords in London eventually produced against Pinochet, they can give confidence to others – as this judgement has now done in Chile – and perhaps have a wider effect.[4]

If left to themselves, of course, 'multilateral institutions' and international courts will do less than many might hope. Delegates of states to the institutions will respond more readily to other delegates, or to more powerful interests in their own states, than they will to popular pressures. Courts will be conservative unless prompted by power and strong contrary opinion. Yet even if the kind of organized pressure which Archibugi envisages were to emerge, it is unlikely to be effective. And for so long as it is not, for so long as it exists 'in parallel' with states, it is unlikely in any but the softest sense to be 'legitimate'. But pressures from below, or beyond, do matter. One of the most striking changes in the conduct of international politics in the past thirty years or so has been the intrusion of organizations that are outside government altogether. Encouraged in the eighties by a UN that had nothing itself to offer a world of debt, and by a World Bank that had come to distrust states and was losing custom to new money's enthusiasm for 'emerging markets', a few of these NGOs – Amnesty International through its publicity, Oxfam International through its lobbying, Greenpeace and *Médecins Sans Frontières* by their actions – have become influential sources of information (and often mischievous disinformation), opinion and pressure. They have not become so, however, by assiduously representing a wide range of interests, or by being responsible to one or another kind of constituency, or even by being noticeably tolerant. They have been single-minded, aggressive, and opportunistic masters of publicity, and have been responsible to no one except themselves and those who choose to finance them. We might be pleased to see them profit from the cosmopolitans who regard them as the centre of a new international 'civil society', bursting with virtue and independent of power. But they are no more virtuous than any other political organization. That is their merit. They simply devise what powers they can to press governments to do more than governments would otherwise do. They do politics.

Archibugi might reply that an international politics of this kind will do little to advance the 'noble tasks' set down for the League of Nations and the UN. 'Cunning diplomats and secret agents' (and now NGOs and the other special interests in the new 'international civil society') will continue to usurp what he regards as the functions of elected representatives, and judicial power will continue to be 'overshadowed by intimidation or reprisal'. 'Threats, wars, accords and diplomacy' will remain the rule. But one should not forget that it is in that state in which foreign policy has, for the past eighty years, been most responsive to public opinion, the United States, that the elected representatives refused even to join the League, and have persistently resisted requests to meet their government's financial obligations to the UN. But there and elsewhere, Archibugi might insist, the opinion of 'the people' can change. If we were but to listen, we might find that it has. And even if it hasn't, we should not despair of enlightening it. Of course. But even if it were to change, it could not express itself in the way that Archibugi imagines. Since people could not negotiate with each other *en masse*, they would have to appoint delegates to do so for them. These delegates, to be successful, would need to be practised in Machiavelli's arts. To practise these arts, they would need to have conventions, rules, procedures, call them institutions, within which to do so, and closed doors behind which they could. Only if everyone, everywhere, was of one right mind would everything be transparent and agreed. Everyone could then stay at home and run the world through Windows. Yet, in a confusion that was exactly Kant's, Archibugi accepts that this would still be a world of states.

The present period of economic and political 'liberalization' is one in which the nominally democratic governments of the ostensibly more successful states try to persuade their own citizens, and the governments and citizens of weaker states, to expect less from politics than before. They would like nothing better than for the governed to go peaceably to work and return home contentedly, to buy things with one button and signal their assent with another. The end of history, they believe, is a fate we should all be pleased to accept. Archibugi is quite right to refuse. We need not less politics, but more. He and those who argue like him are mistaken merely in their picture of what such a politics can be.

## Notes

1. Fredric Jameson, 'Globalization and Political Strategy', and Daniele Archibugi, 'Cosmopolitical Democracy', *New Left Review*, second series, no. 4, July–Aug 2000 (chapter 1 in this volume).

2. Immanuel Kant, *Political Writings*, Hans Reiss, ed., Cambridge 1991, p. 101.

3. For a fuller account, see 'Liberalism since the Cold War: an Enemy to Itself?', in Michael Cox, Ken Booth and Tim Dunne, eds, *The Interregnum: Controversies in World Politics, 1989–99*, Cambridge 1999, pp. 145–60.

4. I elaborate on this in 'Pinochet: The Politics', *International Affairs*, 75 (1999), pp. 253–8.

# 3

# 'International Justice'

## David Chandler

The NATO bombing of Yugoslavia in the spring of 1999 has been saluted as a triumph for 'international justice' over the traditional claims of state sovereignty. The war was in clear breach of international law: waged without UN Security Council authorization, against an elected, civilian government which had not violated any external treaty, justifiable neither as a threat to peace and security, nor in terms of any NATO country's self-defence. It has been welcomed instead as a 'humanitarian' crusade, explicitly setting individual rights above the territorial rights of nation-states. But if the sovereignty of some states – Yugoslavia, Iraq – is to be limited, that of others – the NATO powers – is to be increased under the new order: they are to be given the right to intervene at will. It is, in other words, not sovereignty itself but sovereign equality – the recognition of the legal parity of nation-states, regardless of their wealth or power – which is being targeted by the new interventionists. Yet such equality has been the constitutive principle of the entire framework of existing international law and of all attempts, fragile as they may be, to establish the rule of 'right' over 'might' in regulating inter-state affairs. 'Humanitarian intervention', Daniele Archibugi has written, in his discussion of 'Cosmopolitical Democracy', 'is too precious a concept to be decided on the hoof or, worse still, invoked to mask special interests or designs on power.'[1] This essay will examine the implications of such a right to 'humanitarian' military intervention for the future of inter-state regulation and international law.

The concept of sovereign equality is often understood as an integral part of the long-standing doctrine of state sovereignty. In fact, it is of much more recent provenance than the classic state system which emerged at the end of the Thirty Years War. The Peace of Westphalia of 1648 famously recognized the secular rights of German princelings above the religious claims of the Papacy, legitimating no external power beyond that of the sovereign; it was this formal recognition of the principle of territorial sovereignty which henceforth became the basis of relations between states. There was, however, no international law in the modern sense: such rights of sovereignty were effectively restricted to the major powers and there was no explicit framework of an international community which could formally limit their exercise. Without international law, the regulation of inter-state relations could not extend beyond voluntary agreements between the sovereign states – strategic alliances, aimed at preserving local interests and maintaining a relatively stable balance of power.

The epoch of this classic, 'anarchical' state-system, with no defined limits to the sovereignty of the major powers, was also the era of colonialism. The states included within it were those which could defend their own territory from the claims of other states. It was therefore quite consistent to argue that in countries which could not demonstrate such 'empirical statehood' – the colonies – sovereignty could not apply. Meanwhile, those with sufficient military force to intervene in other states' affairs – in other words, the great powers – continued to do so. During the colonial era, the major powers either regulated their territorial acquisitions directly – as in Africa and India – or, as in China, Japan and the Ottoman Empire, insisted that their own actions could not be fettered by local domestic legislation, claiming the right of extra-territoriality. Under the Westphalian system, then, superior force was the guarantor of effective sovereignty.

The Westphalian model came under attack with the modernization and growing world importance of the leading non-European states. Challenges to Western rule and increasing international instability led to new attempts to regulate inter-state affairs. The Hague Conference of 1899 saw the attendance of China, Japan, the Ottoman Empire, Persia and Siam. In 1905 Japan's defeat of Russia came as a powerful shock to European

imperial confidence, closely bound up with assumptions of racial
superiority. The second Hague Conference of 1907 was the first
gathering of modern states at which Europeans were outnum-
bered by the representatives of other countries. But it was the
watershed of the First World War – bringing in its wake the
collapse of the Russian, Austro-Hungarian and Ottoman empires,
the rise of colonial resistance, the establishment of the Soviet
Union and the threat of new world war – that was decisive in
turning Western policy makers away from the strength-based
Westphalian system and towards a more juridical concept of
sovereignty and a framework of international law.

The principle of national self-determination was proclaimed by
Woodrow Wilson at the 1919 Paris Peace Conference – for the
newly created states of Central Europe. The extension of such a
right to the rest of the world – ringingly affirmed by the Bolshe-
viks' *Declaration of the Rights of the Toiling and Exploited People*
in January 1918 – was held at bay. The expansion of the concept
of territorial sovereignty beyond the principle of 'might is
right' remained highly controversial within policy-making circles.
Robert Lansing, US Secretary of State, recalled his doubts:

> The more I think about the President's declaration as to the right of
> 'self-determination', the more convinced I am of the danger of putting
> such ideas into the minds of certain races. It is bound to be the basis
> of impossible demands on the Peace Conference and create trouble
> in many lands. What effect will it have on the Irish, the Indians, the
> Egyptians, and the nationalists among the Boers? Will it not breed
> discontent, disorder and rebellion? Will not the Mohammedans of
> Syria and Palestine and possibly Morocco and Tripoli rely on it?[2]

This 'danger' was a central concern of the inter-war settlement.
The League of Nations timidly initiated legal restriction of great-
power sovereignty through the introduction of the mandate system, with colonial administrators now deputed to 'advance the
interests' of the subject peoples. The mandates – implying a
recognition that colonial rule could only be temporary – were the
first formal admission that empire was no longer a legitimate
political form. But the concept of sovereign equality remained
confined to a few, the right of self-determination denied to large
sections of the world's population, Japan's attempt to include a
clause on racial equality in the League of Nations Charter firmly

rejected. The development of a universal legal conception of sovereign equality would have to await a further world war.

The 1945 settlement, preserved in the principles of the UN Charter, reflected a new international situation, transformed by the emergence of the Soviet Union as a world power and the spread of national liberation struggles in Asia, the Middle East and Africa. Ideologies of race and empire, too, seemed definitively vanquished with the defeat of the Nazi regime. It was a decisive moment in the transformation of the Westphalian system. In this context, the inter-war consensus on 'the non-applicability of the right to self-determination to colonial peoples' could no longer be sustained. United States policy makers, as they looked forward to assuming the mantle of the now declining British Empire, realized that updated institutions for the management of international relations would have to 'avoid conventional forms of imperialism'.[3] The result was nominal great-power acceptance – however hypocritical – of a law-bound international system.

Central to this new mechanism of international regulation was the conception of sovereign equality. The UN Charter, the first attempt to construct a law-bound 'international community' of states, recognized all its members as equal. Article 2(1) explicitly stressed 'the principle of sovereign equality', while both Article 1(2) and Article 55 emphasized 'respect for the principle of equal rights and self-determination of peoples'. New nations – which would have failed Westphalian tests of 'empirical statehood', and hence been dismissed as 'quasi-states' – were granted sovereign rights,[4] while the sovereignty of the great powers was now, on paper at least, to be restricted. The UN system did not, of course, realize full sovereign equality. In practice, the Security Council overwhelmingly predominated, with each of its self-appointed permanent members – the United States, Britain, France, Russia and China – retaining rights of veto. Still, sovereign equality was given technical recognition in parity of representation in the General Assembly and lip-service to the principle of non-interventionism, setting legal restrictions on the right to wage war.

Under the Westphalian system, the capacity of the most powerful states to use force against the less powerful was a normal feature of the international order. Under the legal framework set up by the Charter, the sovereign's right to go to war (other than by UN agreement or in self-defence) was, for the first time, outlawed – a point sometimes missed by those who would argue that the post-1945 order 'failed to break' with Westphalian norms.[5] The principle of non-intervention was, in fact, a constituting principle of the new international community of states. Just as the rule of law in domestic jurisdictions depends upon the concentration of legalized force in a single authority, and the criminalization of the individual exercise of violence, so within the postwar system of international regulation, the legal monopoly of the use of force resides in the UN.[6] Article 2(4) states:

> All members shall refrain in their international relations from the threat or use of force against the territorial integrity or political independence of any state, or in any manner inconsistent with the purposes of the United Nations.

'We may not appreciate', writes Louis Henkin, 'how remarkable that was, that transformative development in the middle of the twentieth century: "sovereign states" gave up their "sovereign" right to go to war.'[7] It marked, it seemed, the end of the Westphalian system of legitimating great-power domination through the use of force.

The universal recognition of sovereign equality entailed a new conception of states, whose legal authority now derived not from wealth or might but nationhood. Formally speaking, non-Western states from now on had the same standing as Western ones within the international order, despite continuing inequalities of economic and military power.[8] Archibugi is right, of course, to point to the role of the UN in practice, which was repeatedly utilized as an instrument of American hegemony – as he puts it, 'judicial power overshadowed by intimidation or reprisal'.[9] In theory, however, a framework of international law had been created that limited the exercise of state sovereignty – including the right to wage war. In legal terms, at least, might no longer equalled right.

## The new interventionism

Even so mild a form of international regulation is now coming under ferocious attack. The case for the special treatment of some states, and demotion of others, has been put in a variety of registers. British barrister and newspaper pundit Geoffrey Robertson offers a rabid rogue-list: 'The reality is that states are not equal. There can be no "dignity" or "respect" when statehood is an attribute of the governments which presently rule Iraq and Cuba and Libya and North Korea and Somalia and Serbia and the Sudan.'[10] Max Boot, features editor of the *Wall Street Journal*, prefers a swaggering cynicism: 'There is no compelling reason, other than an unthinking respect for the status quo, why the West should feel bound to the boundaries it created in the past.'[11] Brian Urquhart, a former UN undersecretary-general – one of the many British under-labourers for the United States in its bureaucracy – sees sovereign equality as the 'central barrier' to peace and justice, providing a 'cloak of impunity' for every kind of abuse.[12]

Pitted against the concept of international law based on sovereign equality is a new form of global 'justice', formulated in explicit opposition to it. Advocates of this justice herald the emergence of a new, 'human rights'-based order of international relations, arguing that the post-1945 framework – here, 'international society' – is being eclipsed by the ethical demands of global 'civil society'. For Martin Shaw, erstwhile International Socialist, the 'crucial issue'

> is to face up to the necessity which enforcing these principles would impose to breach systematically the principles of sovereignty and non-intervention ... The global society perspective, therefore, has an ideological significance which is ultimately opposed to that of international society.[13]

For Robertson, too, 'the movement for global justice' is 'a struggle against sovereignty'. Sovereign equality is seen by these ideologues as a legal fiction, a mask for the abuse of power. International law is merely an 'anachronism', a historical hangover, while 'some of its classic doctrines – sovereign and diplomatic immunity, non-intervention in internal affairs, non-compulsory submission to the ICJ, equality of voting in the General Assembly – continue to damage the human rights cause'.[14]

The denial of sovereign equality obviously has major consequences for both the form and content of international law. The most prominent is the rise of the idea of a 'duty' of forcible 'humanitarian' intervention – the so-called *devoir d'ingérence*.[15] Its advocates naturally retain the right to decide on whom this obligation falls. Robertson explains that 'humanitarian intervention cannot be the prerogative of the UN' since it cannot be relied upon to act when necessary. The duty of intervention must therefore stand independently: 'UNanimity cannot be the only test of legitimacy.'[16] For Shaw, 'it is unavoidable that global state action will be undertaken largely by states, ad hoc coalitions of states and more permanent regional groupings of states'.[17] In practice, the prosecution of international justice turns out to be the prerogative of the West.

Such is overtly the substance of NATO's new 'strategic concept', promulgated at the Alliance's fiftieth anniversary summit in Washington in late April 1999, at the height of the Balkan War. As US Deputy Secretary of State Strobe Talbott explained,

> We must be careful not to subordinate NATO to any other international body or compromise the integrity of its command structure. We will try to act in concert with other organizations, and with respect for their principles and purposes. But the Alliance must reserve the right and freedom to act when its members, by consensus, deem it necessary.[18]

Similarly, a new study of 'humanitarian intervention' in the wake of the Kosovo war argues explicitly for ad hoc and arbitrary powers to intervene:

> A code of rules governing intervention would be likely in the early twenty-first century to limit rather than help effective and responsible action on the part of the international community . . . Any attempt to get general agreements would be counter-productive . . . It may be inevitable, possibly even preferable, for responses to international crises to unfold selectively.[19]

Ironically, the new 'global' forms of justice and rights protection will be distinctly less universal than those of the UN-policed international society they set out to replace. David Held argues that, 'in the first instance', at least,

> cosmopolitan democratic law could be promulgated and defended by those democratic states and civil societies that are able to muster the necessary political judgement and to learn how political practices and institutions must change and adapt in the new regional and global circumstances.[20]

Rather more bluntly, Shaw explains the rationale of all-round NATO intervention:

This perspective can only be centred on a new unity of purpose among Western peoples and governments, since only the West has the economic, political and military resources and the democratic and multinational institutions and culture necessary to undertake it. The West has a historic responsibility to take on this global leadership.[21]

This line of argument is now increasingly official doctrine. The *Guardian* could hail British military intervention in Sierra Leone as 'the duty owed by a wealthy and powerful nation to, in this case, one of the world's poorest countries'.[22] Here inequality is expressly theorized as the basis of the new world order. Yet the modern system of law (whether international or domestic) depends, both at the basic level of its derivation and in the vital question of its application, on the concept of formal equality between its subjects. All international institutions – whether the UN, OSCE or even NATO itself – derive their authority from inter-state agreements. International law derives its legitimacy from the voluntary assent of nation-states. Without such consent, the distinction between law (based on formal equality) and repression (based on material force) disappears. The equal application of the law entails parity between its subjects, without which it ceases to have meaning. In today's climate, the rights of weaker states can be infringed on the grounds that the law does not fully apply to them, while more powerful states can claim immunity from the law on the grounds that it is they who ultimately enforce it.

The extension of 'international justice' is, in short, the abolition of international law. For there can be no international law without equal sovereignty, no system of rights without state-subjects capable of being its bearers. In a world composed of nation-states, rather than a single global power, universal law can only derive from national governments. Archibugi, arguing that representative governments cannot be trusted with international regulation, proposes instead to 'democratize the international community' through the creation of 'cosmopolitical' institutions – composed, among others, of representatives of NGOs. As part of this 'global extension of democracy', he calls for 'a revision of the powers and functions of states at an international level' to 'deprive them of the oligarchic power they now enjoy'. What he fails to see is that the practical consequences of demolishing the existing – if only juridical – equality between the states can only be to deepen their political inequality. Criticizing the British Prime Minister's shrill calls for 'humanitarian warfare', he rightly points out that Blair 'says nothing about *which* authority may use force to violate state sovereignty, *who* such force should be used against or *which* human rights have to be protected'; but he is insensitive to the dangers of a challenge to the existing framework that cannot specify a realistic constitution of alternative legal subjects.

## The Hague War Crimes Tribunal

Under the cover of 'international justice', a much more direct reflection of the hierarchy of global power is now being set in place, as new Western agencies are given a jurisdiction above international law. The creation of The Hague War Crimes Tribunal for the former Yugoslavia – a supposed model for 'international justice' – is a perfect case in point. Typically, the Serb leader Milan Martić has been indicted for the use of cluster bombs on the Croatian capital Zagreb in May 1995, in which seven civilians were killed and an old people's home and children's hospital damaged. NATO's own use of cluster bombs in its attack on Niš in May 1999, which killed fifteen people and damaged the city's main hospital, was naturally in another category altogether.[23] Who could believe that NATO commanders deliberately made military targets of city bridges, factories, marketplaces, residential neighbourhoods and TV studios, with slight or no military value?

The truth is that the 'impartiality' of the Tribunal is a farce. In brazen breach of Article 16 of the Tribunal's Charter, which states that the prosecutor shall act independently and shall not seek or receive instruction from any government, co-operation between supposedly independent international prosecutors and Western politicians has been close and unconcealed. At a joint press conference with Tribunal prosecutor Louise Arbour, British Foreign Secretary Robin Cook declared, with scant grammar and even less regard for legal propriety, that 'we are going to focus on war crimes being committed in Kosovo and our determination to bring those responsible to justice': as if he and Arbour were part of the same team, deciding who would be held responsible for violations of international law – and naturally ruling himself out from potential charges.[24] James Shea, NATO spokesman during the conflict, was blunter still, replying to a question at a press conference on 17 May 1999 as to the possibility of NATO leaders being investigated for war crimes by the Tribunal: 'Impossible. It was the NATO countries who established the Tribunal, who fund it and support it on a daily basis.'

Arbour herself regularly appeared in public at high-profile meetings with NATO leaders, including Cook and Secretary of State Albright, during the Balkan War. One Tribunal judge, Gabrielle Kirk McDonald, has referred to Albright as the 'Mother of the Tribunal'. President Clinton was personally informed of the indictment of Milošević by Arbour two days before the rest of the world. There have been numerous meetings between the prosecutor and NATO officials, including its Secretary-General, to 'establish contacts and begin discussing modalities of co-operation and assistance' and, in an epic breach of legal norms, NATO – a potential defendant – has been assigned the function of arresting suspects and collecting data. Of course, the Tribunal concerns itself only with the former Yugoslavia. Milošević is to be handed over to 'international justice' without delay. In other parts of the world Montesinos is assured a comfortable refuge, and Sharon received with full honours.

What the jettisoning of the principle of non-interventionism means is the re-legitimation of the right of the great powers to practise what violence they please. Their apologists declare that war is now the 'lesser evil', compared to the new moral crimes of 'indifference' or 'appeasement'. Liberal interventionists have emerged as the biggest advocates of increased military spending.[25] Sycophantic tub-thumpers like Michael Ignatieff extol without inhibition the new militarist values:

> To keep the peace here [Sierra Leone] is to ratify the conquests of evil. It is time to bury peacekeeping before it buries the UN . . . Where peace has to be enforced rather than maintained, what's required are combat-capable warriors under robust rules of engagement, with armour, ammunition and intelligence capability, and a single line of command to a national government or regional alliance . . . the international community has to take sides and do so with crushing force.[26]

Similarly, for Max Boot,

> UN administrators . . . think that no problem in the world is too intractable to be solved by negotiation. These mandarins fail to grasp that men with guns do not respect men with nothing but flapping

gums . . . Just as the US Marine Corps breeds warriors, so the UN's culture breeds conciliators.[27]

For these ideologues, the absolute end of 'international justice' can only be compromised by diplomacy or negotiation. The new professors of Human Rights at the UN University's Peace and Governance Programme are happy to condone those 'good international citizens' who are 'tempted to go it alone' waging war for 'justice', with or without international sanction.[28] Robertson likewise insists that 'a human rights offensive admits of no half-measures'; 'crimes against humanity are, by definition, unforgivable'; 'justice, in respect of crimes against humanity, is non-negotiable'.[29] Such war can know no legal bounds. Bernard Kouchner, UN Civilian Administrator in Kosovo, argues explicitly for pre-emptive attacks – or rather, in the Newspeak so characteristic of the West's 'humanitarian' hawks, for the right to intervene militarily 'against war':

> Now it is necessary to take the further step of using the right to intervention as a preventive measure, to stop wars before they start and to stop murderers before they kill . . . We knew what was likely to happen in Somalia, Bosnia-Herzegovina and Kosovo long before they exploded into war. But we didn't act. If these experiences have taught us anything, it is that the time for a decisive evolution in international consciousness has arrived.[30]

The ability to judge 'murderers before they kill' is an art that relies more on self-interest than science. As Benjamin Schwarz warns, at an April 2000 round table on intervention organized by *The Atlantic*:

> If we choose to be morality's avenging angel in places like Kosovo, we may at first be pleased to see ourselves, like Kurtz in *Heart of Darkness*, as 'an emissary of pity and progress'. But as warriors for right, faced with those we have demonized, we may well succumb to Kurtz's conclusions as well: 'Exterminate the brutes.'[31]

In the Middle East, in Africa and the Balkans, the exercise of 'international justice' signifies a return to the Westphalian system of open great-power domination over states which are too weak to prevent external claims against them.

# Notes

1. See 'Cosmopolitical Democracy', *New Left Review*, second series, no. 4, July–August 2000 (chapter 1 in this volume); and Geoffrey Hawthorn's reply, 'Running the World through Windows', *New Left Review*, second series, no. 5, September–October 2000 (chapter 2 in this volume).

2. Robert Lansing, *The Peace Negotiations: A Personal Narrative*, London 1921, p. 87.

3. Justin Rosenberg, *The Empire of Civil Society*, London 1994.

4. R.H. Jackson, *Quasi-States: Sovereignty, International Relations and the Third World*, Cambridge 1990.

5. David Held, *Democracy and the Global Order*, Cambridge 1995, p. 88.

6. Oliver Ramsbotham and Tom Woodhouse, *Humanitarian Intervention in Contemporary Conflict: A Reconceptualization*, Cambridge 1996, p. 35.

7. Louis Henkin, 'That "S" Word: Sovereignty, and Globalization, and Human Rights, etc.', *Fordham Law Review*, 1999, vol. 68, no. 1, p. 1.

8. Sovereign equality was confirmed in many subsequent UN resolutions, notably the Declaration on the Inadmissibility of Intervention in the Domestic Affairs of States and Protection of their Independence and Sovereignty of 21 December 1965 (Resolution 2131 [XX]) and the Declaration on Principles of International Law Concerning Friendly Relations and Co-operation among States in Accordance with the Charter of the United Nations of 24 October 1970 (Resolution 2625 [XXV]).

9. 'Cosmopolitical Democracy', p. 141.

10. Geoffrey Robertson, *Crimes Against Humanity: The Struggle for Global Justice*, London 1999, p. 372.

11. Max Boot, 'Paving the Road to Hell: The Failure of UN Peacekeeping', *Foreign Affairs*, 2000, vol. 79, no. 2, pp. 143–8.

12. Brian Urquhart, 'In the Name of Humanity', *New York Review of Books*, 27 April 2000.

13. Martin Shaw, *Global Society and International Relations: Sociological Concepts and Political Perspectives*, Cambridge 1994, pp. 134–5.

14. *Crimes Against Humanity*, pp. xviii, 83.

15. Mario Bettati and Bernard Kouchner, *Le Devoir d'ingérence*, Paris 1987.

16. *Crimes Against Humanity*, pp. 382, 72.

17. *Global Society*, p. 186.

18. Cited in B. Simma, 'NATO, the UN and the Use of Force: Legal Aspects', *European Journal of International Law*, 1999, vol. 10, pp. 1–22.

19. Albrecht Schnabel and Ramesh Thakur, eds, Kosovo and the Challenge of Humanitarian Intervention, New York: forthcoming. See www.unu.edu/p&g/kosovo_full.htm

20. *Democracy and the Global Order*, p. 232.

21. *Global Society*, pp. 180–81.

22. 'We Are Right To Be There', *Guardian*, 13 May 2000.

23. R.M. Hayden, *UN War Crimes Tribunal Delivers a Travesty of Justice*, Woodrow Wilson International Center for Scholars, 2000; C. Black and E. Herman, 'Louise Arbour: Unindicted War Criminal', posted to Tribunal Watch, 17 February 2000. Archive available at www.listserve.acsu.buffalo.edu/archives/justwatch-l.html

24. 'Louise Arbour: Unindicted War Criminal'.

25. For example, John Gray, 'Crushing Hatreds', *Guardian*, 28 March 2000; John Lloyd, 'Prepare for a Brave New World', *New Statesman*, 19 April 1999.

26. Michael Ignatieff, 'A Bungling UN Undermines Itself', *New York Times*, 15 May 2000.

27. 'Paving the Road to Hell'.

28. See, for example, *Kosovo and the Challenge of Humanitarian Intervention*.

29. *Crimes Against Humanity*, pp. 73, 260, 268.

30. Bernard Kouchner, 'Perspective on World Politics: Establish a Right to Intervene Against War', *Los Angeles Times*, 18 October 1999.

31. Benjamin Schwarz, *Atlantic* Round Table on Intervention, April 2000, available from www.theatlantic.com/unbound/roundtable/goodfight/schwarz3.htm

# 4

# Cosmopolitanism and Internationalism

*Timothy Brennan*

Daniele Archibugi opens his eloquent case for a 'cosmopolitical democracy' with an important concession. The world's major depositories of power, he observes, remain national states that have 'only increased in the scale and scope of their dominion', within an inter-state system. He is right.[1] But nation-states are a key to understanding our present world not simply because they intractably persist, but also because in significant ways their political valences have altered. Such states continue to represent, as they have always done, jurisdictional acts of enclosure designed to perpetuate class privileges over specified regions. Today, however, they are also the terrains on which new constituencies can work along varied axes of power. They are, in fact, the only effective structures for doing so. National states impose labour discipline on the working poor and adjudicate disputes among local élites. These have always been among their primary functions. But in the current phase of worldwide neo-liberal hegemony, they also offer a manageable (albeit top-heavy) site within which the working poor can make limited claims on power, and have at least some opportunity to affect the way they are ruled.

Since the modern nation-state itself emerged as a domestic response to an imperial redrawing of the map of the planet that brought a chaotic influx of wealth and ideas into the core countries from abroad, and since the discourse of cosmopolitanism necessarily involves a re-theorization of the nation-state, it cannot plausibly treat imperialism as extraneous to its argument, in the way Archibugi does, but ought to see it as intrinsic. Good dialectical sense would suggest that a political form born in the epoch of colonial conquest might play some role in resisting the next stage of imperial hegemony.

Archibugi wishes to 'deprive [states] of the oligarchic power they now enjoy' by a direct appeal to the peoples within states to create a global community with enforceable legal powers. He explains that he prefers the term 'cosmopolitical' to describe his prospect, to avoid the colloquial or vaguely humanist connotations of 'cosmopolitan'. By contrast, I will retain the latter term because I think it indicates the cultural dominant to which his political theory is still unwittingly subject. Archibugi writes from the discipline of international relations, but many of his premises and referents – invocations of 'heterogeneity', 'spontaneity' or 'custom' – are borrowed from the realms of the new urban ethnography and cultural criticism. In considering his construction, I will therefore approach it from the viewpoint of a cultural theory more sensitive to the interdisciplinary flows that have characterized this semantic zone. We need to historicize cosmopolitan discourse. If we do, my argument will be, we can see that cosmopolitanism today is not a new and more supple kind of internationalism, but rather that the two are theoretically incompatible.

## Meanings of cosmopolitanism

Historically, cosmopolitanism has combined two distinct significations. On the one hand, it designates an enthusiasm for customary differences, but as ethical or aesthetic material for a unified polychromatic culture – a new singularity born of a blending and merging of multiple local constituents. Typically, in this conception, a subjunctive 'ought' contains a normative 'is': the suggestion that the period in question is – for the first time in history – already substantially cosmopolitan. On the other hand, cosmopolitanism projects a theory of world government and corresponding citizenship. Here the structure of underlying unity conveyed by the cultural meaning of the term is carried over to the political.[2] The cosmopolitan ideal envisages less a federation or coalition of states than an all-encompassing representative structure in which delegates can deliberate on a global scale. By contrast, internationalism seeks to establish global relations of respect and cooperation, based on acceptance of differences in polity as well as culture. It does not aim to erase such differences juridically, before material conditions exist for doing so equitably. *International*ism does not quarrel with the principle of *national* sovereignty, for there is no other way under modern conditions to secure respect for weaker societies or peoples. If cosmopolitanism springs from a comfortable culture of middle-class travellers, intellectuals and businessmen, internationalism – although based no less on the realities of global interpenetration and homogenization, mass migration and mass culture, under the dominance of capital – is an ideology of the domestically restricted, the recently relocated, the provisionally exiled and temporarily weak. It is addressed to those who have an interest in transnational forms of solidarity, but whose capacities for doing so have not yet arrived.

Archibugi does not call for the abolition of existing states, or the creation of a single world government. He opts instead for a global civil society to monitor the system of states. Yet few of the ironies of historical development season his well-intentioned proposals. States today, he writes, are faced with new kinds of identity politics, separatist movements and immigrant enclaves, which have compelled them to recognize a degree of internal heterogeneity that goes against the grain of their natural drive towards uniformity. But this is a European perspective. What it misses is the extent to which the United States portrays itself as a cynosure of heterogeneity, its characteristic patriotic myths transforming cosmopolitan values into a national ideal. In not dissimilar fashion, Archibugi argues that political parties are still confined to the national level, and – since no international parties exist – calls for new forms of extra-statist political community to fill the gap. But would it not be more realistic to think of contemporary neoliberal orthodoxy as a form of unofficial party organization across national frontiers? It certainly commands a vast network of fellow-thinkers in virtually every country in the world, who speak and act in remarkably similar ways, and can be confident of direct or indirect help from their counterparts abroad. It possesses a firm set of principles and a stable programme that has been put into practice with common results by governments across the globe, whose list lengthens every day. As such, it surely constitutes the core of any future community that could plausibly be called cosmopolitical.

## Simmel and Gramsci

If we turn to the intellectual world, we see a growth of cosmopolitan discourses developing out of approaches to globalization that first appeared in social science/humanities crossover journals of the early 1990s, like *Theory, Culture & Society* and *Public Culture*. Somewhat later the term was picked up in a middlebrow forum sponsored by *The Boston Review*, which offered cosmopolitanism as a progressive alternative to patriotism.[3] But though the notion is now widely bandied about, little or no attempt has been made to reconstruct the historical conjunctures in which it acquired salience in the thought of leading modern social theorists. Among these was Georg Simmel, who argued that cosmopolitanism gave expression to the quasi-colonial expansion of urban centres or metropolitan regions, as a legitimation of their encroachment on geopolitically dispersed and vulnerable outlying territories.[4]

Antonio Gramsci, of course, explored the phenomenon of 'imperial cosmopolitanism' among Italian intellectuals in his *Prison Notebooks* in some detail, looking with a critical eye at the impact of the Catholic universalism of the mediaeval Church, and later of Renaissance humanism, on their outlook. Gramsci understood the familiar barriers to 'national-popular' unity, as he termed it, that could be posed by racial or ethnic divisions, but he also had much to say about the way in which a position of one-time cultural 'centrality', such as that which Italy enjoyed up to the 16th century, could generate a subsequent history of aimless intellectual stasis.[5] Like most of the Marxist intellectuals of his generation, as Michael Löwy has shown, he thought cosmopolitanism an idealist detour away from internationalism, cultivated by certain middle classes under highly specific national conditions.[6]

In the United States, ideas of cosmopolitanism have always been closely linked to notions of pluralism – both invoking mixture and inclusion as vital constituents of a wider unity. Although the constitutional ideology of pluralism, blazoned under the eagle, has local origins, its cultural dimensions ironically derive from the creole nationalisms of Latin America, which often had to be built against the great power to the North. A New World pluralism was first theorized by early Caribbean travellers like Jean-Baptiste Du Tertre and Père Labat, and then forged into a political ethic by Sarmiento, Martí and others in the wake of the nineteenth-century liberation movements, finally issuing into the ideas of José Vasconcelos and Alejo Carpentier in the twentieth century. It was this tradition of thought that was – honourably at first – introduced into North America by the pragmatist philosophers William James and John Dewey in the Gilded Age, to stave off hysterical anti-immigrant sentiment in the US. It was then gradually purged of all trace of its foreign origins, to become officially institutionalized as the creed of the nation. Originally imported from Latin America, the concept of pluralism became part and parcel of the American self-image, ideals of national liberation in the South transformed into embellishments of imperial swagger in the North. Here lie the origins of the contemporary belief that America is the elect among nations – the conviction that the United States is the globally sought-after, the desire of all peoples across the world.[7] Cosmopolitanism of this kind is an identity that depends on others whose originality, even viability, it suppresses.

## Trade and modernity

In Europe, other variants were at work in this period, the most widespread entrusting a cosmopolitan future to the blessings of commerce, in a global system of free trade. This was particularly attractive to British radicals of liberal descent, such as Lowes Dickinson, who in 1908 penned the following paean to the universal dawn he thought capitalism would bring:

> I see the time approaching when the nations of the world, laying aside their political animosities, will be knitted together in the peaceful rivalry of trade; when those barriers of nationality which belong to the infancy of the race will melt and dissolve in the sunshine of science and art; when the roar of the cannon will yield to the softer murmur of the loom, and the apron of the artisan, the blouse of the peasant be more honourable than the scarlet of the soldier; when the cosmopolitan armies of trade will replace the militia of death; when that which God has joined together will no longer be sundered by the ignorance, the folly, the wickedness of man; when the labour and the invention of one will become the heritage of all; and the peoples of the earth meet no longer on the field of battle, but by their chosen

delegates, as in the vision of our greatest poet, in the 'Parliament of Man, the Federation of the World.'[8]

Euphoric visions of this sort came naturally to cosmopolitans in Britain, the centre of a worldwide dominion built on the 'imperialism of free trade'. From more peripheral Portugal, still in possession of the oldest of European colonial empires, but now a disregarded and marginal member of the Western comity of nations, came another version of cosmopolitanism, in which a dream of general modernity compensates for a particular actual backwardness. The poet Fernando Pessoa, setting out a manifesto for the journal *Orpheu* in 1915, wrote:

> What does *Orpheu* want? To create a cosmopolitan art in time and space. Ours is an epoch in which countries, more materially than ever, and for the first time intellectually, all exist within each other; in which Asia, America, Africa and Oceania are Europe and exist within Europe. Any European dock is sufficient . . . to summarize the entire earth. And if I call this *European* rather than American, for example, it is because Europe rather than America is the *source and origin* of this type of civilization which serves as *norm* and *orientation* to the entire world. For this reason true modern art must be totally denationalized; it must integrate all parts of the world within itself. Only thus can you be typically modern.[9]

In this literary variant, cosmopolitanism offers a coming into 'modernity' as the global entrance into a common hybrid self-consciousness by formerly subjugated peoples, without in the least disturbing the self-portraiture of the West. For if we wished to capture the essence of cosmopolitanism in a single formula, it would be this. It is a discourse of the universal that is inherently local – a locality that's always surreptitiously imperial. Its covert appeal is most powerful when, in a double displacement, its political sense is expressed in cultural forms. Typically, cosmopolitanism constructs political utopias in aesthetic or ethical guise, so that they may more effectively play what often proves, on inspection, to be ultimately an economic role.

## A stronger state

Against this background, we can begin to see why the nation is now so often dismissed in 'cultural studies' as obsolete – while

in the same breath it is decried as a complex founded on a
dubious, if not dangerous essentialism, on a coercive form of
statism and welfare paternalism. For political commentators and
think-tank pundits, on the other hand, the nation remains a
resilient reality, forming part of the political landscape of any
foreseeable future, but one best domesticated – or sublimated –
in a Pax Americana dressed up as 'international law'. The general view here could be summed up in the injunction: let us have
less nation and more *state* – but not a state that micro-manages
corporations or regulates business at the expense of growth.
Fear-mongering cameos of 'tribal' bloodletting in barbaric back-
lands are combined with sober-sided arguments for freeing the
market from government interference in the homelands (and
everywhere else). In this agenda, however, deregulating the market and privatizing public assets does not mean a weaker state.
What is in prospect is a *stronger* state in matters of surveillance
and repression: chipping at *habeas corpus* or trial by jury, increasing prison sentences, stepping up border patrols – not to speak
of adding a new wing of government which, for most purposes,
functions as an extension of the state, while furiously proclaiming its independence from it, and so escaping even the formali-
ties of democratic control: the fourth estate. Above all, this is a
state capable of making absolutely certain that today's heightened mobility of capital is not matched by any comparable
mobility of labour. Globalization means a tightening of border
controls.[10]

## A manageable community

These developments should serve to remind us of a long-standing
historical reality. Nation-states are not only, as we customarily
hear today, imagined communities: they are also, and no less
fundamentally, *manageable* communities. The state as coercive
negotiator presides over a community that it must, by definition,
be capable of managing. What it is capable of managing becomes
inexorably what must be ruled. Cultural theory has become
inordinately fixated on the ideology of nationalism in recent
decades, dwelling on the diffusion of communications media or
images of ethnic belonging or patriarchal privileges, whose affec-
tive combination can cast individuals or groups under the

national spell, passively or hysterically. However disturbing, these dimensions of nation-making have nonetheless been overstated. Fascinated by the narrative layerings and polysemic ambiguities of political myth and representation, cultural theory radically underestimates the practical issues of management at stake in the making of nations. Here the sober concerns of international relations are a salutary corrective.

For viewed organizationally, nations may be as much a matter of practical default as of ideal enchantment, or manipulation. For a long historical epoch there has been no alternative to them, because no coercive or hegemonic apparatus of rule – notwithstanding imperial efforts by Egyptians, Macedonians, Turks, Mongols, Mughals, Romans, Britons, Germans and latterly North Americans – was capable of managing the entire earth. Nation-states, of course, only emerged quite late in this process, when capitalism had come into the world. The transition from various kinds of tributary state to the modern nation-state – which dates essentially from the Romantic period – could be seen as the end-product of a management crisis created by foreign conquest and the wealth that it generated, the result of three centuries of primitive accumulation based on slave labour, the *encomienda* system, overseas plunder and the creation of entirely new global markets (rather than the penetration of existing ones). The passage from what historians traditionally call colonialism to imperialism proper, in the late nineteenth century, consolidated this political form. Fences had to be fortified at home to clarify jurisdiction over the spoils abroad. The massive cultural confrontations of global settlement and exploitation bred a reactive fear of difference, not as an irrational xenophobia or support of psychic identity, but rather as a rational line of demarcation between home and abroad, owners and owned, occupiers and occupied. Administratively, nations today continue to be discrete units for the organization of profit-making, resource extraction, and the perpetuation of unequal social relations. But they are also, within a world system in which enormous disparities in national power persist, structures that give some chance to local or indigenous peoples to draw a boundary between what is theirs and what lies beyond, between what is open to the outside and what is sheltered from it. Nations are 'manageable' in both directions. They allow the state to manage the subalterns and the subalterns to petition the state, with a rhetoric of the 'popular' that appeals to a shared cultural identity.

Debates about the future of the nation-state today, with few exceptions, make no distinction between those created by imperial expansion and those created by peoples resisting that expansion. But the effect of arguments that the national state should be subsumed in a more democratic international polity is to give succour to those who would like to replace many states (most of them deemed pathetically belated, fictive or unviable) with one or two: a 'world state' not explicitly built in the name of any existing power, but factually serving its interests in decently mediated guise. The cosmopolitan fancy that once beguiled Dante or Kant would now take shape in the *Realpolitik* of rapid deployment forces, carrier jets, cruise missiles and satellite surveillance. A world recreated in the image of America as a 'universal nation' – hegemonized through popular culture, fashion and the internet – can be imagined for the first time. We are at last within sight, many argue, of Kant's perpetual peace. The real question, though it is never put in these terms, is this: is the globe now manageable?

Archibugi's proposal of a 'cosmopolitical democracy' suggests that, hopefully, it is. But though it is clearly inspired by the admirable ideals that produced the Universal Declaration of Human Rights proclaimed by the United Nations over half a century ago, postmodernity has in practice given us a universal of another kind – the universality of electronic media with global reach and instantaneous penetration, cosmopolitan masters of the ether. We need to be very cautious in contemplating any cosmopolis that would short-circuit the existing nation-states in the name of the people: on that imaginary terrain, too many powerful interests are already entrenched. There are alternatives to a standoff between a suspect utopianism of the cosmopolitical community and a blinkered defence of the existing nation-state system. It is better to view the latter as a transitional arena, which for the moment contains the only structures through which transnational forms of solidarity might emerge in the only way they can – slowly and over many generations. Fredric Jameson has put the needed case for the nation-state with characteristic power in these pages.[11] Internationalism should not be mistaken for its dialectical other, the cosmopolitanism that is a product of politi-

cal tendencies historically opposed to it. The answer to Archibugi's proposal is not mere critique, but a different proposal. We
should be encouraging popular efforts in Southern Mexico,
Colombia, Indonesia or Palestine – and so many other parts of
the world – to establish a modicum of real sovereignty, rather
than constructing intricate theoretical edifices liable to weaken
the very ability to imagine it. That does not clash with the need
for new forms of cross-border mobilization, radical cultural combination, international campaigns for civic solidarity and labour
protection. The two responsibly imply each other.

## Notes

1. See Daniele Archibugi, 'Cosmopolitical Democracy', *New Left Review*,
second series, no. 4, July–Aug 2000 (chapter 1 in this volume); and responses
by Geoffrey Hawthorn, 'Running the World through Windows', *New Left
Review*, second series, no. 5, Sept–Oct 2000 (chapter 2 in this volume), and
David Chandler, '"International Justice"', *New Left Review*, second series, no.
6, Nov–Dec 2000 (chapter 3 in this volume).
2. I have explored these issues at some length in *At Home in the World:
Cosmopolitanism Now*, Cambridge, MA 1997.
3. See Martha Nussbaum et al., 'Patriotism or Cosmopolitanism', *The
Boston Review*, October–November 1994.
4. See David Frisby and Mike Featherstone, eds, *Simmel on Culture*,
London 1997, pp. 81–2.
5. Antonio Gramsci, *Quaderni del Carcere*, vol. 1, Turin 1975, p. 371.
6. See Michael Löwy, *Fatherland or Mother Earth? – Essays on the National
Question*, London 1998, pp. 5–29, who notes ambiguities in the earlier Marxist
tradition.
7. For critical reflections on this world-view, see Enrique Dussel, *The
Underside of Modernity*, New York 1996; Roberto Retamar, *Caliban and Other
Essays*, Minneapolis, MN 1989; and Arif Dirlik, *The Postcolonial Aura*, Boulder,
CO 1997.
8. Goldsworthy Lowes Dickinson, in *A Modern Symposium*, London 1908,
pp. 26–7. Cited in Bernard Porter, *Critics of Empire: British Radical Attitudes to
Colonialism in Africa 1895–1914*, London 1968, p. 331. Similar sentiments
found organized expression across the Atlantic. The Cosmopolitan Club,
appealing to 'ideals of world brotherhood', published a series of pamphlets
whose authors included William Howard Taft (refreshed by his massacres in
the Philippines) on 'The Dawn of World Peace', and Norman Angells's more
academic (and contemporary-sounding) 'The Mirage of the Map: an Interrog-
ation'; see *Documents of the American Association for International Conciliation*,
New York 1911. After the Second World War, Hollywood personalities like
Clifton Fadiman and Oscar Hammerstein held fund-raisers for *World Government News*, performing skits to expose the 'myth of national sovereignty' on
behalf of a strong UN. Today Walter Cronkite's World Federalist Association

preaches 'sustainable development' and 'a strong international court of justice'. This is a movement that never really dies.

9. See Anthony Geist and José Monleón, eds, *Modernism and its Margins*, New York 1999, pp. 282–3.

10. The single currency and Schengen zone in the European Union have been accompanied by much stricter regulations governing the entry into the EU of people from Africa, Asia and the Caribbean; just as NAFTA has seen the intensification of border patrols and surveillance by the INS along the frontier between Mexico and the USA.

11. See 'Globalization and Political Strategy', *New Left Review*, second series, no. 4, July–Aug 2000.

# 5

# The New Liberal Cosmopolitanism

## *Peter Gowan*

Over the past decade a strong ideological current has gained prominence in the Anglo-American world, running parallel to the discourse of globalization and rhetorically complementing it. Indeed, in official parlance it is the more insistent of the two, and seems likely to become all the more clamorous in the aftermath of September 11 2001. We may call it the new liberal cosmopolitanism, as distinct from the more democratic cosmopolitanism defended here by Daniele Archibugi.[1] Its theorists are for the most part to be found in international relations departments of the Anglophone universities, though some have been seconded to offices of the UN Secretariat or NATO protectorate in Bosnia.[2] Viewed historically, the new doctrine is a radicalization of the Anglo-American tradition that has conceived itself as upholding a liberal internationalism, based on visions of a single human race peacefully united by free trade and common legal norms, led by states featuring civic liberties and representative institutions. Such liberal internationalism sought to create a global order that could enforce a code of conduct on the external relations between states. But it still essentially accepted the Westphalian system that granted states jurisdiction over their own territories.

The new liberal cosmopolitanism, by contrast, seeks to overcome the limits of national sovereignty by constructing a global order that will govern important political as well as economic aspects of both the internal and external behaviour of states. This is not a conception advocating any world government empowered to decide the great international issues of the day. Rather, it proposes a set of disciplinary regimes – characteristically dubbed, in the oleaginous jargon of the period, 'global governance' – reaching deep into the economic, social and political life of the states subject to it, while safeguarding international flows of finance and trade. In this system, sovereignty is reconceived as a partial and conditional licence, granted by the 'international community', which can be withdrawn should any state fail to meet the domestic or foreign standards laid down by the requirements of liberal governance.[3]

Significant ideological shifts are always in some measure responses to changes in the real world. The new liberal cosmopolitanism is no exception. Its theories have arisen against the background of a whole set of new pressures on the internal organization of weaker states, and new patterns of interaction among stronger ones. Victory in the Cold War has made it easier for the Western powers to dispense with client dictatorships that were once loyal allies in the battle against Communism, and to proclaim liberal democracy a general value, to be upheld even in less favoured parts of the world. Domestic economic law and property relations have been steadily realigned, across continents, to harmonize with directives of the IMF, WTO or relays at regional level. States outside the rich core have been remarkably ready to make such internal, 'behind the border' changes. Strategically, the collapse of the USSR has not led to any revival of major conflicts between the Western powers, but on the contrary to a reinforcement of what Michael Doyle extols as the 'Pacific Union' of our day – the military alliance that fought the Gulf War, launched the attack on Yugoslavia and, at the time of writing, appears to be gearing up for an onslaught in West Asia. The multiplication of UN military missions involving the major powers tells the same story. The theorists of the new liberal cosmopolitanism (henceforward NLC) are on firm ground in pointing to all these developments as a sea change in international relations. When, however, they attempt to explain them, we quickly enter the realm of apologetic euphemism.

### First among unequals

Crucial to the NLC version of today's world is the claim, not just that the 'Pacific Union' has remained united, but that its members have broken with power politics as their governing impulse. What this, of course, represses is the central fact of contemporary international relations: one single member of the Pacific Union – the United States – has acquired absolute military dominance over every other state or combination of states on the entire planet, a development without precedent in world history. The US government, moreover, has shown no sign whatever that it is ready to relinquish its global dominance. American defence spending, as high today as it was in the early 1980s, is increasing, and a consensus across the Clinton and Bush administrations has developed in favour of scrapping the Anti-Ballistic Missile Treaty. The underlying reality of the Pacific Union is a set of bilateral, hub-and-spokes military alliances under US leadership. In the past liberal theorists usually explained the forging of these alliances as responses to powerful Communist and Soviet threats to demo-cratic values and regimes. Yet, though liberalism and democracy are now widely held to be a prevailing norm, and the Warsaw Pact has vanished, these 'defensive' alliances have not quit the stage. On the contrary, Washington has worked vigorously to reorganize and expand them during the 1990s.

NLC theorists protest that the United States has, nevertheless, abandoned egoistic national interest as its strategic guideline. After all, are not liberal-democratic values tirelessly lauded and expounded in the speeches of US leaders – most imperishably, by former President Clinton? Such declarations are no novelty – ringing proclamations of disinterested liberal principle go back to the days of classical nineteenth-century power politics and Lord Palmerston. If, on the other hand, we turn to actual policy guidelines for US diplomacy in the 1990s, we find them wholly dedicated to the calculations of power politics.[4] Where such documents refer to the icons of free trade and liberal democracy, they are presented as conditions for the advancement of US power and prosperity.

Do these power-political instruments and orientations at least exempt other members of the Pacific Union (i.e. the union of liberal democratic and capitalist states) from the calculus of domination? By no means. Hegemonic military alliances have two faces – one external and one internal: the first directed against potential enemies, the second serving to keep auxiliaries in line. Lord Ismay, the first Secretary-General of NATO, expressed this duality with crystal clarity when he famously remarked in the 1950s that the purpose of NATO was keep the Russians out and the Germans down. The same dual objective has remained at the centre of American Grand Strategy for the post-Cold War epoch – witness the Pentagon's forthright injunction, in a document leaked to the *New York Times* early in 1992, that the US 'discourage the advanced industrialized nations from even aspiring to a larger global or regional role'.[5] Conventional apologias for the American-led war against Yugoslavia as a disinterested rescue mission for human rights, free of any power-political consideration, ignore the regimenting function of the Balkan intervention within NATO itself – the demonstration effect on European allies of overwhelming US military might in their own borderlands, consolidating the unequal structure of the Atlantic Pact internally.[6]

In these respects, realist accounts of the nineties are clearly superior to the prospectuses of the new liberal cosmopolitans. Zbigniew Brzezinski has summed up the actual nature of Doyle's Pacific Union with characteristic bluntness, remarking that compared to the British Empire of the nineteenth century,

> the scope and pervasiveness of American global power today are unique ... Its military legions are firmly perched on the western and eastern extremities of Eurasia, and they also control the Persian Gulf. American vassals and tributaries, some yearning to be embraced by even more formal ties to Washington, dot the entire Eurasian continent.[7]

Brzezinski offers us a map of 'US geopolitical preponderance and other areas of US political influence'. The whole of Western Europe, Japan, South Korea, Australia and New Zealand, as well as some parts of the Middle East and Canada fall into the category of US 'preponderance' – not just influence. The main zones with the resource capacities to challenge US hegemony are precisely those where the US has most firmly established its political sway.

Brzezinski's map also indicates the large parts of the planet which are of little strategic interest to the US. There can, of course, be objections to Brzezinski's selection of areas of vital concern and areas of relative neglect, marked as it is by his own geopolitical preoccupations – others might wish to emphasize a more 'geo-economic' pattern of power-projection, with greater priority accorded to the most important centres of capital accumulation or natural resources (above all petroleum). Yet such a stress would also reveal a highly selective focus (and one that scarcely differed from Brzezinski's). Although the United States and other Pacific Union governments publicly stress the need for the global spread of liberal rights and regimes, their policies actually obey a double derogation. In 'strategic backwaters', such as most of sub-Saharan Africa today, even real genocide can be casually covered or countenanced, as the experience of Rwanda has shown. Where delinquent states are pivotal to American strategic interests, on the other hand, they are vigilantly shielded from human rights pressures, as the cases of Saudi Arabia, Israel, Turkey or Indonesia, to name only the most flagrant examples, have long made clear.

## World institutions

Any form of liberal cosmopolitan project for a new world order requires the subordination of all states to some form of supra-state planetary authority. NLC occlusion of the role of the US in the Pacific Union is compounded by a misrepresentation of the relationship between the US and the various institutions of 'global governance' that are either in place or being canvassed. There is no evidence that these institutions have strengthened their juris-diction over the dominant power in the international system. If anything, the evidence of the 1990s suggests a trend in the opposite direction, as most of these organizations are able to function effectively only insofar as they correspond to the per-ceived policy priorities of the United States, or at least do not contradict them; indeed, in many instances they should rather be viewed as lightly disguised instruments of US policy.

The United Nations is a striking case in point. With the end of the Cold War, the US has been able to utilize the UN for its own ends in a style not seen even in the days of the Korean War. The expedition of Desert Storm in 1991, followed by a decade of sanctions against Iraq, in which UN 'inspection missions' have been openly colonized by the CIA, and the Balkan War, whose violation of the UN Charter was rewarded with the promotion of NATO to UN subcontractor, have only been the most prominent examples of the submission of the Security Council to American dictates. The Secretary-General holds office only at US pleasure.

When Boutros-Ghali proved insufficiently malleable – 'unable to understand the importance of cooperation with the world's first power' in the words of White House factotum James Rubin – he was summarily removed in favour of an American placeman, Kofi Annan, who regularly makes public assertions of the need for the UN to cater to the pre-eminence of Washington at which Trygve Lie himself would have blushed. None of this, of course, has meant that the US feels it necessary even to pay its dues to the UN. In similar spirit, the United States has set up a War Crimes Tribunal under the UN label to punish those it views as its enemies in the Balkans, and protect those it deems its friends, while at the same time declining to sign up to an international court of Human Rights, on the grounds that members of its own armed services might unseasonably be charged before it, or too visibly given special exemption from legal sanction under the escape clause carefully crafted for the US in the treaty.

If we turn to international financial institutions, the pattern is even starker. The IMF is so completely an agency of American will that when the Mexican debt crisis struck in 1995, the Treasury in Washington did not even bother to consult European or Japanese members of the Fund, but – in brazen contravention of its Charter – simply instructed the IMF overnight to bail out American bond-holders, while appropriating additional funds, not even tenuously at its disposal, from the Bank of International Settlements in Basle for the same purpose. The East Asian crisis of 1997–98 offers further evidence, if it were needed, of the ability of the US Treasury to use the IMF as an instrument of its unilateralism, most flagrantly and coercively in the South Korean case. The latest arrival in the panoply of 'global governance', the World Trade Organization, repeats the pattern.

Ratification of the WTO Treaty was explicitly made conditional upon the WTO proving 'fair' to US interests, which since the late 1980s has always meant an unabashed rejection of any rule deemed 'unfair' to those interests – an approach the impeccably orthodox economist Jagdish Bhagwati has called 'aggressive uni-lateralism'. Bhagwati highlights the creation and use of so-called Super 301 and Special 301 laws, but to these could be added 'anti-dumping' provisions and countervailing duties. Such meas-ures have been far from marginal in US international economic policy: as Miles Kahler points out, 'the number of actions brought against "unfair" trading practices increased dramatically' during the 1990s.[8] According to another authority, 'no other economic regulatory programme took on such an increase in case-loads'.[9] Alongside this refusal to be bound by cosmopolitan economic law, meanwhile, there have been vigorous attempts to extend the jurisdictional reach of US domestic law internationally, applying it to non-American corporations operating outside the United States, in the notorious Helms–Burton pursuit of foreign firms trading with Cuba.

In short, the reality is an asymmetrical pattern of change in the field of state sovereignty: a marked tendency towards its erosion in the bulk of states in the international system, accompanied by an accumulation of exceptional prerogatives on the part of one state. We must, in other words, make a sharp distinction between the members of the Pacific Union: the United States has not exhibited any discernible tendency either to abandon power politics or to subordinate itself to supra-state global authorities. Expressions of official enthusiasm for norm-based cosmopolitanism as an institutionalized order, although by no means wanting in Washington (the majority of NLC theorists are, after all, American), have been more profuse on the other side of the Atlantic. During the 1990s, as the European Union committed itself to developing a Common Foreign and Security Policy, and prepared for enlargement to the East in the wake of NATO expansion, it started to lay ever greater emphasis on applying its ideological and legal regimes to external partner states. Today, the EU regularly outdoes the US itself in lecturing other states on the inseparability of the free market from the rule of law and democratic government, and in posing as guardian of universal liberal principles. In practice, however, it has consistently acted as a regional subordinate of the US, save where narrow trade, investment and production interests are concerned – still liable to spark contention at a lower level.

The various West European states would all prefer the US to proceed with less unilateralism. But their conception of what passes for 'multilateral' – essentially a matter of style rather than substance – remains sufficiently minimal not to present any threat to American hegemony. At no period since the end of the Second World War has Western Europe been so closely aligned, ideologically and politically, with the United States as today. The anxiety with which the incoming Bush administration was greeted in European capitals was a sign of dependence rather than distance. The days of Adenauer and De Gaulle, or even Edward Heath and Helmut Schmidt, are long past.

## Trade regimes

Let us counter-factually suppose, however, that the allies of the United States could inveigle it into a more collegial form of Pacific Union dominance. Is there any evidence that such a configuration would usher in a liberal cosmopolitan order subordinating the sovereignty of national states to universalist liberal norms and institutions, applied equally to all? To answer this question, we need to ask: what are the social and economic transformations that are now jointly promoted by the Pacific Union, and how do these affect the international system of states? The theorists of NLC present the fundamental changes under way as, firstly, steady progress towards a global free market, subject to negotiated regulation, and secondly, the spread of liberal democracy across the earth, unifying the peoples of the world in representative government, monitored by global institutions protecting human rights. These are large claims. Let us begin by looking at the economic prospectus held out by NLC.

The common notion, taken more or less for granted by NLC theorists, that the companies of Pacific Union states inaugurated economic globalization by escaping the control of their own states, ignores the fact that the patterns of international economic exchange have continued to be shaped in large measure by state diplomacy, establishing the legal and institutional framework for the operation of markets. NLC doctrine tends to assume that the regulatory and market-shaping impulses of states have been and are geared towards liberal free-trade regimes. Contemporary evidence suggests that this is misleading: the drift of the international economic policy of core countries in the 1990s has been marked by resistance to free-trade principles in sectors of critical importance to economies outside the core – agricultural products, steel, textiles and apparel – and by moves towards managed trade and 'reciprocity' in a number of others. Examples include various key aspects of US–Japanese trade, where the total range of imports or exports to be achieved in various sectors is specified in

advance; the use of Voluntary Export Restraints, pricing agreements and other non-tariff barriers by the EU to control the level
of imports from Eastern Europe; and so-called 'rules of origin'
designed to exclude from free entry into a given market goods
produced with varying amounts of inputs from third countries.
The effect of such protectionist and mercantilist methods is,
typically, to generate chronic trade and current account deficits
on the part of less developed countries – a near universal problem
facing East European states – exacerbating already huge debts,
and making peripheral governments increasingly desperate to
gain supposedly compensating inflows of capital from the core
states. This is a pattern that all too often renders them vulnerable
and unstable, hence incapable of generating sustained improvement in the well-being of their populations.

Furthermore, the bulk of the economic changes of the 1990s
and early 2000s do not concern international trade at all.
Although described in the Western media as 'trade regimes' or
'trade negotiations', they have been overwhelmingly about the
property rights of foreign capitals in other states: that is, the
ability of foreign operators to gain ownership of domestic assets,
or establish businesses within states on the same terms as domestic
companies, to move money in and out of the country freely, and
to enforce monopoly rents on intellectual property. The public-
policy issues raised in these areas concern such matters as the
costs and benefits of allowing global oligopolies to gain ownership
of domestic assets and integrate them into their profit streams;
of ending controls on the free movement of private finance;
of privatizing (mainly into foreign ownership) domestic social-
service provisions and utilities; and last, but by no means least,
the costs and benefits of making domestic financial systems – and
thereby entire national economies – highly vulnerable to sudden
and massive gyrations in global monetary relations and in international financial markets.

Current trends in international trade and in the internal
transformations of non-core political economies are thus very far
from guaranteeing virtuous circles of cosmopolitan economic and
social gains for the world's populations. There is overwhelming
evidence of a huge and growing polarization of wealth between
the immiserated bulk of humanity and extremely wealthy social
groups within the core countries. Neither is there the slightest

indication that, were its allies within the Pacific Union to subordinate the US to a more collegial system, this pattern of economic
relations would alter in any way. Indeed, one of the main bases
for perceptions of common cause between the US and its allies is
precisely their joint interest in perpetuating this drive for control
of new profit streams from non-core economies.

## Permeable sovereignty

NLC theorists confuse juridical forms with social substance. They
depict the world as a fragmented system of state sovereignties on
one side, and a proliferating number of regional, international
and global regimes and institutions on the other. In the midst of
these institutional patterns they perceive a swelling mass of individuals, increasingly free to maximize their welfare in markets.
This juridical perspective provides the basis for hoping that global
regimes can encase state sovereignties in a legally egalitarian,
cosmopolitan rule of law in which citizens of the world can unite
in free exchange. If, however, we view this same international
order from the angle of social power, it looks more like a highly
centralized pyramid of capitalist market forces dominated by the
Pacific Union states and strongly supported by their state officials.
This reality is captured by Justin Rosenberg's notion of an 'empire
of civil society'.[10] In this empire, we find substantial unity between
the states and market forces of the core countries, rather than
the antagonism suggested by theorists of globalization and liberal
cosmopolitanism. We also find substantial unity across the societies of the Pacific Union, whose empire is guarded not by any
supra-state authority, but by a single hegemon.

We do not have ready to hand a language for describing this
pattern of global social power. We are used to thinking of both
state sovereignty and international markets as the opposites of
imperialism. This could be said to have been true of the various
European colonialisms of the nineteenth and first half of the
twentieth centuries, for these were largely juridical empires claiming sovereign legal power over conquered territories and peoples.
But the distinctive feature of the Pax Americana has been the
enlargement of US social control within the framework of an
international order of juridically sovereign states. Samuel

Huntington has provided the classic statement of how US imperial expansion has worked:

> Western Europe, Latin America, East Asia, and much of South Asia, the Middle East and Africa fell within what was euphemistically referred to as 'the Free World', and what was, in fact, a security zone. The governments within this zone found it in their interest: a) to accept an explicit or implicit guarantee by Washington of the independence of their country and, in some cases, the authority of the government; b) to permit access to their country to a variety of US governmental and non-governmental organizations pursuing goals which those organizations considered important . . . The great bulk of the countries of Europe and the Third World found the advantages of transnational access to outweigh the costs of attempting to stop it.[11]

During most of the Cold War, as Huntington notes, the principal lever of US expansion was the security pact. Since the beginning of the 1980s a second instrument has supplemented it: financial and market-access pacts for states facing financial crisis. These pacts not only allow entry of Atlantic capitals into lesser sovereign states; they also allow national and international market structures to be redesigned so as to favour systematically the market dominance of Atlantic multinational corporations. In liberal thought, the rejection by the dominant core states of formalized legal authority over territory can seem to suggest a far weaker form of political power than the European juridical empires of old. This is because liberal approaches often tend to conceive power as 'command'. But he who takes legal command over a territory assumes responsibility for everything that happens on it – frequently a heavy burden and potentially a dangerous one. On the other hand, he who shapes the relevant environment of a given state authority can ensure that it acts in ways conducive to his interests. The emergent global system is geared to shaping the environments of sovereign states so that developments within them broadly match the interests of the Pacific Union – while responsibility for tackling these developments falls squarely on the governments of the sovereign states concerned. This new type of international order, then, does not make the system of penetrated sovereign states a legal fiction. They remain crucial cornerstones of the world order, but their role becomes above all that of maintaining political control over the populations within their jurisdiction.

## Domestic liberalization

The second principal basis for NLC optimism lies in the spread of liberal democratic forms of polity across the globe. Yet, paradoxically, severe pressures on the foundations of many newly liberal-democratic states have come from the very Pacific Union seen by liberal cosmopolitans as the fount of international harmony. States are forced to open their economies to monetary and financial movements to which the employment conditions of their citizens become extremely vulnerable. Their élites are encouraged to impose policies which widen the gap between rich and poor. Economically weak countries are driven to compete for the entry of foreign capital by reducing taxes on the business classes – thereby undermining their capacity to maintain social and educational services. All these pressures have been taking their toll: as Geoffrey Hawthorn has noted, states under strain or in disintegration, the emergence of shadow states or outright state collapse are becoming common sights in the contemporary world. In such conditions liberal girders burst, and groups will often increasingly turn to organized crime or break with the homogenizing national political values of the state, demanding exit as national minorities.

These trends are not confined to polities outside the Pacific Union. They are also reflected in a general malaise within the 'consolidated' liberal democracies of the core, well captured by Philippe Schmitter:

> Privatization of public enterprises; removal of state regulations; liberalization of financial flows; conversion of political demands into claims based on rights; replacement of collective entitlements by individual contributions; sacralization of property rights; downsizing of public bureaucracies and emoluments; discrediting of 'politicians' in favour of 'entrepreneurs'; enhancement of the power of 'neutral technical' institutions, like central banks, at the expense of 'biased political' ones – all these modifications have two features in common: 1) they diminish popular expectations from public choices, and 2) they make it harder to assemble majorities to overcome the resistance of minorities, especially well-entrenched and privileged ones.

Schmitter goes on to note the decline in democratic participation in those advanced liberal democracies 'most exposed to the "more liberalism" strategy', commenting:

whether this process of 'dedemocratization' can continue is, of course, the all-important question. Its justification rests almost exclusively on the superior economic performance that is supposed to accrue to a liberalized system of production and distribution – along with the deliberate effort to foster a strong normative rejection of politics as such.[12]

Finally, of course, NLC theorists welcome military intervention at large by the Pacific Union in the name of human rights – or even 'civilization' – as an inspiring step forward towards the realization of a world ruled by liberal principles rather than power. On closer inspection, however, these expeditions offer a model of power-projection that virtually inverts this description. When constitutional polities descend into civil war, liberal procedures collapse – as liberal theory acknowledges, allowing for emergency situations when liberal norms are suspended. Typically, in such crisis conditions, both sides to a political conflict will accuse the other of violating provisions of the law, which becomes a largely rhetorical token in a struggle over other issues, such as separatism, irredentism, or confessional division. During the 1990s, states of the Pacific Union intervened in several such conflicts, proclaiming the need to uphold liberal norms, while taking no political position on the issues that have caused them. The NATO attack on Yugoslavia in 1999, lauded by NLC theorists as a triumph of humanitarian principle, should rather be seen as an example of politically unprincipled, arbitrary imperial government. The conflict between the Yugoslav government and the Kosovar Albanians concerned the right of the latter to secede from Yugoslavia. The Pacific Union states in effect declared this political issue irrelevant and themselves incapable of laying down any general principle to resolve it, resorting instead to an arbitrary 'pragmatism' that seems set to repeat itself in any such future operations. The revenge attacks being planned in the wake of the destruction of the World Trade Center seem unlikely to be aimed at mitigating the tensions racking Saudi Arabian society – home to the majority of the hijackers – whose extraordinarily repressive confessional regime has, as noted, long been smiled upon by the Pacific Union.

For even if the Pacific Union states were to overcome all tensions amongst themselves and merge into a minority condominium over the planet, there is every reason to suppose that they would continue to place contradictory demands upon the system over which they currently preside. On the one hand, they demand internal arrangements within those states which suit the interests of the 'empire of civil society'. But on the other they rely upon those states to preserve domestic order and control their local populations. These incompatible policy requirements stem from an essentially arbitrary attitude towards enforcing universalist liberal norms of individual rights.

The evidence mustered by the supporters of the new liberal cosmopolitanism to claim that humanity is finally on the verge of being united in a single, just world order is not convincing. The liberal-individualist analytical corset does not fit the world as it is: it fails to strap American power into its prognosis of a supra-state order. The cosmopolitan project for unifying humanity through the agency of the dominant capitalist states – on the normative basis that we are all individual global citizens with liberal rights – will not work: it is more likely to plunge the planet into increasingly divisive turmoil.

There is another version of cosmopolitanism abroad today, which places at the centre of its conception of a new world order the notion of a democratic global polity. This comes in a number of different editions, some scarcely distinguishable from liberal cosmopolitanism save for more voluble democratic piety. But in its most generous version, exemplified by Daniele Archibugi's essay in these pages, this is a programme with the great merit of seeking to subordinate the rich minority of states and social groups to the will of a global majority, in conditions where the bulk of the world's population remains trapped in poverty and powerlessness. Yet even its best proposals suffer from two crippling weaknesses. They focus too narrowly on purely political institutions, while ignoring the fact that a Herculean popular agency would be required to realize even these against the united colours of the Pacific Union. Any prospect of bringing humanity towards genuine unity on a global scale would have to confront the social and economic relations of actually existing capitalism with a clarity and trenchancy from which most representatives of this current shrink; and any hope of altering these can only be nullified by evasion or edulcoration of the realities of the sole superpower. Timothy Brennan has criticized the self-deceptions of a complacent cosmopolitanism of any stripe. The best antidote to them comes from clear-minded advocates of the present order itself. As Robert Kagan and William Kristol wrote, with tonic accuracy, in *The National Interest* (Spring 2000):

> Today's international system is built not around a balance of power but around American hegemony. The international financial institutions were fashioned by Americans and serve American interests. The international security structures are chiefly a collection of American-led alliances. What Americans like to call international 'norms' are really reflections of American and West European principles. Since today's relatively benevolent circumstances are the product of our hegemonic influence, any lessening of that influence will allow others to play a larger part in shaping the world to suit their needs . . . American hegemony, then, must be actively maintained, just as it was actively obtained.

In other words, US power will not come to an end until it is actively detained. No scheme for universal harmony, however long-term, is credible if it tries to sidestep it.

## Notes

1. See 'Cosmopolitical Democracy', *New Left Review*, second series, no. 4 (chapter 1 in this volume); and the subsequent discussions of it in Geoffrey Hawthorn, 'Running the World through Windows', *New Left Review*, second series, no. 5 (chaper 2 in this volume); David Chandler, 'International Justice', *New Left Review*, second series, no. 6 (chapter 3 in this volume); Timothy Brennan, 'Cosmopolitanism and Internationalism', *New Left Review*, second series, no. 7 (chapter 4 in this volume). I will return to the relations between 'liberal' and 'democratic' versions at the end of this article.

2. For leading statements of this current, see Michael Doyle, 'A Liberal View: Preserving and Expanding the Liberal Pacific Union', in T.V. Paul and John Hall, eds, *International Order and the Future of World Politics*, Cambridge 1999 and Michael Doyle, 'Kant, Liberal Legacies and Foreign Affairs', *Philosophy and Public Affairs*, vol. 12, nos. 3 and 4, 1983; see also Seyom Brown, *New Forces, Old Forces and the Future of World Politics*, Glenview, IL 1988; James Rosenau, 'Citizenship in a Changing Global Order', in James Rosenau and Ernst-Otto Czempiel, eds, *Governance without Government: Order and Change in World Politics*, Cambridge 1992; Larry Diamond, 'The Globalisation of Democracy', in Ray Kiely and Phil Marfleet, eds, *Globalisation and the Third World*, London 1998; Paul Taylor, 'The United Nations in the 1990s: Proactive Cosmopolitanism and the Issue of Sovereignty', *Political Studies*, vol. 47, 1999, pp. 538–65; Richard Falk, *Positive Prescriptions for the Near Future*, Princeton Center for International Studies, Paper No. 20, 1991. Doyle has served as an observer in Bosnia, Falk as a consultant to Annan.

3. Paul Taylor, 'The United Nations in the 1990s'.

4. See, for example, The White House, *A National Security Strategy for a New Century*, Washington, DC 1998.

5. This was the 1992 Draft of the Pentagon Defense Planning Guidance.

6. See 'The Twisted Road to Kosovo', *Labour Focus on Eastern Europe*, Special issue, May 1999.

7. See Zbigniew Brzezinski, *The Grand Chessboard. American Primacy and its Geostrategic Imperatives*, New York 1997, p. 23.

8. Miles Kahler, *Regional Futures and Transatlantic Economic Relations*, New York 1995, p. 46.

9. Pietro Nivola, *Regulating Unfair Trade*, Washington, DC 1993, p. 21.

10. Justin Rosenberg, *The Empire of Civil Society*, London and New York 1995.

11. Samuel Huntington, 'Transnational Organizations in World Politics', *World Politics*, vol. 25, no. 3, 1973, p. 344.

12. Philippe Schmitter, 'Democracy's Future: More Liberal, Preliberal or Postliberal?', *Journal of Democracy*, vol. 6, no. 1, January 1995.

# 6

# Can Cosmopolitical Democracy Be Democratic?

*Nadia Urbinati*

What follows is a critical reading of cosmopolitical democracy, or cosmopolitanism as a *project of global government*.[1] I use the term 'criticism' in its theoretical and analytical, rather than polemical sense. I do not question the aspiration to make the economic and political global order more respectful of the life and dignity of the world's inhabitants. The Kantian maxims commanding us to seek peace and respect individual rights have enriched classical cosmopolitanism with a practical goal all humans are responsible for realizing. Post-Kant, the burden of proof is on those who want to argue against cosmopolitan civil rights. My main objection to cosmo*political* democracy is its translation of the Kantian maxims into the project of devising global decision-making procedures that are actually the province of states. My objection interrogates in the name of democratic premises the cogency and desirability of making the cosmos into a unified political space. Theorists of cosmopolitical democracy do not simply claim for democracy 'within' and 'between' states. Much more radically, they deem it necessary to construct a supranational political body endowed with the power of legislation, administration, and military intervention/coercion. *Cosmopolis* is a project of centralization and unification of power, not decentralization or mere cooperation. It adds power to the already existing *loci* of power. Thus, despite their pledge of allegiance to Kant's plane of perpetual peace, theorists of cosmopolitical democracy *de facto* violate the Kantian *lex aurea* according to which cosmopolitan civil rights entail the containment of political power, not its *supererogation*. Recognizing the value and essence of liberal democracy should alert us to the anti-democratic risk contained in the idea of a *spaceless* democracy. As Jürgen Habermas has recently argued, postnational democracy can hardly aim at more than 'weak forms of legitimation' (moral and normative) to retain a democratic character.

## The European paradigm of cosmopolitan democracy

Cosmopolitanism is a composite family of ancient lineage. Its liberal humanist branch is rooted in classical Stoicism and the modern doctrine of natural rights. Its neo-liberal branch has grown from the theory of the free market and the liberation of civil society from the fetters of feudalism and state absolutism. Thus cosmopolitanism can mean the aspiration for global justice and the universalization of human rights, as well as an uncritical celebration of globalization.[2] Their differences notwithstanding, both liberal and neo-liberal cosmopolitanism view national sovereignty as an obstacle because it resists outside interference and obstructs transnational exchange and/or cooperation. In their humanist, liberal, and economic versions, scholars of different disciplines, countries, and political orientation share remarkably similar cosmopolitan ideals. Liberal cosmopolitanism is itself a cosmopolitan phenomenon.[3] 'Democratic cosmopolitanism' presents an interestingly different case, however.

*Democratic* cosmopolitanism bills itself as a political response to the acknowledged fact of globalization. Unlike its neo-liberal counterpart, however, it does not see globalization as a natural like and self-regulating phenomenon. As an ideal, democratic cosmopolitanism represents the reluctance of politics to capitulate in the face of the so-called 'spontaneity' of global economic competition. It reaffirms the power of associated individuals and peoples to shape their lives.[4] Thus despite its affiliation with the 'utopian' legacy of perpetual peace, its aspiration to reassert the place of politics puts democratic cosmopolitanism in the camps of Rousseau and Hegel. Not because, like Rousseau and Hegel, it opts for autonomous sovereign city-republics or nation-states, but because in its proponents' eyes, the liberty envisioned by global civil society falls short, and they aspire to create a space for political liberty at the global level. They make their case in the name of citizenship, not simply of humanity. And they propose cosmopolitan political institutions in the name of citizenship as a status, not simply as a symbolic or moral value.

So it is their view of the relationship between civil society and politics that distinguishes the various interpretations of democratic cosmopolitanism. In one view, democracy's natural place is civil society; in the other, the political realm. The former approach shares a liberal anti-coercive view of politics and interprets democracy more as a civic culture of association, participation and mobilization than as a political process of decision-making. This is Richard Falk's position. His writings convey a deep discontent with the statist form of collective behaviour. Falk's theoretical and ideal background is libertarian insofar as it stresses one particular aspect of democratic action, the one that values spontaneous public practice from below. Here civil society is the most genuine place of participation and freedom because it resists organized power, and above all state power. Cosmopolitan democracy is identified with a postmodernist view of democracy as post-state based.[5]

The political approach to democratic cosmopolitanism, on the contrary, is much more attentive to the actual and potential relationship between civil society and the political sphere. It acknowledges social movements and non-governmental organizations as fundamental components of global democracy but it also believes that in the absence of institutionalized procedures of decision and control, social movements and NGOs can be both exclusionary and hierarchical. The writings of Daniele Archibugi and David Held approach cosmopolitan democracy from this perspective, and envision international political organisms empowered to enact enforceable legal collective decisions in response to globalization and human rights violations. Their cosmopolitanism rests on the assumption that civil society lacking the generality of citizenship will revert to a 'state of nature' where liberty thrives at the expense of equality and economic power at the expense of justice. As the Eastern European states' exit from Communism demonstrates, a healthy civil society and secure individual freedoms need a legal and governmental system that enjoys institutional autonomy from social interests and operates under rules of impartiality and rational efficiency.[6] Thus a world democratic polis should aspire to govern the entity Falk sees as emerging through *self*-governing social actors and movements, which represents the growing opportunity for peoples and individuals to assert their influence over their natural and social environment.

The political branch of democratic cosmopolitanism is a largely European phenomenon, both in its deliberative-discourse version (Habermas) and in its political-institutional one (Archibugi and Held). In both cases, the moral justification for a global democratic order is derived from the Kantian premise that a degree of association among the peoples of the world is needed to protect human rights and successfully oppose their violation. Both conceive a postnational democratic order as the most advanced answer to the challenge posed by the erosion of state sovereignty and the international and domestic order set up by the Westphalia Treaty. Whereas in the past, international issues were 'interstate' issues, or 'boundary matters' resolved 'by pursuing reasons of state, backed, ultimately, by coercive force', today, the source of contemporary international issues is largely transnational actors that states are wholly unfit to face. 'Overlapping spheres of influence, interference and interest create dilemmas at the center of democratic thought' because democracy has been associated with the state form.[7]

The erosion of state sovereignty visibly accelerated with the end of the Cold War equilibrium and two concomitant factors. First, a *centrifugal* dissemination of non-political powers as an effect of the extraordinary expansion of financial and communication networks beyond the borders of the states. Second, a *centripetal* process of political integration among European countries. Both are phenomena of transnationality but point in very different, if not opposite, directions. In particular, the latter has become the theatre of the tension between the neo-liberal and the democratic trajectories of cosmopolitanism. The European Union is the paradigm of the political approach to democratic cosmopolitanism.[8]

The European integration actualizes the ideal of radical and democratic European intellectuals to make their continent the laboratory of a world order alternative to other hegemonic models: first national-socialism, then communism, and presently a deregulated global capitalism. It is the daughter of the vision of a peaceful Europe inhabited by democratic nations that inspired

European intellectuals from the age of the Enlightenment to the age of the democratic revolutions of 1848. As a subterranean current, this vision linked together Kant's cosmopolitan liberalism and Giuseppe Mazzini's cosmopolitan law of nations.[9] The European political integration gives this old idea a new rebirth and, furthermore, inspires theorists of democratic cosmopolitanism. The institutional and legal networks that have been enveloping European states and peoples since 1950 have served as the template for a bolder view of transnationality.[10] It is no coincidence that the pioneers of cosmopolitical and postnational democracy are mainly European.

Twentieth-century Europe has witnessed both the most tremendous *cosmopolitan* civil war and the renaissance of the ideal of *cosmopolitan* perpetual peace. It has also witnessed the extraordinary event of a military victory (1945) that sought legal justice in order to win a total and indisputable legitimacy over the peoples of the Continent, including the defeated. It sought a kind of legitimacy that might and military victory alone could not deliver. The defeat of Nazi-fascism could not have been total if it was only military. Both the rule of might *and* the rule of law defeated Nazi-fascism. Of the two, the latter has become the backbone of European democracy and democratic thought, and above all of the process of Continental unification.

European democratic theorists are at the cutting edge of efforts to resist international 'realism' and to disassociate democracy from 'national interest'. Just consider the theoretical trajectories of the two main contemporary political theorists, the American John Rawls and the German-European Jürgen Habermas. The former ties universal principles of right and liberty to the national-constitutional context in a way that has become progressively stronger, and has culminated in a theory of international justice firmly anchored to national-territorial states. The latter ties those principles to a 'discourse-theoretical understanding of democracy' that in and of itself configures a de-nationalized view of democracy. In Hegel's language, one might say that Habermas' deliberative democracy is the philosophical consciousness of the political trajectory of European integration. His model is theoretically predisposed to envision a postnational legal order and a postnational democratic public sphere in a way that Rawls' is not. By the same token, the European Union is predisposed to become the paradigm for cosmopolitan democracy in a way that the United States is not. '[T]he EC has had the bold idea of disconnecting nationality from citizenship, and this idea may well evolve to a general principle which ultimately transforms the ideal of cosmopolitan citizenship into a reality.'[11]

The cosmo*political* version of cosmopolitan thought radicalizes the European paradigm by challenging the process of globalization from the perspective of a world citizenship whose affiliation transcends cultural belonging and territorial specificity, and assumes political status. Rather than retaining the post-French Revolution model of democracy, this version of cosmopolitanism constitutes a radical revision of it. This is what distinguishes Held's and Archibugi's approach from Habermas'. *Cosmopolitical* democracy and *postnational* democracy differ in respect to the form and depth each ascribes to the association of the peoples of the world. Their differences spring from different judgements about the role of the nation-state in the processes of both domestic and international democratization.

Habermas faces the challenges of globalization from the perspective of the emancipatory experiences 'articulated in the ideas of popular sovereignty and human rights'. He is posing the problem of how to legitimate postnational democratic decisions without creating a 'civil solidarity' at the global level. 'Civic solidarity is rooted in particular collective identities; cosmopolitan solidarity has to support itself on the moral universalism of human rights alone.' Unless we change the definition and practice of democratic self-determination (or citizenship) we cannot make a spaceless cosmos the home of democracy because '[a]ny political community that wants to understand itself as a democracy must at least distinguish between members and non-members'. Democratic self-determination cannot exist without the 'inside'/ 'outside' dialectics.[12] Unlike liberal universalism, democratic universalism refers to a specific demos made up of people who are united by something more concrete than humanity and reason. This is why anyone can claim to be a citizen of the world, but no one can claim to be, say, an American citizen without being one. The institutional analog of citizenship is 'power' and legal-political obligation, not mere moral duty. The thoroughly voluntary character of cosmopolitan citizenship is matched by its lack of a direct political recognition and legitimation.

This is why Habermas situates himself in the tradition of Hans Kelsen and can bind cosmopolitan law to legitimacy without grounding them in an anterior political identity. Cosmopolitan democratic legitimacy has multiple, interconnected sources: democratic states that give birth to agreements and conventions along with a public sphere populated by non-governmental organizations and critical public opinion grounded in circuits of communication. The cosmopolitan horizon utilizes, and in fact stresses democracy's deliberative character, but drops the ambition to become political in the way 'particular collective identities' are political.[13] At most the world can become a 'community' devoid of 'sociological' or concrete subjects and inhabited by legal persons each state commits itself to acknowledge and respect. The precondition for this multi-layered system of legitimation and control is the gradual democratization of states and their civil societies. This legalistic (via states-jurisdiction) *plus* public opinion solution is the most advanced option a democrat should hope for at the global level. It recognizes the inherent complexity of normative frameworks and the integration of political status (citizenship) and legal status (legal personhood), where the former remains territorial and the latter gives birth to the multiplicity of legal and public instances comprising the institutions of the international order.[14] Quite appropriately, scholars have equated this postnational network of overlapping authorities and multiple loyalties with a neomedievalism.[15]

Held and Archibugi propose going beyond this, though. They want to create a new political status of world citizenship independent of the mediation of states. Moreover, they want citizens to be represented in a world parliament (see also Falk and Strauss, chapter 11 in this volume); they propose not only instituting an international criminal court with effective enforcement power, but also reforming the United Nations Security Council to transform it into an effective executive organ.[16] Finally, and more disturbing, they propose the creation of a civilian *and* military peace force 'at the disposal of the Security Council'.[17] Even if they do not call for the overcoming of states, their cosmopolitical order resembles very much a state-like sovereign.[18] Furthermore, the institutional design they propose is a quasi state with a low democratic standard because its parliament would hold only a consultative function and no checking power over the Council.

This executive-unbalanced power relation seems to confirm the fact that the cosmopolis project is inspired first of all by the prospect of military intervention and coercion. Whereas *existing* intergovernmental institutions are ruled by principles of non-intervention and multilateralism (intervention being an exception), the new Cosmopolitical executive (the Security Council) will be empowered not only to 'compel' members to comply with the basic norms (Universal Declaration of Human Rights) but also to decide to use military force against them. The former have a negative or preventive function, the latter will have a positive and active function.[19] The discretionary power of the world executive, while it poses serious problems of democratic deficit, is the undesirable but predictable consequence of a *political* (thus interventionist) cosmopolitanism. This explains Archibugi's insistence on the need to compensate for the inherent limits of a nationally based citizenship, and finally his strategic rhetorical use of a negative picture of states. His strong criticism of state sovereignty and his understandable alarm at the deterioration of the international arena in the light of the demise of the Cold War equilibrium, reveal both his impatience with Kant's perspective of the *longue durée*, and his interventionist inclinations.

## The violation of the Kantian model

Archibugi is unclear about who should take the initiative to overcome the existing world *dis*order and open the way for cosmopolis. He appeals to the peoples within states to mobilize and demand global democracy. However, at the moment peoples *en masse* have been more active in signalling the crisis of the existing state order than in advancing a postnational democratic alternative. In fact, most of the time, their reactions have been retrogressive rather than progressive. The lessons of the violent dissolution of the federation of Yugoslavia or the milder regional chauvinism in Northern Italy are that peoples have precipitated the erosion of state sovereignty in favour of a state form that is mono-ethnic and more exclusionary. It is perhaps the awareness of the discrepancy between people's potential and people's actual democratic role that induces Archibugi to seek more selective company. What was true two centuries ago remains true today: cosmopolitical democracy is inspired not by the masses but by the tiny minority of intellectuals who try to educate public opinion and influence 'the politicians sitting at the negotiating tables'. The *philosophes* are the enlightened minds that feel responsible for, and are able to foresee, 'often centuries in advance', the new order and propagate it among rulers and ruled.[20] In a Platonist, and even Jacobean vein, theorists of cosmopolitical democracy hope for a bottom-up movement while proposing a top-down strategy. If cosmopolis will succeed, it will hardly be through democratic means.

Intellectual aspiration for a world order modelled according to the principles of a 'perpetual peace' is neither new nor original. In fact it was the most audacious expression of the universalistic ideals of the Enlightenment and a consistent liberal proposal. The moral foundations of the many schemes for a perpetual peace are to be found in the contractarian justification of political authority and the theory of natural rights. That only consent can give political power legitimacy was the logical conclusion of the assumption that the individual has a value in herself, and in fact is the primary source of value in relation to which all other goods – material and symbolic – ought to be judged and esteemed. Modern cosmopolitanism sprang from liberalism. Its normative principle entails the limitation of the prerogative of political power. It proclaims individual rights and pertains to the sphere of justice. It aspires to subject politics to morals by transforming political power from might to legality. Its natural referees are courts of justice rather than parliaments. As Kant argued, cosmopolitan civil rights refer to the legal sphere not the spheres of the good and politics. Indeed, that legal sphere entails rights rather than philanthropy, and concerns politics only insofar as it demands that states limit their jurisdiction so as to make the surface of the earth relatively open to individuals' choices to move without abjuring their national belonging.

Like the basic rights to property and life, cosmopolitan 'civil' rights are claimed in the name of a pre-political entity, that is to say the individual – 'but the *right to visit*, to associate, belongs to all men by virtue of their common ownership of the earth's surface'. As such, they are conceived as a claim *against* the unrestrained power of states. They are not 'political rights'. For them to be respected, all states should include them in their legal codes and make them into positive public law. This would allow individuals to claim for them and appeal to justice for their enforcement. Just as with the bills of right within national constitutions, cosmopolitan civil rights imply self-constraint on the part of political power.[21]

Kant's model for a perpetual peace had a *negative* character in the sense that its purpose was to prevent states from exercising their sovereignty outside or against the basic moral principle of individual rights. If Kant did not propose a world government it was because his aim was not to bypass states but to induce them to cooperate voluntarily and thus to accept restraints on their power. Hence his conclusion that if all states complied with the consent legitimacy proviso – if they became republican – they would be complying with cosmopolitan civil rights. Peace was imperative. Kant implies that the permanent possibility of war is responsible for autocracy. In a life-threatening scenario, the defence of security justifies the use of excessive force and the adoption of exceptional means that can also violate individual rights (*nomos*) in order to guarantee survival (*bios*). The enactment of emergency laws by the American government to cope with the terrorist threat validates Kant's paradigm concerning the tension between the argument of security and that of civil rights.

Kant's perpetual peace was a project of liberty (because it was a project of security) not democracy. It was a project of political containment, rather than political building. This becomes clear once we remember that Kant resorted to the logic of an invisible hand explanation or a philosophy of world history in order to justify his model. He chose a *longue durée* perspective and did not call on political actors to take direct initiative to enact a legal world order. Nor did he think, like contemporary theorists of cosmopolitical democracy, that 'voluntary association' among states should give some the power to sanction others. He believed that as economic, moral and communicative global interaction and interdependence among individuals developed, states would gradually proceed toward a form of legal integration that did not compromise their sovereignty. This meant that no one state could have more power than another. Mutual agreement requires an *egalitarian* distribution of power among the associate states. Kant's logic was exactly the same as the one he employed to explain the original social contract by which individuals exited the state of nature and created the commonwealth.

Theorists of cosmopolitical democracy violate the Kantian model on three counts. First, they question the idea that the democratic transformation of states should come first. Indeed, while they are impatient with Kant's *longue durée*, they don't want 'to make people democratic against their will'. 'Starting from the top' (from cosmopolitical institutions) seems to them less 'paternalistic' than expanding democracy.[22] However, it is unclear why they should worry about being paternalistic if they deny the principle of sovereign autonomy. Second, they doubt that democracy 'within states' will bring about democracy 'between states' and a world order more respectful of human rights.[23] However, it is counterintuitive to think that global citizenship and cosmopolitical institutions would produce these outcomes even if a portion of world citizens lives under non-democratic regimes. Would the United States still be a democratic republic if some of its state members were not democratic?[24] Finally theorists of cosmopolitical democracy defy Kant's egalitarian proviso and underestimate the fact that within an international scenario dominated by one nation-state that holds a quasi-imperial power, cosmopolis would be not only impossible, but dangerous.[25] Indeed, it would either be hegemonized by the strongest, or it would need to mobilize an extraordinarily great power in order to subject the stronger.[26] In either case, there would hardly be room for a cosmopolitical democracy. 'Viewed historically, Kant's reticence concerning the project of a *constitutionally* organized community of nations was certainly realistic' and sensitive to the political condition of Europe after the French Revolution.[27] Contemporary theorists of cosmopolitical democracy seem to lack Kant's realism when they aspire to be more assertive and politically interventionist. Their project is deaf to eighteenth-century warnings about the despotic potential of a world government.[28]

## Sovereignty surrendered and the 'vices' of parliamentary democracy retained

The two main challenges faced by cosmopolitical democracy are territorially localized political power and globally diffused economic power. Its proponents argue that states are powerful enough to harm their subjects but insufficiently powerful to protect their own people from the harm wrought by the new global actors.

While economic globalization does not erode the coercive power of the state, it gravely diminishes states' power to pursue the politics of social justice. The paradox of our time, Archibugi and Held argue, is that the extraordinary escalation of economic globalization tends to make all states less democratic, or rather to reduce their potential for a broader democratic politics. This paradox induces them to long for something more than 'inter-state' democracy. Archibugi proposes an international power endowed with enough strength to 'interfere in domestic affairs', something that coordination among autonomous states, even democratic ones, cannot guarantee.[29] As the argument goes, while there is no certainty that the Kantian strategy would change the nature of international relations, there is no doubt that it would *not* change the logic of the international order because national sovereignty would still prevail. The expansion of the geo-social space calls for the construction of an expanded geo-political space. Finally, the traditionally circumscribed space within which democracy has been contained all along demands radical change.[30]

Theorists of cosmopolitical democracy base their proposals on a strong critique of the state form. States are 'the world's major depositories of power' responsible for a coerced national, cultural and religious homogenization. 'It is states that have armed forces; control police; mint currency; permit or refuse entrance to their lands; states that recognize citizens' rights and impose their duties.'[31] However, it is unclear, and Archibugi does not clarify, why these state's prerogatives are a negative fact, above all if one thinks that the alternative could be private corporations or churches minting currency and refusing entrance to their lands. The emancipation of the legal and political power of the state from patrimonialism and religion should be carefully disassoci-ated from the long history of the arbitrary use of force and the law that has been perpetrated by state rulers throughout the centuries. In this regard, bureaucratic emancipation from feudal rule and subsequent democratic constitutionalism represented a true revolution in the structure and form of the state, not merely an 'evolution'. By the same token, the welfare state transformation of the democratic states has not merely been an additional 'instrument of service' states used to mitigate what they are, so much as a 'tool of domination'.[32]

Archibugi's picture suggests that it is the link between democracy and 'national interests' that vitiates democracy. 'It can be
argued that it is consistent with the interests of the French people
for a democratic French government to carry out nuclear experiments in the Pacific Ocean, if all the advantages go to France
and the radioactive waste only harms people in another hemisphere.'[33] Hence, his conclusion that a global government involving 'the world's citizens' would be able to rid democracy of the
selfishness it inherited from the nation-state. It is unclear, though,
why and how a French citizen would overcome his national
selfishness in voting for a global parliament. Does cosmopolitical
citizenship entail self-forgetting?

The source of the problems I have been posing is the interpretation of sovereignty adopted by theorists of cosmopolitical
democracy. Archibugi refers to sovereignty as an all-powerful and
absolute entity. While this view may perhaps be functional to his
justification of cosmopolitical democracy, it is very problematic.
Sovereignty inhabits an international juridical order and a permanent relationship of inter-state recognition. It is difficult to
even talk of sovereignty apart from the grammar of the international norms sovereignty inhabits. The conceptual pair
'inside'/'outside' designates a dialectical back and forth between
states and the international order, rather than a barrier delimiting
two distinct spatial dimensions. The international order is not an
empty space located outside states, in which atom-like states
fluctuate and conflict like in the Epicurean void, but an organism
comprising each and every state, outside of which states are
unthinkable. As per Kelsen, 'the legal order of each State, each
national legal order, is organically connected with the international legal order and through this order with every national
legal order, so that all legal orders merge into an integrated legal
system'.[34] According to this legal, and thus relational, conception
of sovereignty, each state exists within a delimited normative
order. Because it implies the presence of others, state sovereignty,
like individual sovereignty, is always limited. This is the very
condition of its existence. How would a cosmopolitical order
situate itself in relation to this comprehensive network of norms?
Would it be an additional agreement that obligates states morally,
or would it be a super-political decision-making entity that rules
over states and, if necessary, against them? In the latter case, it

would lack any peer to relate to, making it an unlimited sovereign, which is just as difficult to consider in the global sphere as it is in the case of single states. What makes the idea of cosmopolitical democracy so problematic is the nature of the global scene. As a political space, the global scene comprises interrelated issues rather than an integrated demos. Issues, not citizens, are or can become global. This fact is reflected in the vocabulary employed by scholars of globalization. Quite understandably, they prefer the word 'governance' to 'government'. Governance entails an explicit reference to 'mechanisms' or 'organized' and 'coordinated activities' appropriate to the solution of some specific problems.[35] Unlike government, governance refers to 'policies' rather than 'politics' because it is not a binding decision-making structure.[36] Its recipients are not 'the people' as a collective political subject, but 'the populations' that can be affected by global issues such as the environment, migration or the use of natural resources. Global governance is represented by a network of associations and interest groups; it relies on specific abilities and expertise, and refers to specific publics. In a word, its actors are united as a result of the problem(s) they are affected by and that they aim at solving. Interest groups, not the 'citizens of the world', are their multiple agencies. The desire for efficiency, security, justice and better organization drives the resolution to set up oversight bodies to screen decisions in particular vital areas. But these imperatives do not require a supranational government. They indicate the need for democracy 'within states' and 'between states' and the adoption of incentives to facilitate the democratic transitions of non-democratic states or to impede authoritarian involvement in weak democracies.[37] Moreover, they require the reform of international economic and financial institutions, which must be more responsive to the actual needs of the world's populations, and the evolution of international norms regulating modalities of global economic justice.[38]

    In conclusion, let me briefly mention a further set of problems that theorists of cosmopolitical democracy must approach with great care, as Robert Dahl has effectively and convincingly argued.[39] The word democracy may be used to define both a form of government as well as a political practice of participation. In its descriptive sense, democracy denotes a system of rules of the game that set and regulate the inclusion, whether direct or indirect, in the decision-making process of those who are supposed to obey the law, and the procedures according to which decisions are made, checked, implemented, and revised. So in this sense democracy refers to voting and electoral selection, entails majority rule, and presumes a view about what and how representation should represent, whether interests or persons. In any case, democracy is directly tied to the state.[40]

As the name of a political practice, however, the word democracy has a prescriptive meaning enriched by moral content in that it gives participation a formative and educative function. The value of the theory of public deliberation – which encompasses both the moment of decision and the process of consent formation and expression of ideas – is that it captures the complexity of democracy. It allows us to refer to democracy as a comprehensive world incorporating politics and civil society, government and social movements, political rights and civil rights, and the autonomous decision of a political community to deal with the problems it deems relevant to the maintenance of its democratic constitution.[41] The theory of deliberative democracy recognizes and justifies the role of public criticism and action on all the domestic and global decisions taken. This is the rationale for postnational democracy as global public opinion sphere.

However, although theorists of cosmopolitical democracy refer to the deliberative view in order to justify their proposals, they apply the descriptive definition and tie democracy to state-like institutions for decision-making practices. They propose to globalize parliamentary democracy and even political parties. They don't clarify how, given their reasonable dissatisfaction with the functioning of state-based democracies, a world order would be able to make democracy work better. Indeed, extension of territory has been a key factor contributing to the unsatisfactory performance of representative democracy. When representation and political parties are transferred to the world level – as Archibugi proposes – all the 'vices' that have plagued modern parliamentary democracy since its inception would be transferred along with those institutions.[42] These 'vices' include the problem of enforcing accountability of elected representatives, the potential for development of an elected oligarchy, and the growth of hierarchical structures of consent formation.[43] As the process of European integration shows, the extension of democracy beyond state borders implies the following unavoidable paradox: it allows for more participation, but can also give rise to a proliferation of powers that *de facto* decrease the chance of an effective control and coordination, and finally participation itself.[44] Wouldn't 'the citizens of the world' just legitimate an extraordinarily powerful distant elite that is exceptionally free from control? Theorists of cosmopolitical democracy should take Dahl's admonishment seriously on the obstacles to democratic accountability, and thus the risks of an unchecked delegated politics, that a global extension of the political space is likely to imply. A 'democratic' cannot 'in good conscience support such delegation of power and authority by democratic countries to international organizations and institutions. . . To speak in this case of "delegating authority" would simply be a misleading fiction useful only to the rulers.'[45]

## Notes

1. Daniele Archibugi, 'Cosmopolitical Democracy', *New Left Review*, second series, no. 4, July–Aug 2000, p. 144 (chapter 1 in this volume).

2. 'Typically, in this conception, a subjunctive "ought" contains a normative "is"'; Timothy Brennan, 'Cosmopolitanism and Internationalism,' *New Left Review*, second series, no. 7, January–February 2001, p. 76 (chapter 4 in this volume).

3. On the cultural interchange and global interdependence as enrichment of the culture of individuality as a value, see Jeremy Waldron, 'Minority Cultures and the Cosmopolitan Alternative', in Will Kymlicka, ed., *The Rights of Minority Cultures*, Oxford 1995, pp. 93–121.

4. Jürgen Habermas, 'The Postnational Constellation and the Future of Democracy', in id., *The Postnational Constellation: Political Essays*, trans. Max Pensky, Cambridge, MA 2001, p. 59.

5. Richard Falk, *On Human Governance: Toward a New Global Politics*, University Park, PA 1995, and 'The United Nations and Cosmopolitan Democracy: Bad Dream, Utopian Fantasy, Political Project', in Daniele Archibugi, David Held and Martin Köhler, eds, *Re-imagining Political Community*, Cambridge 1998, pp. 309–31.

6. On the 'cost' of individual rights in terms of governmental agencies capable of providing each citizen for 'an opportunity to be heard before an impartial body' and an effective public system borne by the taxpayers, and thus subject to public accountability see Stephen Holmes and Cass R. Sunstein, *The Cost of Rights: Why Liberty Depends on Taxes*, New York & London 1999, in particular pp. 35–76.

7. David Held, 'Democracy and Globalization', in *Re-imagining Political Community*, p. 22.

8. The 'exemplary case of the European Union' is used 'to test the conditions for a democratic politics beyond the nation-state'; Habermas, 'The Postnational Constellation and the Future of Democracy', p. 62.

9. The threshold between democratic nationality (as the basic condition for a democratic Europe) and nation-state nationalism was established in 1849, when the unification of the main Continental countries was achieved by monarchical armies through the repression of the democratic movements for national self-determination. Fascism grew up precisely in those countries (Italy and Germany) that conquered state unity by means of a violent disassociation of nationality and democracy. See Nadia Urbinati, ' "A Common Law of Nations": Giuseppe Mazzini's democratic nationality', *Journal of Modern Italian Studies*, vol. 1, no. 2, 1996, pp. 197–222.

10. Jürgen Habermas, 'Why Europe needs a Constitution', *New Left Review*, no. 11, September–October 2001, pp. 3–26.

11. Ulrich K. Preuss, 'Citizenship in the European Union: A Paradigm for Transnational Democracy?,' in *Re-imagining Political Community*, p. 149.

12. Habermas, 'The Postnational Constellation and the Future of Democracy', pp. 107–10.

Similar is the view of Will Kymlicka who thus insists on the need to distinguish between democratic nationality and nationalism, and to reconcile the former with cosmopolitanism (*Politics in the Vernacular: Nationalism, Multiculturalism, and Citizenship*, Oxford 2001, chapters 10 and 11).

13. Hence, Habermas' cosmopolitan Kelsenianism is a strategy that aims at preserving the national articulation of democracy rather than dissolving it. This emerges from a comparison of two of his most recent essays on cosmopolitanism: 'Kant's Idea of Perpetual Peace: At Two Hundred Years' Historical Remove' (in *The Inclusion of the Other: Study in Political Theory*, edited by Ciaran Cronin and Pablo De Greiff, Cambridge, MA 1999, pp. 167–201) and the already mentioned 'The Postnational Constellation and the Future of Democracy'. Habermas' acknowledgment that democracy cannot avoid a 'self-referential' concept of collective self-determination' situates him in a position of mediation between Carl Schmitt and Hans Kelsen. But the point of view that Habermas' readers seem keener to stress is the 'antagonism' between him and the Crown Jurists of the Third Reich; see, for instance, Brett R. Wheeler, 'Law and Legitimacy in the Work of Jürgen Habermas and Carl Schmitt', *Ethics & International Affairs*, vol. 15, 2001, pp. 175–9.

14. See Jean Cohen, 'Changing Paradigms of Citizenship and the Exclusiveness of the Demos', *International Sociology*, vol. 14, 1999, p. 260.

15. Hedley Bull, *The Anarchical Society: A Study of Order in World Politics*, New York 1977, p. 254.

16. Held, *Democracy and the Global Order*, pp. 267–87 and 'Democracy and Globalization', in *Re-imagining Political Community*, p. 25.

17. Daniele Archibugi, 'Principles of Cosmopolitan Democracy', in *Re-imagining Political Community*, p. 221.

18. 'The extension of "international justice" is, in short, the abolition of international law. For there can be no international law without equal sovereignty, no system of right without state-subjects capable of being its bearers. In a world composed of nation-states, rather than a single global power, universal law can only derive from national governments'; David Chandler, ' "International Justice" ', *New Left Review*, second series, no. 6, November–December 2000, p. 63 (chapter 3 in this volume).

19. Archibugi, 'Principles of Cosmopolitan Democracy', p. 218. For a discussion on principles of non-intervention and intervention in relation to

the UN peacemaking strategies and international law, see Michael Doyle, 'The New Interventionism', *Metaphilosophy*, vol. 32, 2001, pp. 212–35.

20. Archibugi, 'Principles of Cosmopolitan Democracy', p. 199.

21. Immanuel Kant, *Perpetual Peace: A Philosophical Sketch* (1795), in *Political Writings*, edited by Hans Reiss, Cambridge 1991, pp. 105–106.

22. Archibugi, 'Cosmopolitical Democracy', pp. 138–9.

23. Ibid., pp. 143–5.

24. See Norberto Bobbio, 'Democracy and the International System', in Daniele Archibugi and David Held, eds, *Cosmopolitan Democracy: An Agenda for a New World Order*, Cambridge 1995, pp. 17–18.

25. Chandler, ' "International Justice" ', pp. 60–62.

26. Theorists of cosmopolitical democracy might face this objection by resorting to the 'power of numbers' over that of might. Whereas in a *disordered* international order, the military superiority of the United States is unbridled, in a world parliament where only votes count, the United States would have to face the fact that it does not dispose of numerical majority. However, as the history of state sovereignty shows, for votes to have an effective power a Leviathan must first 'confiscate all weapons'. (I thank Daniele Archibugi for discussing this issue with me.)

27. Habermas, 'Kant's Idea of Perpetual Peace', p. 170.

28. On the autocratic implications of cosmopolis see Danilo Zolo, *Cosmopolis: Prospects for World Government*, trans. David McKie, Cambridge 1997.

29. Archibugi, 'Cosmopolitical Democracy', pp. 145 and 149; David Held, 'The Transformation of Political Community: Rethinking Democracy in the Context of Globalization', in Ian Shapiro and Casiano Hacker-Cordón, eds, *Democracy's Edges*, Cambridge 1999, pp. 91–102.

30. Daniele Archibugi, David Held and Martin Köhler, Introduction to *Re-imagining Political Community*, p. 4.

31. Archibugi, 'Cosmopolitical Democracy', p. 137.

32. Ibid., pp. 137–8.

33. Ibid., p. 145.

34. Hans Kelsen, *General Theory of Law and State*, trans. Anders Wedberg, Cambridge, MA 1945, p. 354. 'Even if all international law had the character of contractual law, it would not be possible to maintain the idea that States are sovereign because they are not subject to a superior legal order restricting its will. For the rule *pacta sunt servanda*, the legal basis of all international treaties, as a rule of positive international law, corresponds only in a limited way to the principle of autonomy.'

35. James N. Rosenau, 'Governance and Democracy in a Globalizing World', in *Re-imagining Political Community*, pp. 30–32.

36. John S. Dryzek, *Deliberative Democracy and Beyond: Liberals, Critics, Contestations*, Oxford 2000, p. 120.

37. See, for instance, the proposals elaborated by Thomas Pogge, 'Achieving Democracy', *Ethics and International Affairs*, vol. 15, 2001, pp. 3–23.

38. Andrew Hurrell, 'Global Inequality and International Institutions', *Metaphilosophy*, vol. 32, 2001, pp. 34–57; but see the entire issue which is dedicated to 'Global Justice'.

39. Robert Dahl, 'Can International Organizations be Democratic? A Skeptic's View', in *Democracy's Edges*, pp. 19–36.

40. Norberto Bobbio, *Democracy and Dictatorship*, trans. Peter Kennealy,

Cambridge 1989, pp. 133–55. Bobbio's minimal procedural definition or descriptive definition has been endorsed by Adam Pzreworski, *Democracy and the Market: Political and Economic Reforms in Eastern Europe and Latin America*, Cambridge 1997, pp. 10–14.

41. Literature on deliberative democracy is vast. I limit myself to mention two of Habermas' most recent articles on the subject: 'Three Normative Models of Democracy' and 'On the Internal Relation between the Rule of Law and Democracy', in *The Inclusion of the Other*, pp. 239–64.

42. Geoffrey Hawthorn, 'Running the World through Windows', *New Left Review*, second series, no. 5, September–October 2000, pp. 103–104 (chapter 2 in this volume).

43. John Dunn, 'Situating Democratic Political Accountability', in Adam Przeworski, Susan C. Stokes, Bernard Manin, eds, *Democracy, Accountability, and Representation*, Cambridge 1999, pp. 329–43.

44. See Dennis Thompson, 'Democratic Theory and Global Society', *Journal of Political Philosophy*, vol. 7, no. 2, 1999, pp. 111–25.

45. Dahl, 'Can International Organizations be Democratic?', p. 22.

# 7

# The Class Consciousness
# of Frequent Travellers:
# Towards a Critique of Actually
# Existing Cosmopolitanism[1]

*Craig Calhoun*

Some claim that the world is gradually becoming united, that it will grow into a brotherly community as distances shrink and ideas are transmitted through the air. Alas, you must not believe that men can be united in this way.

Fyodor Dostoevsky, 1880

A certain attenuated cosmopolitanism had taken place of the old home feeling.

Thomas Carlyle, 1857

Among the great struggles of man – good/evil, reason/ unreason, etc. – there is also this mighty conflict between the fantasy of Home and the fantasy of Away, the dream of roots and the mirage of the journey.

Salman Rushdie, 2000

On September 11 2001, terrorists crashing jets into the World Trade Center and the Pentagon struck a blow against cosmopolitanism – perhaps more successfully than against their obvious symbolic targets, the unequal structures of global capitalism and political power. They precipitated a renewal of state-centred politics and a 'war on terrorism' seeking military rather than law enforcement solutions to crime. Moved by Wahabbi Islamic Puritanism and sheltered by Afghanistan's Taliban, they seemed to exemplify a simplistic opposition between backward traditionalists and Western modernism. That Muslims had long been stereotyped as the bad other to globalization only made it easier for Westerners to accept this dubious framing of the events, and made it harder for them to see a clash between different modernist projects, to miss the evidently popular message that 'technology can be our weapon too'.

One need be no friend to terrorism to be sorry that the dominant response to the terrorist attacks has been framed as a matter of war rather than crime, an attack on America rather than an attack on humanity. What could have been an occasion for renewing the drive to establish an international criminal court and multilateral institutions needed for law enforcement quickly became an occasion for America to demonstrate its power and its allies to fall into line with the 'war against terrorism'. Militarism gained and civil society lost not only on September 11 but in the response that followed.[2] This was true domestically as well as internationally, as the US and other administrations moved to sweep aside protections for the rights of citizens and immigrants alike and strengthen the state in pursuit of 'security'.

In this context, the cosmopolitan ideals articulated during the 1990s seem all the more attractive but their realization much less immanent. It is important not only to mourn this, but to ask in what ways the cosmopolitan vision itself was limited – overoptimistic, perhaps, more attentive to certain prominent dimensions of globalization than to equally important others. In the wake of the Cold War, it seemed to many political theorists and public actors that the moment had finally arrived not just for Kantian perpetual peace but for cosmopolitanism to extend beyond mere tolerance to the creation of a shared global democracy. It seemed easy to denigrate states as old-fashioned authorities of waning influence and to extol the virtues of international civil society. It was perhaps a weakness of this perspective that the myriad dimensions of globalization all seemed evidence of the need for a more cosmopolitan order, and therefore the tensions among them were insufficiently examined. Likewise, the cosmopolitanism of democratic activists was not always clearly distinct from that of global corporate leaders, though the latter would exempt corporate property from democratic control. Just as protesters against the WTO often portrayed themselves as 'anti-globalization', even though they formed a global social movement, advocates of cosmopolitan institutions often sounded simply pro-globalization rather than sufficiently discriminating among its forms.

In a sense, the non-cosmopolitan side of globalization struck back on September 11. Migrants whose visions of their home cultures were more conservative and ideological than the original settlers figured prominently. Indeed, most of the terrorists were Arabs who had spent a considerable time studying in the West – even at seemingly cosmopolitan Oxford, in the case of Osama bin Laden. A dark side to globalization was brought to light: criminal activity and flows of weapons, people, ideas, money and drugs that challenged state authority but hardly in the name of international civil society, and sometimes financed terrorist networks. At the same time, the sharp inequalities masked by cosmopolitan ideals – and especially the use of cosmopolitan rhetoric by neo-liberal corporate leaders whose actions contribute to those inequalities – challenged efforts to 'solve' terrorism as a problem separate from others.

This paper is an effort to examine some of the limits and biases of the cosmopolitan theory that flourished in the 1990s. It is written not in rejection of cosmopolitanism, but as a challenge to think through more fully what sorts of social bases have shaped cosmopolitan visions and what sorts of issues need more attention if advances in democracy are to be made. What experiences make cosmopolitan democracy an intuitively appealing approach to the world? What experiences does it obscure from view? I want also to consider how much the political theory of cosmopolitanism is shaped by liberalism's poorly drawn fight with communitarianism and thus left lacking a strong account of solidarity. This impedes efforts to defend the achievements of previous social struggles against neo-liberal capitalism, or to ground new political action. Finally, I wish to offer a plea for the importance of the local and particular – not least as a basis for democracy, no less important for being necessarily incomplete. Whatever its failings, 'the old home feeling' helped to produce a sense of mutual obligations, of 'moral economy', to borrow the phrase Edward Thompson retrieved from an old tradition.[3]

## Cosmopolitanism, old and new

Cosmopolitanism today partly resumes its own old tradition. Cosmopolitan ideals flourished as calls for unity among ancient Greek city-states, though in fact these were often at war. Rome was more cosmopolitan if less philosophical than Greece. Cosmopolitanism has been a project of empires, of long-distance trade, and of cities. Christianity offered a cosmopolitan framework to medieval Europe, though it equally informed a non-cosmopolitan rejection of those it deemed heretics and heathens. The Ottoman Empire offered a high point of cosmopolitanism, and European empires their own often less tolerant versions. But the cosmopolitanism of Church and empire depended on the distinction of merchants and clerics from rulers. It is thus an innovation to see cosmopolitanism as a political project and especially to speak of 'cosmopolitan democracy'. The tolerance of diversity in great imperial and trading cities has always reflected, among other things, precisely the absence of need or opportunity to organize political self-rule.

A new cosmopolitanism flourished in the Enlightenment. This once again involved relative élites without a responsibility for ruling. It did nonetheless influence rulers, not least by encouraging a courtly cosmopolitanism in the later years of the ancient regime. There were also cosmopolitan links among democrats and other insurgents, and these contributed to the ideals of the late eighteenth-century public sphere. Nationalism and cosmopolitanism met in certain strands of the American and French revolutions and linked to democracy in figures like Thomas Paine. But eighteenth-century cosmopolitanism, especially its élite variants, was hostile to religion, and in opposing reason to prejudice often imagined a collective life free of traditional loyalties rather than incorporating them in heterogeneous form. Philosophical cosmopolitans of the Enlightenment imagined a world reflecting their lives and intellectual projects. During the same period, though, European colonial projects were becoming increasingly important. They informed both the development of nationalism and that of cosmopolitanism, the view of both home and away. While some nineteenth-century thinkers embraced cosmopolitanism as an urban aesthetic ideal, others, like Thomas Carlyle, were ambivalent about cosmopolitanism. They worried that it was somehow an 'attenuated' solidarity by comparison to those rooted in more specific local cultures and communities.

Today's cosmopolitans need to confront the same concerns. Many rightly point to the limits and dangers of relying on nation-states to secure democracy in a world which is ever-more dramatically organized across state borders. Yet they – we – imagine the world from the vantage point of frequent travellers, easily entering and exiting polities and social relations around the world, armed with visa-friendly passports and credit cards. For such frequent travellers cosmopolitanism has considerable rhetorical advantage. It seems hard not to want to be a 'citizen of the world'. Certainly, at least in Western academic circles, it is hard to imagine preferring to be known as parochial. But what does it mean to be a 'citizen of the world'? Through what institutions is this 'citizenship' effectively expressed? Is it mediated through various particular, more local solidarities? Does it present a new, expanded category of identification as better than older, narrower ones (as the nation has frequently been opposed to the province or village) or does it pursue better relations among a diverse range of traditions and communities? How does this citizenship contend with global capitalism and with non-cosmopolitan dimensions of globalization?

A thoroughgoing cosmopolitanism might indeed bring concern for the fate of all humanity to the fore, but a more attenuated cosmopolitanism is likely to leave us lacking the old sources of solidarity without adequate new ones. Much cosmopolitanism focuses on the development of world government or at least global political institutions. These, advocates argue, must be strengthened if democracy is to have much future in a world where nation-states are challenged by global capitalism, cross-border flows and international media and accordingly less able to manage collective affairs.[4] At the same time, these advocates see growing domestic heterogeneity and newly divisive subnational politics as reducing the efficacy of nation-states from within. While most embrace diversity as a basic value, they simultaneously see multiculturalism as a political problem. In the dominant cosmopolitan theories, it is the global advance of democracy that receives most attention and in which most hopes are vested. But cosmopolitanism without the strengthening of local democracy is likely to be a very élite affair. And advances in global democracy are challenged by fragmented solidarities at both intermediate and local levels.

## Place and perspective

Cosmopolitanism is often presented simply as global citizenship. Advocates offer a claim to being without determinate social bases that is reminiscent of Mannheim's idea of the free-floating intellectual. In offering a seeming 'view from nowhere', cosmopolitans commonly offer a view from Brussels (where the postnational is identified with the strength of the European Union rather than the weakness of, say, African states), or from Davos (where the postnational is corporate), or from the university (where the illusion of a free-floating intelligentsia is supported by a relatively fluid exchange of ideas across national borders).

Cosmopolitanism is a discourse centred in a Western view of the world.[5] It sets itself up commonly as a 'Third Way' between rampant corporate globalization and reactionary traditionalism or nationalism. If Giddens' account of the Third Way is most familiar, the trope is still more widespread. Barber's notion of a path beyond 'Jihad vs. McWorld' is an example brought to renewed prominence (and the best-seller lists) following the September 11 attacks.[6] Such oppositions oversimplify at best, though, and often get in the way of actually achieving some of the goals of cosmopolitan democracy. In the first place, they reflect a problematic denigration of tradition, including ethnicity and religion. This can be misleading in even a sheer factual sense – as for example Barber's description of Islamism as the reaction of small and relatively homogeneous countries to capitalist globalization. The oppositions are also prejudicial. Note, for example, the tendency to treat the West as the site of both capitalist globalization and cosmopolitanism but to approach the rest of the world through the category of tradition. More generally, cultural identities and communal solidarities are treated less as creative constructions forged amid globalization than as inheritances from an older order. They should be available to people, much cosmopolitan thought implies, as lifestyle choices. As Brennan puts it, cosmopolitanism 'designates an enthusiasm for customary differences, but as ethical or aesthetic material for a unified polychromatic culture – a new singularity born of a blending and merging of

multiple local constituents'.[7] This vision of unity amid difference
echoes on a grander scale that of great empires and great
religions, and it underwrites the cosmopolitan appeal for all-
encompassing world government.[8]

Cosmopolitanism also reflects an élite perspective on the
world. Certainly few academic theories escape this charge, but it
is especially problematic when the object of theory is the potential
for democracy. The top ranks of capitalist corporations provide
exemplars of a certain form of cosmopolitanism, though not of
democracy. Likewise, a large proportion of global civil society –
from the World Bank to non-governmental organizations setting
accountancy standards – exists to support capitalism not pursue
democracy. Even the ideas of cosmopolitan democracy and
humanitarian activism, however, reflect an awareness of the world
that is made possible by the proliferation of non-governmental
organizations working to solve environmental and humanitarian
problems, and by the growth of media attention to those problems. These are important – indeed vital – concerns. Nonetheless,
the concerns, the media, and the NGOs need to be grasped
reflexively as the basis for an intellectual perspective. It is a
perspective, for example, that makes nationalism appear one-
sidedly as negative. This is determined first perhaps by the
prominence of ethnonationalist violence in recent humanitarian
crises, but also by the tensions between states and international
NGOs. It is also shaped by specifically European visions and
projects of transnationalism. Nationalism looks different from,
say, an African vantage point. And it is often the weakness of
states which seems the most pressing problem, even if tyrants
control those relatively weak states.

The cosmopolitan ideals of global civil society can sound
uncomfortably like those of the civilizing mission behind colonialism, especially when presented as a programme from the outside borne by global NGOs rather than an opportunity for local
development. In this connection, we should recall how recent,
temporary, and ever incomplete the apparent autonomy and
closure of 'nation' is. In Europe, the invocation of 'nation' may
sound conservative and traditional (though it was not always so).
Looked at from the standpoint of India, say, or Ethiopia, it is not
at all clear whether 'nation' belongs on the side of tradition or
on that of developing cosmopolitanism. Or is it perhaps distinct

from both – a novel form of solidarity and a basis for political claims on the state, one which presumes and to some extent demands performance of internal unity and external boundedness?

The very idea of democracy suggests that it cannot be imposed from above, simply as a matter of rational plan. Democracy must grow out of the lifeworld; it must empower people not in the abstract but in the actual conditions of their lives. This means to empower them within communities and traditions, not in spite of them, and as members of groups not only as individuals. This does not mean accepting old definitions of all groups; there may be struggle over how groups are constituted. For example, appeals to aboriginal rights need not negate the possibility of struggle within 'traditional' groups over such issues as gender bias in leadership.[9] Cosmopolitan democracy – refusing the unity of simple sameness and the tyranny of the majority – must demand attention to differences – of values, perceptions, interests, and understandings.

Yet it is important that we recognize that legitimacy is not the same as motivation. We need to pay attention to the social contexts in which people are moved by commitments to each other. Cosmopolitanism that does so will be variously articulated with locality, community, and tradition, not simply a matter of common denominators. It will depend to a very large extent on local and particularistic border crossings and pluralisms, not universalism.

Such cosmopolitanism would both challenge the abandonment of globalization to neo-liberalism (whether with enthusiasm or a sense of helpless pessimism) and question the impulse to respond simply by defending nations or communities that experience globalization as a threat. Nonetheless, the power of states and global corporations and the systemic imperatives of global markets suggest that advancing democracy will require struggle. This means not only struggle against states or corporations, but struggle within them to determine the way they work as institutions, how they distribute benefits, what kinds of participation they invite. The struggle for democracy, accordingly, cannot be only a cosmopolitan struggle from social locations that transcend these domains, it must be also a local struggle within them. It would be a mistake to imagine that cosmopolitan ethics – universally applied – could somehow substitute for a multiplicity of political, economic, and cultural struggles. Indeed, the very struggle may be an occasion and source for solidarity.

## Liberalism and belonging

Contemporary cosmopolitanism is the latest effort to revitalize liberalism.[10] It has much to recommend it. Aside from world peace and more diverse ethnic restaurants, there is the promise to attend to one of the great lacunae of more traditional liberalism. This is the assumption of nationality as the basis for membership in states, even though this implies a seemingly illiberal reliance on inheritance and ascription rather than choice, and an exclusiveness hard to justify on liberal terms.

Political theory has surprisingly often avoided addressing the problems of political belonging in a serious, analytic way by presuming that nations exist as the prepolitical bases of state-level politics. I do not mean that political theorists are nationalists in their political preferences, but rather that their way of framing analytic problems is shaped by the rhetoric of nationalism and the ways in which this has become basic to the modern social imaginary.[11] 'Let us imagine a society', theoretical deliberations characteristically begin, 'and then consider what form of government would be just for it.' Nationalism provides this singular and bounded notion of society with its intuitive meaning.

Even so Kantian, methodologically individualistic, and generally non-nationalist a theorist as John Rawls exemplifies the standard procedure, seeking in *A Theory of Justice* to understand what kind of society individuals behind the veil of ignorance would choose – but presuming that they would imagine this society on the model of a nation-state. Rawls modifies his arguments in considering international affairs in *Political Liberalism* and *The Law of Peoples*, but continues to assume something like an idealized nation-state as the natural form of society. As he writes:

> ... we have assumed that a democratic society, like any political society, is to be viewed as a complete and closed social system. It is complete in that it is self-sufficient and has a place for all the main purposes of human life. It is also closed, in that entry into it is only by birth and exit from it is only by death.[12]

Rawls is aware of migration, war, and global media, of course, even while he rules them out of theory and even though it is striking how little he considers the globalization of economic foundations for his imagined society. For Rawls, questions of international justice seem to be just as that phrase and much diplomatic practice implies: questions 'between peoples', each of which should be understood as unitary. Note also the absence of attention to local or other constituent communities within this conception of society. Individuals and the whole society have a kind of primacy over any other possible groupings. This is the logic of nationalism.[13]

This is precisely what cosmopolitanism contests – at least at its best – and rightly so. Indeed, one of the reasons given for the very term is that it is less likely than 'international' to be confused with exclusively intergovernmental relations.[14] Advocates of cosmopolitanism argue that people belong to a range of polities of which nation-states are only one, and that the range of significant relationships formed across state borders is growing. Their goal is to extend citizenship rights and responsibilities to the full range of associations thus created. In David Held's words,

> people would come, thus, to enjoy multiple citizenships – political membership in the diverse political communities which significantly affected them. They would be citizens of their immediate political communities, and of the wider regional and global networks which impacted upon their lives.[15]

Though it is unclear how this might work out in practice, this challenge to the presumption of nationality as the basis for citizenship is one of the most important contributions of cosmopolitanism (and cosmopolitanism is strongest when it takes this seriously, weakest when it recommends the leap to a more centralized world government).

The cosmopolitan tension with the assumption of nation as the prepolitical basis for citizenship is domestic as well as international. As Jürgen Habermas puts it,

> the nation-state owes its historical success to the fact that it substituted relations of solidarity between the citizens for the disintegrating corporative ties of early modern society. But this republican achievement is endangered when, conversely, the integrative force of the nation of citizens is traced back to the prepolitical fact of a quasi-

natural people, that is, to something independent of and prior to the
political opinion- and will-formation of the citizens themselves.[16]

But pause here and notice the temporal order implied in this
passage. *First* there were local communities, guilds, religious bodies, and other 'corporative bonds'. *Then* there was republican
citizenship with its emphasis on the civic identity of each citizen.
*Then* this was undermined by ethnonationalism. What this misses
is the extent to which each of these ways of organizing social life
existed simultaneously with the others, sometimes in struggle and
sometimes symbiotically. New 'corporative ties' have been created,
for example, notably in the labour movement and in religious
communities. Conversely, there was no 'pure republican' moment
when ideas of nationality did not inform the image of the republic
and the constitution of its boundaries.

As Habermas goes on, however, 'the question arises of whether
there exists a functional equivalent for the fusion of the nation of
citizens with the ethnic nation'.[17] We need not accept his idealized history or entire theoretical framework to see that this raises
a basic issue. That is, for polities not constructed as ethnic nations,
what makes membership compelling? This is a question for the
European Union, certainly, but also arguably for the United States
itself, and for most projects of cosmopolitan citizenship. Democracy requires a sense of mutual commitment among citizens that
goes beyond mere legal classification, holding a passport, or even
respect for particular institutions. As Charles Taylor has argued
forcefully, 'self-governing societies' have need 'of a high degree
of cohesion'.[18]

Cosmopolitanism needs an account of how social solidarity and
public discourse might develop enough in these wider networks
to become the basis for active citizenship. So far, most versions of
cosmopolitan theory share with traditional liberalism a thin conception of social life, commitment, and belonging. They imagine
society – and issues of social belonging and social participation –
in too thin and casual a manner. The result is a theory that suffers
from an inadequate sociological foundation. Communitarianism
is more sociological in inspiration, but often suffers from an
inverse error, a tendency to elide the differences between local
networks of social relationships and broad categories of belonging
like nations.

The cosmopolitan image of multiple, layered citizenship can helpfully challenge the tendency of many communitarians to suggest not only that community is necessary and/or good, but that people normally inhabit one and only one community.[19] It also points to the possibility – so far not realized – of a rapprochement between cosmopolitanism and communitarianism. As Bellamy and Castiglione write, hoping to bridge the opposition between cosmopolitanism and communitarianism, 'a pure cosmopolitanism cannot generate the full range of obligations its advocates generally wish to ascribe to it. For the proper acknowledgement of "thin" basic rights rests on their being specified and overlaid by a "thicker" web of special obligations'.[20] They would strengthen Held's suggestion that persons inhabit not only rights and obligations, but also relationships and commitments within and across groups of all sorts including the nation.

More often, however, cosmopolitans have treated communitarianism as an enemy, or at least used it as a foil.[21] Despite this, advocates of cosmopolitan democracy find themselves falling back on notions of 'peoples' as though these exist naturally and prepolitically. They appeal, for example, for the representation of peoples – not only states – in various global projects including an eventual world parliament.[22] This poses deeper problems than is commonly realized. Not only is the definition of 'people' problematic, the idea of representation is extremely complex. Representing peoples has been one of the primary functions of modern states – however great the problems with how they do it. Advocates for 'peoples' represent them in the media and claim to represent them even in terrorist action. But it is the legal and political procedures of states and the relatively cohesive public spheres associated with them that provide effective checks on unstated claims to represent others and tie mediatic images to concrete policy choices. Absent state-like forms of explicit self-governance, it is not clear how the representation of peoples escapes arbitrariness.

Cosmopolitan democracy requires not only a stronger account of representation, but also a stronger account of social solidarity and the formation and transformation of social groups. If one of its virtues is challenging the idea that nationality (or ethnic or other identities understood as analogous to nationality) provides people with an unambiguous and singular collective membership, one of its faults is to conceptualize the alternative too abstractly and vaguely. Another is to underestimate the positive side of nationalism, the virtues of identification with a larger whole. This can indeed be oppressive and anti-democratic. But it can also be the source of mutual commitment and solidarity underpinning democracy and uniting people across a range of differences. Moreover, whatever its limits, the nation-state has proved more open to democratization than religions or some other kinds of large groupings.

## Solidarity

In cosmopolitanism as in much other political theory and demo-cratic thought generally, there is a tendency to assume that social groups are created in some prepolitical process – as nations, for example, ethnicities, religions, or local communities. They reflect historical accident, inheritance, and necessity. They result per-haps from the accumulation of unintended consequences of purposive action, but they are not in themselves chosen. Surely, though, this is not always so.

The social solidarity that makes social commitments compel-ling is indeed shaped by forms of integration, like markets, that link people systemically, by force of necessity, or as it were 'behind their backs'. It is also shaped by material power, as for example modern economic life is a matter not only of markets but of corporations and state regulation. Clearly, it is informed by shared culture and by categorical identities like race, ethnicity, class, and nation. And crucially it is built out of networks of directly inter-personal social relations, such as those basic to local community. The last already suggests the importance of choice: community is not just inherited, it is made and remade – and interpersonal relationships are also basic to social movements. More generally, though, we should recognize the importance of public discourse as a source of social solidarity, mutual commitment, and shared interest. Neither individuals nor social groups are fully or finally formed in advance of public discourse. People's identities and understandings of the world are changed by participation in public discourse. Groups are created not just found and the forms of group life are at least potentially open to choice.[23]

Public discourse is not simply a matter of finding pre-existing common interests, in short, nor of developing strategies for acting on inherited identities; it is also in and of itself a form of solidarity. The women's movement offers a prominent example; it transformed identities, it did not just express the interests of women whose identities were set in advance. It created both an arena of discourse among women and a stronger voice for women in discourses that were male dominated (even when they were ostensibly gender neutral). The solidarity formed among women had to do with the capacity of this discourse meaningfully to bridge concerns of private life and large-scale institutions and culture. We can also see the inverse, the extent to which this gendered production of solidarity is changed as feminist public discourse is replaced by mass-marketing to women and the production of feminism's successor as a gendered consumer identity in which liberation is reduced to freedom to purchase.

In short, there are a variety of ways in which people are joined to each other, within and across the boundaries of states and other polities. Theorists of cosmopolitan democracy are right to stress the multiplicity of connections. But we need to complement the liberal idea of rights with a stronger sense of what binds people to each other. One of the peculiarities of nation-states has been the extent to which they were able to combine elements of each of these different sorts of solidarity. They did not do so perfectly, of course. Markets flowed over their borders from the beginning, and some states were weak containers of either economic organization or power. Not all states had a populace with a strong national identity, or pursued policies able to shape a common identity among citizens. Indeed, those that repressed public discourse suffered a particular liability to fissure along the lines of ethnicity or older national identities weakly amalgamated into the new whole; the Soviet Union is a notable case. Conversely, though, the opportunity to participate in a public sphere and seek to influence the state was an important source of solidarity within it.

Actually existing international civil society includes some level of each of the different forms of solidarity I listed. In very few cases, however, are these joined strongly to each other at a transnational level. There is community among the expatriate staffs of NGOs; there is public discourse on the Internet. But few of the categorical identities that express people's sense of themselves are matched to strong organizations of either power or community at a transnational level. What this means is that international civil society offers a weak counterweight to systemic integration and power. If hopes for cosmopolitan democracy are to be realized, they depend on developing more social solidarity.

As I have emphasized, such solidarity can be at least partially chosen through collective participation in the public sphere. It is unlikely, however, that solidarity can be entirely a matter of choice. This is the import of Habermas' question about whether the nation of citizens can fully replace the ethnic nation. It is a problem to rely heavily on a purely political conception of human beings. Such a conception has two weak points. First, it does not attend enough to all the ways in which solidarity is achieved outside of political organization, and does not adequately appreciate the bearing of these networks on questions of political legitimacy. Second, it does not consider the extent to which high political ideals founder on the shoals of everyday needs and desires – including quite legitimate ones. The ideal of civil society has sometimes been expressed in recent years as though it should refer to a constant mobilization of all of us all the time in various sorts of voluntary organizations.[24] But in fact one of the things people quite reasonably want from a good political order is to be left alone some of the time – to enjoy a non-political life in civil society. In something of the same sense, Oscar Wilde famously said of socialism that it requires too many evenings. We could say of cosmopolitanism that it requires too much travel, too many dinners out at ethnic restaurants, too much volunteering with *Médecins Sans Frontières*. Perhaps not too much or too many for academics (though I wouldn't leap to that presumption) but too much and too many to base a political order on the expectation that everyone will choose to participate – even if they acknowledge that they *ought* to.

A good political order must deal fairly with the fact that most people will not be politically active most of the time. That actually existing politics turn many people off only makes the issue more acute. But for cosmopolitan democracy, scale is the biggest issue. Participation rates are low in local and national politics; there is good reason to think that the very scale of the global ecumene will make participation in it even narrower and more a province of élites than participation in national politics. Not only does

Michels' law of oligarchy apply, if perhaps not with the iron force he imagined, but the capacities to engage cosmopolitan politics – from literacy to computer literacy to familiarity with the range of acronyms – are apt to continue to be unevenly distributed. Indeed, there are less commonly noted but significant inequalities directly tied to locality. Within almost any social movement or activist NGO, as one moves from the local to the national and global in either public actions or levels of internal organization one sees a reduction in women's participation. Largely because so much labour of social reproduction – child care, for instance – is carried out by women, women find it harder to work outside of their localities. This is true even for social movements in which women predominate at the local level.[25]

## Rationalism and difference

Contemporary cosmopolitan theory is attentive to the diversity of people's social engagements and connections. But this cosmopolitanism is also rooted in seventeenth- and eighteenth-century rationalism with its ethical universalism.[26] Modern cosmopolitanism took shape largely in opposition to traditional religion and more generally to deeply rooted political identities. Against the force of universal reason, the claims of traditional culture and communities were deemed to have little standing. These were at best particularistic, local understandings that grasped universal truths only inaccurately and partially. At worst, they were outright errors, the darkness which the Enlightenment challenged. Certainly, the sixteenth- and seventeenth-century wars of faith seemed to cry out for universalistic reason and a cosmopolitan outlook. Yet, nationalism was as important a result as cosmopolitanism and the two developed often hand-in-hand. Religion sometimes divided nations, but nations also provided a secular framework for achieving unity across religious lines.

Early modern rationalism was also rich with contractarian metaphors and embedded in the social imaginary of a nascent commercial culture. It approached social life on the basis of a proto-utilitarian calculus, an idea of individual interests as the basis of judgement, and a search for the one right solution. Its emphasis on individual autonomy, whatever its other merits, was deployed with a blind eye to the differences and distortions of private property. The claims of community appeared often as hindrances on individuals. They were justified mainly when community was abstracted to the level of nation, and the wealth of nations made the focus of political as well as economic attention. Much of this heritage has been absorbed into contemporary liberalism, including the political theory of cosmopolitan democracy.

Like the earlier vision of cosmopolis, the current one responds to international conflict and crisis. It offers an attractive sense of shared responsibility for developing a better society and transcending both the interests and intolerance that have often lain behind war and other crimes against humanity. However, this appears primarily in the guise of ethical obligation, an account of what would be good actions and how institutions and loyalties ought to be rearranged. Connection is seldom established to any idea of political action rooted in immanent contradictions of the social order. From the liberal rationalist tradition, contemporary cosmopolitanism also inherits suspicion of religion and rooted traditions; a powerful language of rights that is also sometimes a blinder against recognition of the embeddedness of individuals in culture and social relations; and an opposition of reason and rights to community. This last has appeared in various guises through three hundred years of contrast between allegedly inherited and constraining local community life, on the one hand, and the ostensibly freely chosen social relationships of modern cities, markets, associational life, and more generally cosmopolis, on the other.

Confronting similar concerns in the mid-twentieth century, Theodor Adorno wrote:

> An emancipated society . . . would not be a unitary state, but the realization of universality in the reconciliation of differences. Politics that are still seriously concerned with such a society ought not, therefore, propound the abstract equality of men even as an idea. Instead, they should point to the bad equality today . . . and conceive the better state as one in which people could be different without fear.[27]

This is very inadequately achieved at the level of the nation-state, to be sure, but it seems harder, not easier, to develop in a global polity. Indeed, the projection of nationality to a global scale is a major motivation behind repression of difference. This is not to say that cultural and social differences provoke no conflict in villages or urban neighbourhoods. They do, but face-to-face relations also provide for important forms of mediation. Ethnic violence in cities and villages commonly reflects organized enmity on a larger scale rather than being its basis.

The tension between abstract accounts of equality and rooted accounts of difference has been renewed in the recent professional quarrels between liberal and communitarian political theorists. For the most part, cosmopolitans model political life on a fairly abstract, liberal notion of person as a bearer of rights and obligations.[28] This is readily addressed in rationalist and indeed proceduralist terms. And however widely challenged in recent years, rationalism retains at least in intellectual circles a certain presumptive superiority. It is easy to paint communitarian claims for the importance of particular cultures as irrational, arbitrary, and only a shade less relativist than the worst sort of postmodernism.[29] But immanent struggle for a better world always builds on particular social and cultural bases.[30] Moreover, rationalist universalism is liable not only to shift into the mode of 'pure ought' but to approach human diversity as an inherited obstacle rather than as a resource or a basic result of creativity.

Entering this quarrel on the liberal side, but with care for diversity, Held suggests that national communities cease to be treated as primary political communities. He does not go so far as some and claim that they should (or naturally will) cease to exist, but rather imagines them as one sort of relevant unit of political organization among many. What he favours is a cosmopolitan democratic community:

> a community of all democratic communities must become an obligation for democrats, an obligation to build a transnational, common structure of political action which alone, ultimately, can support the politics of self-determination.[31]

In such a cosmopolitan community, 'people would come . . . to enjoy multiple citizenships – political membership in the diverse political communities which significantly affected them'.[32] Sovereignty would then be 'stripped away from the idea of fixed borders and territories and thought of as, in principle, malleable time-space clusters . . . it could be entrenched and drawn upon in diverse self-regulating associations, from cities to states to corpo-rations'.[33] Indeed, so strong is Held's commitment to the notion that there are a variety of kinds of associations within which people might exercise their democratic rights that he imagines 'the formation of an authoritative assembly of all democratic states and agencies, a reformed General Assembly of the United Nations . . .' with its operating rules to be worked out in 'an international constitutional convention involving states, IGOs, NGOs, citizen groups and social movements'.[34] The deep question is whether this all-embracing unity comes at the expense of cultural particularity – a reduction to liberal individualism – or provides the best hope of sustaining particular achievements and openings for creativity in the face of neo-liberal capitalism.

Various crises of the nation-state have set the stage for the revitalization of cosmopolitanism. The crises were occasioned by acceleration of global economic restructuring in the 1990s, new transnational communications media, new flows of migrants, and proliferation of civil wars and humanitarian crises in the wake of the Cold War. The last could no longer be comprehended in terms of the Cold War, which is one reason why they often appeared in the language of ethnicity and nationalism. Among their many implications, these crises all challenged liberalism's established understandings of (or perhaps wilful blind spot towards) the issues of political membership and sovereignty. They presented several problems simultaneously: (1) Why should the benefits of membership in any one polity not be available to all people? (2) On what bases might some polities legitimately inter-vene in the affairs of others? (3) What standing should organiza-tions have that operate across borders without being the agents of any single state (this problem, I might add, applies as much to business corporations as to NGOs and social movements) and conversely how might states appropriately regulate them?

Enter cosmopolitanism. Borders should be abandoned as much as possible and left porous where they must be maintained. Intervention on behalf of human rights is good. NGOs and transnational social movements offer models for the future of the world. These are not bad ideas, but they are limited ideas.

## Capitalism

The current enthusiasm for global citizenship and cosmopolitanism reflects not just a sense of its inherent moral worth but also the challenge of an increasingly global capitalism. It is perhaps no accident that the first cited usage under 'cosmopolitan' in the Oxford English Dictionary comes from John Stuart Mill's *Political Economy* in 1848: 'Capital is becoming more and more cosmopolitan.'[35] Cosmopolitan, after all, means 'belonging to all parts of the world; not restricted to any one country or its inhabitants'. As the quotation from Mill reminds us, the latest wave of globalization was not required to demonstrate that capital fit this bill. Indeed, Marx and Engels wrote in the *Communist Manifesto*:

> the bourgeoisie has through its exploitation of the world market given a cosmopolitan character to production and consumption in every country. . . All old-established national industries have been destroyed or are daily being destroyed. . . In place of the old local and national seclusion and self-sufficiency, we have intercourse in every direction, universal inter-dependence of nations. And as in material so also in intellectual production. The intellectual creations of individual nations become common property. National one-sidedness and narrow-mindedness become more and more impossible, and from the numerous national and local literatures, there arises a world literature.[36]

This is progress, of a sort, but not an altogether happy story. 'The bourgeoisie', Marx and Engels go on, 'by the rapid improvement of all instruments of production, by the immensely facilitated means of communication, draws all, even the most barbarian, nations into civilisation. . . It compels all nations, on pain of extinction, to adopt the bourgeois mode of production; it compels them to introduce what it calls civilization into their midst, i.e., to become bourgeois themselves. In one word, it creates a world after its own image.'[37] It is not clear that these new commonalties are necessarily a basis for harmony, though, and Marx and Engels stressed the contradictions within capitalism and the inevitable clashes among capitalist powers.

The rise of the modern capitalist world system was not simply a progress of cosmopolitanism. It marked a historical turn against empire, and capitalist globalization has been married to the dominance of nation-states in politics.[38] Capitalist cosmopolitans have indeed traversed the globe, from early modern merchants to today's World Bank officials and venture capitalists. They have forged relations that cross the borders of nation-states. But they have also relied on states and a global order of states to maintain property rights and other conditions of production and trade. Their passports bear stamps of many countries, but they are still passports and good cosmopolitans knew which ones get them past inspectors at borders and airports.

Not least of all, capitalist cosmopolitanism has offered only a weak defence against reactionary nationalism. This was clearly déclassé so far as most cosmopolitans were concerned. But Berlin in the 1930s was a very cosmopolitan city. If having cosmopolitan élites were a guarantee of respect for civil or human rights, then Hitler would never have ruled Germany, Chile would have been spared Pinochet, and neither the Guomindang nor the Communists would have come to power in China. Cosmopolitanism is not responsible for empire or capitalism or fascism or communism, but neither is it an adequate defence.

Even while the internal homogeneity of national cultures was being promoted by linguistic and educational standardization (among other means), the great imperial and trading cities stood as centres of diversity. Enjoying this diversity was one of the marks of the sophisticated modern urbanite by contrast to the 'traditional' hick. To be a cosmopolitan was to be comfortable in heterogeneous public space. Richard Sennett cites (and builds on) a French usage of 1738: 'a cosmopolite ... is a man who moves comfortably in diversity; he is comfortable in situations which have no links or parallels to what is familiar to him.'[39] Yet there is a tendency for commercial capitalism and political liberalism to tame this diversity. While cities can be places of creative disorder, jumbling together ethnicities, classes, and political projects, most people claim only familiar parts of the diversity on offer. The difference between a willingness to enter situations truly without parallels or familiarity and a willingness to experience diversity as packaged for consumer tastes is noteworthy. While Sennett's strong sense of cosmopolitanism calls for confrontation with deep and necessarily contentious differences between ways of life, there is a tendency for a soft cosmopolitanism to emerge. Aided by the frequent flyer lounges (and their extensions in 'international standard' hotels), contemporary cosmopolitans meet others of different backgrounds in spaces that retain familiarity.

The notion of cosmopolitanism gains currency from the flourishing of multiculturalism – and the opposition those who consider themselves multiculturally modern feel to those rooted in monocultural traditions. The latter, say the former, are locals with limited perspective, if not outright racists. It is easier to sneer at the far right, but too much claiming of ethnic solidarity by minorities also falls foul of some advocates of cosmopolitanism. It is no accident either that the case against Salman Rushdie began to be formulated among diasporic Asians in Britain or that cosmopoliticians are notably ambivalent towards them. Integrationist white liberals in the United States are similarly unsure what to make of what some of them see as 'reverse racism' on the part of blacks striving to maintain local communities. Debates over English as a common language reveal related ambivalence towards Hispanics and others. It is important for cosmopolitan theorists to recognize, though, that societies outside the modern West have by no means always been 'monocultural'. On the contrary, it is the development of the European nation-state that most pressed for this version of unity. And it is often the insertion of migrants from around the world into the Western nation-state system that produces intense 'reverse monoculturalism', including both the notion that the culture 'back home' is singular and unified and pure and sometimes the attempt by political leaders on the home front to make it so. Such projects may be simply reactionary, but even when proclaimed in the name of ancient religions, they often pursue alternative modernities. An effectively democratic future must allow for such different collective projects – as they must allow for each other. It must be built in a world in which these are powerful and find starting points within them; it cannot be conceptualized adequately simply in terms of diversity of individuals.

This complexity is easy to miss if one's access to cultural diversity is organized mainly by the conventions of headline news or the packaging of ethnicity for consumer markets. In the world's global cities, and even in a good many of its small towns, certain forms of cosmopolitan diversity appear ubiquitous. Certainly Chinese food is now a global cuisine – both in a generic form that exists especially as a global cuisine and in more 'authentic' regional versions prepared for more cultivated global palates. And one can buy Kentucky Fried Chicken in Beijing. Local taste cultures that were once more closed and insular have indeed opened up. Samosas are now English food just as pizza is American and Indonesian curry is Dutch. Even where the hint of the exotic (and the uniformity of the local) is stronger, one can eat internationally – Mexican food in Norway, Ethiopian in Italy. This is not all 'McDonaldization' and it is not to be decried in the name of cultural survival. Nonetheless, it tells us little about whether to expect democracy on a global scale, successful accommodation of immigrants at home, or respect for human rights across the board. Food, tourism, music, literature and clothes are all easy faces of cosmopolitanism. They are indeed broadening, literally after a fashion, but they are not hard tests for the relationship between local solidarity and international civil society.

Despite the spread of consumerist cosmopolitanism, too many states still wage war or take on projects like ethnic cleansing that an international public might constrain or at least condemn. Profit, moreover, is pursued not only in 'above board' trading and global manufacturing, but in transnational flows of people, weapons and drugs. The 'legitimate' and 'illegitimate' sides of global economics life are never fully separable – as is shown for example by the role of both recorded and unrecorded financial transfers in paving the way for the September 11 attacks. The cosmopolitan project speaks to these concerns, suggesting the need not only for multilateral regulatory agreements but for new institutions operating as more than the sum – or net outcome – of the political agendas of member states. It may be that 'legitimate' businesses have an interest in such institutions and that this will help to compensate for their weak capacity to enforce agreements. Trying to secure some level of democratic participation for such transnational institutions will remain a challenge, though, for reasons suggested above. So too will avoiding a predominantly technocratic orientation to global governance projects. Not least, there will be important tensions between liberal cosmopolitan visions that exempt property relations from democratic control and more radical ones that do not. If this is not addressed directly, it is easy for the rhetoric of cosmopolitanism – and indeed cosmopolitan democracy – to be adopted by and become a support for neo-liberal visions of global capitalism.

Cosmopolitanism – though not necessarily cosmopolitan democracy – is now largely the project of capitalism, and it flourishes in the top management of multinational corporations and even more in the consulting firms that serve them. Such cosmopolitanism often joins élites across national borders while ordinary people live in local communities. This is not simply because common folk are less sympathetic to diversity – a self-serving notion of élites. It is also because the class structuring of public life excludes many workers and others. This is not an entirely new story. One of the striking changes of the nineteenth and especially twentieth centuries was a displacement of cosmopolitanism from cities to international travel and mass media. International travel, moreover, meant something different to those who travelled for business or diplomacy and those who served in armies fighting wars to expand or control the cosmopolis. If diplomacy was war by other means, it was also war by other classes who paid less dearly for it.

Deep inequalities in the political economy of capitalism (as earlier of empire) mean that some people labour to support others whose pursuit of global relations focuses on acquisition and accumulation. Cosmopolitanism does not in itself speak to these systemic inequalities, any more than did the rights of bourgeois man that Marx criticized in the 1840s. If there is to be a major redistribution of wealth, or a challenge to the way the means of production are controlled in global capitalism, it is not likely to be guided by cosmopolitanism as such. Of course, it may well depend on transnational – even cosmopolitan – solidarities among workers or other groups. But it will have to contend with both capitalism's economic power and its powerful embeddedness in the institutional framework of global relations.

The affinity of cosmopolitanism to rationalist liberal individualism has blinded many cosmopolitans to some of the destructions neo-liberalism – the cosmopolitanism of capital – has wrought and the damage it portends to hard-won social achievements. Pierre Bourdieu has rightly called attention to the enormous investment of struggle that has made possible relatively autonomous social fields – higher education, for example, or science – and at least partial rights of open access to them.[40] Such fields are organized largely on national bases, at present, though they include transnational linkages and could become far more global. This might be aided by the 'new internationalism' (especially of intellectuals) that Bourdieu proposes in opposition to the globalization of neo-liberal capitalism. The latter imposes a reduction to market forces that undermines both the specific values and autonomy of distinctive fields – including higher education and science – and many rights won from nation-states by workers and others. In this context, defence of existing institutions including parts of national states is not merely reactionary. Yet it is commonly presented this way, and cosmopolitan discourse too easily encourages the equation of the global with the modern and the national or local with the backwardly traditional.

Neo-liberalism presents one international agenda simply as a force of necessity to which all people, organizations and states have no choice but to adapt. Much of the specific form of integration of the European Union, for example, has been sold as the necessary and indeed all but inevitable response to global competition. This obscures the reality that transnational relations might be built in a variety of ways, and indeed that the shifting forces bringing globalization can also be made the objects of collective choice. Likewise, existing national and indeed local institutions are not mere inheritances from tradition but – at least sometimes – hard-won achievements of social struggles. To defend such institutions is not always backward.

The global power of capitalism, among other factors, makes the creation of cosmopolitan institutions seem crucial. But it would be a mistake for this to be pursued in opposition to more local solidarities or without adequate distinction from capitalism. Appeals to abstract human rights in themselves speak to neither – or at least not adequately as currently pursued. Building cosmopolitanism solely on such a discourse of individual rights – without strong attention to diverse solidarities and struggles for a more just and democratic social order – also runs the risk of substituting ethics for politics. An effective popular politics must find roots in social groups and networks of ties among them.

## Conclusion

The current pursuit of cosmopolitan democracy flies in the face of a long history in which cosmopolitan sensibilities thrived in market cities, imperial capitals, and court society while democracy was tied to the nation-state. Cosmopolitanism flourished in Ottoman Istanbul and old regime Paris partly because in neither were members of different cultures and communities invited to organize government together. It was precisely when democracy became a popular passion and a political project that nationalism flourished. Democracy depends on strong notions of who 'the people' behind phrases like 'we the people' might be, and who might make legitimate the performative declarations of constitution-making and the less verbal performances of revolution.[41]

One way of looking at modern history is as a race in which popular forces and solidarities are always running behind. It is a race to achieve social integration, to structure the connections among people and organize the world. Capital is out in front. Workers and ordinary citizens are always in the position of trying to catch up. As they get organized on local levels, capital and power integrate on larger scales. States come close to catching up, but the integration of nation-states is an ambivalent step. On the one hand, state power is a force its own right – not least in colonialism – and represents a flow of organizing capacity away from local communities. On the other hand, democracy at a national level constitutes the greatest success that ordinary people have had in catching up to capital and power. Because markets and corporations increasingly transcend states, there is new catching up to do. This is why cosmopolitan democracy is appealing.

Yet, as practical projects in the world (and sometimes even as theory), cosmopolitanism and democracy have both been intertwined with capitalism and Western hegemony. If cosmopolitan democracy is to flourish and be fully open to human beings of diverse circumstances and identities, then it needs to disentangle itself from neo-liberal capitalism. It needs to approach both cross-cultural relations and the construction of social solidarities with deeper recognition of the significance of diverse starting points and potential outcomes. It needs more discursive engagement across lines of difference, more commitment to reduction of material inequality, and more openness to radical change. Like many liberals of the past, advocates of cosmopolitan democracy often offer a vision of political reform attractive to élites partly because it promises to find virtue without radical redistribution of wealth or power. This is all the more uncomfortable for the left in the advanced capitalist countries because those advocating more radical change typically challenge Western culture and values – including much of liberalism – as well as global inequality.

The answer clearly does not lie with embracing illiberal nationalisms or 'fundamentalisms'. These may be voices of the oppressed without being voices for good. But not all nationalism is ugly ethnonationalism; not all religion is fundamentalism. Both can be sources of solidarity and care for strangers as well as xenophobia or persecution of heretics. They are also in conflict with each other as often as they are joined together. But if cosmopolitan democracy is to be more than a good ethical orientation for those privileged to inhabit the frequent traveller lounges, it must put down roots in the solidarities that organize most people's sense of identity and location in the world. To appeal simply to liberal individualism – even with respect for diversity – is to disempower those who lack substantial personal or organizational resources. It is also disingenuous, if would-be cosmopolitans don't recognize the extent to which cosmopolitan appreciation of global diversity is based on privileges of wealth and perhaps especially citizenship in certain states. Cosmopolitan democracy depends on finding ways to relate diverse solidarities to each other rather than trying to overcome them.

This is surely a matter of robust public communication in which ordinary people can gain more capacity to shape both the societies within which they live and the global forces that shape the options open to them. But it is important to recognize that relations across meaningful groups are not simply matters of rational-critical discourse but involve the creation of local hybrid cultures, accommodations, collaborations and practical knowledge. Equally, it is important to see that attenuated cosmopolitanism won't ground mutual commitment and responsibility. Not only tolerance but solidarity is required for people to live together and join in democratic self-governance.

Still, feeling at home can't be an adequate basis for life in modern global society. Exclusive localism is neither empowering nor even really possible, however nostalgic for it people may feel. Cosmopolitanism by itself may not be enough; a soft cosmopolitanism that doesn't challenge capitalism or Western hegemony may be an ideological diversion; but some form of cosmopolitanism is needed.

## Notes

1. Earlier versions of this paper were presented to the conference, 'The Future of Cosmopolitanism', University of Warwick, April 2000; to the International Studies Association, February 2001; to the University of North Carolina Conference on Local Democracy and Globalization, March 2001; and at Candido Mendes University, May 2001. I am grateful for comments on all these occasions and especially from Pamela DeLargy, Saurabh Dube, Michael Kennedy, Laura MacDonald, Thomas McCarthy and Kathryn Sikkink.

2. See Mary Kaldor, 'Beyond Militarism, Arms Races and Arms Control', forthcoming in Craig Calhoun, P. Price and A. Timmer, eds, *Understanding September 11*, New York 2002, for a good analysis of this.

3. Edward P. Thompson, 'The Moral Economy of the English Crowd in the Eighteenth Century', *Past and Present*, vol. 50, 1971, pp. 76–136.

4. See David Held, *Democracy and the Global Order*, Cambridge 1995; Daniele Archibugi and David Held, eds, *Cosmopolitan Democracy: An Agenda for a New World Order*, Cambridge 1995; Daniele Archibugi, David Held and Martin Köhler, eds, *Re-imagining Political Community: Studies in Cosmopolitan Democracy*, Stanford, CA 1998. Held, Archibugi and colleagues conceptualize democratic cosmopolitan politics as a matter of several layers of participation in discourse and decision-making, including especially the strengthening of institutions of global civil society, rather than an international politics dominated by nation-states. Less layered and complex accounts appear in Falk's call for global governance and Nussbaum's universalism. See Richard Falk, *Human Rights Horizons: The Pursuit of Justice in a Globalizing World*, New York 2000, and Martha Nussbaum, *Cultivating Humanity*, Cambridge, MA 1998.

5. One is reminded of Malaysian Prime Minister Mahathir Mohamad's account of human rights as the new Christianity. It makes Europeans feel entitled, he suggested, to invade countries around the world and try to subvert their traditional values, convert them, and subjugate them. Mahathir was of course defending an often abusive government as well as local culture, but a deeper question is raised.

6. 'Jihad and McWorld operate with equal strength in opposite directions, the one driven by parochial hatreds, the other by universalizing markets, the one re-creating ancient subnational and ethnic borders from within, the other making war on national borders from without. Yet Jihad and McWorld have this in common: they both make war on the sovereign nation-state and thus undermine the nation-state's democratic institutions.' Benjamin Barber, *Jihad vs. McWorld*, New York 1995, p. 6. David Held similarly

opposes 'traditional' and 'global' in positioning cosmopolitanism between the two 'Opening Remarks' to the Warwick University Conference on 'The Future of Cosmopolitanism'.

7. Timothy Brennan, 'Cosmopolitanism and Internationalism', *New Left Review*, second series, no. 7, January–February 2001, p. 76 (chapter 4 in this volume). Arguing against Archibugi's account of the nation-state, Brennan rightly notes the intrinsic importance of imperialism, though he ascribes rather more complete causal power to it than history warrants.

8. The call for world government is more important to some cosmopolitans – notably Richard Falk – than others. See, e.g., Richard Falk, *Human Rights Horizons*, cit.

9. This is a central issue in debates over group rights. See, for example, Will Kymlicka, *Multicultural Citizenship*, New York 1995.

10. Liberalism of course embraces a wide spectrum of views in which emphases may fall more on property rights or more on democracy. So too cosmopolitanism can imply a global view that is liberal not specifically democratic. Archibugi prefers 'cosmopolitics' to 'cosmopolitan' in order to signal just this departure from a more general image of liberal global unity. See 'Cosmopolitical Democracy', *New Left Review*, second series, no. 4, July–August 2000, pp. 137–50 (chapter 1 in this volume).

11. On the predominance of nationalist understandings in conceptions of 'society', see Calhoun, 'Nationalism, Political Community, and the Representation of Society: Or, Why Feeling at Home Is Not a Substitute for Public Space', *European Journal of Social Theory*, vol. 2, no. 2, 1999, pp. 217–31.

12. John Rawls, *Political Liberalism*, New York 1993, p. 41.

13. See Calhoun, *Nationalism*, Minneapolis 1997.

14. Daniele Archibugi, 'Principles of Cosmopolitan Democracy', in D. Archibugi, D. Held and M. Köhler, eds, *Re-imagining Political Community*, pp. 198–228.

15. David Held, *Democracy and the Global Order*, p. 233. Held's book remains the most systematic and sustained effort to develop a theory of cosmopolitan democracy.

16. *The Inclusion of the Other* (ed. C. Cronin and P. De Greiff), Cambridge, MA 1998, p. 115.

17. Ibid., p. 117. Note that Habermas tends to equate 'nation' with 'ethnic nation'.

18. 'Modern Social Imaginaries', *Public Culture*, vol. 14, no. 1, 2002.

19. It is this last tendency which invites liberal rationalists occasionally to ascribe to communitarians and advocates of local culture complicity in all manner of illiberal political projects from restrictions on immigration to excessive celebration of ethnic minorities to economic protectionism. I have discussed this critically in 'Nationalism, Political Community, and the Representation of Society'.

20. Richard Bellamy and Dario Castiglione, 'Between Cosmopolis and Community', in Daniele Archibugi, David Held and Martin Köhler, eds, *Re-imagining Political Community*, pp. 152–78.

21. See, e.g., Janna Thompson, 'Community Identity and World Citizenship', in Daniele Archibugi, David Held and Martin Köhler, eds, *Re-imagining Political Community*, pp. 179–97.

22. Archibugi, 'Cosmopolitical Democracy', p. 146.

23. I have developed this argument about public discourse as a form of or basis for solidarity and its significance for transnational politics further in 'Constitutional Patriotism and the Public Sphere: Interests, Identity, and Solidarity in the Integration of Europe', in Pablo De Greiff and Ciaran Cronin, eds, *Global Ethics and Transnational Politics*, Cambridge, MA 2002, pp. 275–312.

24. This hyperTocquevillianism appears famously in Robert Putnam's *Bowling Alone*, New York 2000, but has in fact been central to discussions since at least the 1980s, including prominently Robert Bellah *et al.*, *Habits of the Heart*, Berkeley 1984. The embrace of a notion of civil society as centrally composed of a 'voluntary sector' complementing a capitalist market economy has of course informed public policy from America's first Bush administration with its 'thousand points of light' forward. Among other features, this approach neglects the notion of a political public sphere as an institutional framework of civil society; see Jürgen Habermas, *Structural Transformation of the Public Sphere*, Cambridge, MA 1989. It grants a high level of autonomy to markets and economic actors; it is notable for the absence of political economy from its theoretical bases and analyses. As one result, it introduces a sharp separation among market, government and voluntary association (non-profit) activity that obscures the question of how social movements may challenge economic institutions, and how the public sphere may mobilize government to shape economic practices.

25. On how global NGOs actually work, see Margaret Keck and Kathryn Sikkink, *Activists Beyond Borders*, Ithaca, NY 1998.

26. See Stephen Toulmin's analysis of the seventeenth-century roots of the modern liberal rationalist worldview in *Cosmopolis: The Hidden Agenda of Modernity*, New York 1990. As Toulmin notes, the rationalism of Descartes and Newton may be tempered with more attention to sixteenth-century forebears. From Erasmus, Montaigne and others we may garner an alternative but still humane and even humanist approach emphasizing wisdom that included a sense of the limits of rationalism and a more positive grasp of human passions and attachments.

27. Theodor W. Adorno, *Minima Moralia*, London 1974, p. 103.

28. Amartya Sen, in *Development as Freedom*, New York 2000, lays out an account of 'capacities' as an alternative to the discourse of rights. This is also adopted by Martha Nussbaum in her most recent cosmopolitan arguments in *Women and Human Development*, Cambridge 2000. While this shifts emphases in some useful ways (notably from 'negative' to 'positive' liberties in Isaiah Berlin's terms), it does not offer a substantially 'thicker' conception of the person or the social nature of human life. Some cosmopolitan theorists, notably David Held, also take care to acknowledge that people inhabit social relations as well as rights and obligations.

29. See, for examples, 'Struggles for Recognition in the Democratic Constitutional State', Habermas' surprisingly sharp-toned response to Charles Taylor's 'The Politics of Recognition', both in Amy Gutman, ed., *Multiculturalism: Examining the Politics of Recognition*, Princeton, rev. edn, 1994; or Janna Thompson's distorting examination of 'communitarian' arguments, 'Community Identity and World Citizenship', in Daniele Archibugi, David Held and Martin Köhler, eds, *Re-imagining Political Community*.

30. This has been an important theme in the work of Ashis Nandy. See,

among many, *Exiled at Home*, Oxford 1998, and *Traditions, Tyranny and Utopias*, Oxford 1993.

31. *Democracy and the Global Order*, p. 232.

32. Ibid., p. 233.

33. Ibid., p. 234.

34. Ibid., pp. 273–4. The theme is developed in Richard Falk and Andrew Strauss (chapter 11 in this volume).

35. This is a point made also by Bruce Robbins in *Secular Vocations: Intellectuals, Professionalism, Culture*, London 1993, p. 182. See also his 'The Village of the Liberal Managerial Class', in Vinay Dharwadker, ed., *Cosmopolitan Geographies: New Locations in Literature and Culture*, New York 2001, pp. 15–32.

36. Karl Marx and Friedrich Engels, 'Manifesto of the Communist Party', in *Collected Works*, London 1976, p. 488.

37. Ibid. Marx and Engels, remarkable as their insight is, were fallible observers. Not much later in the *Communist Manifesto* they reported that modern subjection to capital had already stripped workers of 'every trace of national character', p. 494.

38. This is a central point of Immanuel Wallerstein, *The Modern World System*, vol. 1, New York 1974.

39. Richard Sennett, *The Fall of Public Man*, New York 1977, p. 17.

40. See the essays in Pierre Bourdieu, *Acts of Resistance*, New York 1999, and *Contre-feux II*, Paris 2001.

41. See Charles Taylor, 'Modern Social Imaginaries'.

# 8

# The Influence of the Global Order on the Prospects for Genuine Democracy in the Developing Countries[1]

*Thomas W. Pogge*

There is much rhetorical and even some tangible support by the developed states for democratization processes in the poorer countries. Most people there nevertheless enjoy little genuine democratic participation or even government responsiveness to their needs. This fact is commonly explained by indigenous factors, often related to the history and culture of particular societies. My essay outlines a competing explanation by reference to global institutional factors, involving fixed features of our global economic system. It also explores possible global institutional reforms that, insofar as the offered explanation is correct, should greatly improve the prospects for democracy and responsive government in the developing world.

## Evidence of inequality

Broadly considered, our world appears to be in top condition, economically. At $31,171 billion in the year 2000,[2] aggregate global income is higher than ever before. And even if inflation and population growth are taken into account, global economic growth has been impressive: even while humankind has doubled during the past 40 years, from 2,994 million people[3] to 6,054 million,[4] real (i.e., inflation-adjusted) global aggregate income has nearly quadrupled in the same period, so that the global *per capita* income now ($5,149) is almost twice what it was in 1960 ($2,714).[5] Looking forward one might add that, following the end of the Cold War, global military expenditures have been cut by nearly one half – from 4.7 per cent of the global product in 1985[6] to 2.4 per cent thereof in 1996[7] – a decline that currently releases some $700 billion annually (the so-called 'peace dividend') for more productive purposes. Is the world we are handing over to the humanity of the new millennium then an idyllic paradise in which milk and honey flow freely?

This Panglossian view is disturbed by the fact that large segments of humankind are hardly participating in our economic progress and prosperity. At the bottom, in the poorest quintile (fifth), conditions continue to be desperate: over 1,200 million persons live below the international poverty line, 'that income or expenditure level below which a minimum, nutritionally adequate diet plus essential non-food requirements are not affordable'.[8] The World Bank currently specifies this line in terms of $392.88 PPP (purchasing power parities) 1993:[9] people count as poor if their income per person per year has less purchasing power than $392.88 had in the US in 1993, which corresponds roughly to the purchasing power of $483 in the US in the year 2001.[10] As a consequence of such severe poverty, 826 million are undernourished, 968 million lack access to safe water, 2,400 million lack access to basic sanitation, and 854 million adults are illiterate;[11] more than 880 million lack access to basic health services;[12] approximately 1,000 million have no adequate shelter and 2,000 million no electricity.[13] 'Two out of five children in the developing world are stunted, one in three is underweight and one in ten is wasted.'[14] 250 million children between 5 and 14 do wage work outside their household – often under harsh or cruel conditions: as soldiers, prostitutes or domestic servants, or in agriculture, construction, textile or carpet production.[15] Roughly one third of all human deaths, some 50,000 daily, are due to poverty-related causes,[16] easily preventable through better nutrition, safe drinking water, vaccines, cheap re-hydration packs, and antibiotics. If the European Union had its proportional share of all this misery, we would have over 51 million malnourished people and over 1.1 million poverty-related deaths each year.

Of course, severe poverty is nothing new. What is new is the extent of global inequality. Genuine affluence is no longer confined to a tiny minority. Hundreds of millions are enjoying a high standard of living with lots of free time during and after their working years, allowing ample opportunities to enjoy travel, education, cars, household appliances, computers and so on. The so-called 'high-income countries' – 32 affluent states plus Hong Kong – contain 14.9 per cent of the world's population, but have 79.7 per cent of aggregate global income.[17] National income *per capita* in these countries averages $27,510.[18] By contrast, the people in the poorest quintile live, on average, 30 per cent below the international poverty line.[19] Thus they have, on average, $338 PPP 2001 per person per year. Since the purchasing power attributed to them by the World Bank is on average about four times their actual income,[20] the people of the poorest quintile have at current exchange rates about $85 per person per year – collectively $103 billion annually or one third of one per cent of aggregate global income.[21] In short: 1/240 of the collective national incomes of the high-income countries would suffice to double all incomes in the bottom quintile.

Such extreme inequality is a recent phenomenon: 'The income gap between the fifth of the world's people living in the richest countries and the fifth in the poorest was 74 to 1 in 1997, up from 60 to 1 in 1990 and 30 to 1 in 1960. [Earlier] the income gap between the top and bottom countries increased from 3 to 1 in 1820 to 7 to 1 in 1870 to 11 to 1 in 1913.'[22] A detailed study of the development of income inequality among *persons* world-wide shows the same dramatic trend: 'World inequality has increased . . . from a Gini (statistical coefficient) of 62.5 in 1988 to 66.0 in 1993. This represents an increase of 0.6 Gini points per year. This is a very fast increase, faster than the increase experienced by the US and UK in the decade of the 1980s . . . The bottom 5 percent of the world grew poorer, as their real incomes decreased by one quarter, while the richest quintile grew richer. It gained 12 percent in real terms, that is it grew more than twice as much as mean world income (5.7 percent).'[23]

Inequalities in wealth are significantly greater than inequalities in income. Well-off persons typically have more net worth than annual income, while the poor typically own less than one annual income. The huge fortunes of the ultra-rich have been specially

highlighted in recent *Human Development Reports*: 'The world's 200
richest people more than doubled their net worth in the four
years to 1998, to more than $1 trillion. The assets of the top three
billionaires are more than the combined GNP of all least developed countries and their 600 million people.'[24] 'The additional
cost of achieving and maintaining universal access to basic education for all, basic health care for all, reproductive health care
for all women, adequate food for all and safe water and sanitation
for all is . . . less than 4% of the combined wealth of the 225
richest people in the world.'[25]

## Explaining the evidence

One is tempted to react to such facts with moral condemnation.
But it is more important, first of all, to explain these facts. How
does it come about that there is so much desperate poverty in a
world that, in aggregate, is rather affluent? And why is global
economic inequality consistently and rapidly increasing? I am well
aware that such questions do not fall within the purview of the
ordinary tasks and competencies of a mere philosopher. I want to
address them nonetheless, because I believe that economists and
political scientists have not taken them seriously enough and have
thus far given only incomplete, and even misleading accounts of
the causes of current global poverty and inequality.

Let us begin with points of agreement. First, there is little
controversy about the facts. Indeed, most of the data I have
presented come, directly or indirectly, from the economists at the
World Bank who, however, understandably prefer to dwell on the
positive. Second, economists deplore the widespread persistence
of severe poverty and the accumulation of enormous global
inequalities in income and wealth. Third, economists agree that
these facts have social causes. That so many people subsist in life-
threatening poverty is not due to their own laziness, wastefulness,
greater needs, or lesser natural endowments, but due to social
factors over which they have no control. If these same people had
been born in Italy or Norway, they would lead just as long and
healthy and happy lives as those who actually did have the good
fortune to be born in those places.

What then are the social causes of the persistence of poverty?
Here economists divide into two main schools of thought. The

libertarians on the right – also called freshwater economists because they tend to live in Chicago – argue that poverty persists because most poor countries do not follow the examples of Japan and the Asian tigers (Hong Kong, Taiwan, Singapore and South Korea). These success stories show, so say the libertarians, that the best way to expel human misery is economic growth, and the best way to achieve economic growth is to foster free enterprise with a minimum in taxes, regulations and red tape.

The other, left-leaning school of thought, represented by Amartya Sen, also has its favourite poster-child: Kerala, a state in India. Kerala is a poor state, but its socialist government gives priority to fulfilling basic needs. And so the people of Kerala do much better in terms of health, education and life expectancy than the people of other, more affluent Indian states.[26]

Economists disagree then quite sharply about the causal roles of various *local* social factors in the reproduction of poverty. One side argues that poverty persists because poor countries have too much government: taxes, regulations and red tape. The other side argues that poverty persists because poor countries have too little government: schools, hospitals and infrastructure. As this issue is surely important, our attention is diverted from what both sides take for granted: that the social causes of poverty, and hence the key to its eradication, lie in the poor countries themselves. We find this shared belief all the more appealing because it reinforces our ever so dear conviction that we and our governments and the global economic order we impose are not substantial contributors to the horrendous conditions among the global poor. So we get drawn into believing that the crucial variable for the explanation and avoidance of severe poverty is the decision-making in the developing countries: with the right organization and developmental policies any poor country can over time meet the basic needs of its people.[27] Yet severe poverty remains widespread, because the poor countries have bad economic institutions and bad economic policies which are generally due to the incompetence and corruption of their political leaders and public officials. This is the picture that both right-wing and left-wing economists present, and this is the view that our politicians and the general public accept and repeat.

This popular view of global poverty is quite correct in what it asserts. The eradication of severe poverty in the developing countries indeed depends strongly on their governments and political institutions. It depends on how their economies are structured and also on whether there exists a genuine competition for political office which gives politicians an incentive to be responsive to the interests of the poor majority.

But the popular explanation of global poverty is nonetheless deeply misleading, because it portrays the faulty institutions and policies and the corrupt élites prevalent in the developing world as an exogenous fact: as a fact that explains, but does not itself stand in need of explanation. 'Some developing countries manage to give themselves reasonable political institutions, but many others fail or do not even try. This is just the way things are.' An explanation that runs out at this point does not explain very much.

An adequate explanation of global poverty must not merely adduce the prevalence of faulty institutions and policies and of corrupt and oppressive élites in the developing world but must also provide an explanation for this prevalence. In order to understand the persistence of massive and severe poverty worldwide, we need an explanation for why incompetent, oppressive and corrupt governments which are unresponsive to the needs and interests of 'their' populations are so very frequent in the developing world.

Explanations offered in this vein generally point to the culture and/or history of particular countries. A cultural explanation might assert, for instance, that corruption or dictatorial rule are endemic to the culture of certain countries, widely accepted by the population as a familiar feature of their way of life.[28] A historical explanation may, for instance, trace Cambodia's lack of progress during the last 30 years back to the fact that this country was dragged into the Vietnam War and that its population was therefore victimized first by a pro-American military dictatorship with civil war and then, after the US withdrawal, by a crazy communist nationalism of the Khmer Rouge (who had become popular through the earlier military repression). Likewise, one might explain the frequency of corrupt élites in Africa by reference to the fact that national borders there were drawn during the colonial era without regard for tribal and linguistic boundaries. This has led to ethnically and linguistically heterogeneous states whose internal communities feel much distrust and little solidarity for one another. As a consequence, many African politicians are supported only by members of their own linguistic or ethnic community. Since such politicians must then rely on this community for their political power, they are beholden to it and obliged to favour it unfairly, which in turn reinforces mutual resentment and distrust among the various communities.

Such cultural and historical explanations are not always correct. This is especially true of cultural explanations, from which one can often learn more about the prejudices of their authors than about the countries in question. Indonesia, for instance, has long been a favourite example of a corrupt culture – but only among those who were blind to the hatred and contempt ordinary Indonesians have been feeling for their ruling élite until these feelings finally burst forth in the late 1990s.

Historical explanations, insofar as they are correct, usefully complement and relativize the conventional analysis according to which responsibility for world poverty lies with 'the poor countries themselves'. But historical explanations also conveniently localize the affluent countries' contributions to world poverty in the past – when the US was still making war in South East Asia or when European states still had colonies in Africa. Such explanations therefore do not upset the popular opinion that *we now* are not involved in the reproduction of global poverty and can do only very little toward mitigating this problem.

Precisely this popular opinion is undermined when our explanation of oppression and poverty takes account of present global factors. I do not have in mind here merely (what one might call) negative factors, such as the absence of initiatives through which the rich countries *could* promote greater democratic responsiveness and economic justice. For the absence of possible causal factors can generally contribute to the explanation of actual phenomena only in a somewhat metaphysical sense. Nor am I referring to the numerous cases in which significant support from governments and secret services of powerful countries has enabled allied but domestically unpopular and corrupt groups to gain or to maintain power. Rather, I want to highlight aspects of the prevailing *global* economic and political order that contribute actively to the perpetuation of poverty.

Two such aspects are obvious, so a brief mention will suffice. The rules of our global order are shaped through negotiations among governments representing the interests of their countries and populations. It is therefore not surprising that these rules reflect the existing huge international differentials in bargaining power and expertise. This fact helps us understand the above-documented fact: that international economic inequality is steadily increasing. The affluent states use their greater bargaining power to shape the rules of the global economic order in their own favour. These skewed rules in turn allow them to procure the lion's share of the benefits of global economic growth. This increases international economic inequality and thereby further strengthens the bargaining power of the affluent states, allowing them to shape the rules even more strongly in their favour. And so the cycle continues.[29]

The other obvious aspect involves the negative externalities of our affluent lifestyle: the populations of poor countries suffer from the pollution produced in the developed countries during the last 200 years – while they are, unlike us, excluded from the benefits. They suffer the effects of global warming and ozone depletion caused by our emissions of greenhouse gases. They suffer the effects of the drug trade fuelled by the huge demand for drugs in the US and Europe and of the war on drugs waged by the US and European governments. They suffer from the depletion of natural resources such as crude oil and metals, which are scarcer and dearer than they would be if the affluent countries were prepared to moderate their consumption. They suffer from disease strains that have become resistant to ordinary drugs because of treatment practices in the developed countries. They suffer from the AIDS epidemic which is exacerbated by patent rules that permit drug companies to suppress cheaper generic versions of medications they have patented.

Leaving these more obvious aspects aside, I will focus on showing how our global order plays an important part in sustaining oppression and corruption in the poorer countries. These phenomena are especially significant because they cause not only poverty in the developing world, but also moral detachment among the affluent. We do not feel responsibility, but only condescending pity for peoples who somehow never get their act together and allow themselves to be ruled by incompetent kleptocrats who ruin their economies. Showing this picture's inadequacy is crucial, then, for overcoming that moral detachment.

A paradigm case of corruption is bribery. Bribes play a major role in the awarding of public contracts in the developing countries, which suffer staggering losses as a result. These losses arise in part from the fact that bribes are 'priced in': bidders on contracts must raise their price in order to get paid enough to pay the bribes. Additional losses arise as bidders can afford to be non-competitive, knowing that the success of their bid will depend on their bribes more than on the price they offer. The greatest losses probably arise from the fact that officials focused on bribes pay little attention to whether the goods and services they purchase on their country's behalf are of good quality or even needed at all. Much of what developing countries have imported over the decades has been of no use to them – or even harmful, by promoting environmental degradation or violence (bribery is especially pervasive in the arms trade). May we then conclude that poverty in developing societies is the fault of their own tolerance of corruption and of their own leaders' venality?

This comfortable conclusion is upset by the fact that, until 1999, most developed states have not merely legally authorised their firms to bribe foreign officials, but have even allowed these firms to deduct such bribes from their taxable revenues, thereby providing financial inducements and moral support to the practice of bribing politicians and officials in the developing countries.[30] Bribes encouraged by such rules divert the loyalties of officials in developing countries and also make a great difference to which people are motivated to scramble for public office in the first place. There is hope that the recently adopted *Convention on Combating Bribery of Foreign Officials in International Business Transactions*[31] will make blatant bribery less frequent. But this Convention cannot undo the pervasive culture of corruption that is now deeply entrenched in many developing countries thanks to the extensive bribery they were subjected to during their formative years.

Moreover, huge asymmetries in other incentives remain in place. The political and economic élite of a poor country interacts both with its domestic population and with foreign governments and corporations. These two constituencies differ enormously in wealth and power. The former – poorly educated and heavily preoccupied with the daily struggle for their families' survival –

can do little by way of resisting or rewarding their local and national rulers. The latter, by contrast, have vastly greater rewards and penalties at their disposal. Politicians with a normal interest in their own political and economic success can therefore be expected to cater to the interests of foreign governments and corporations rather than to the interests of their much poorer compatriots. And this, of course, is what we find: there are plenty of developing-country governments that came to power or stay in power only thanks to foreign support. And there are plenty of developing-country politicians and bureaucrats who, induced or even bribed by foreigners, work against the interests of their people: *for* the development of a tourist-friendly sex industry (whose forced exploitation of children and women they tolerate and profit from), *for* the importation of unneeded, obsolete or overpriced products at public expense, *for* the permission to import hazardous products, wastes, or productive facilities, against laws protecting employees or the environment, and so on.

To be sure, there would not be such huge asymmetries in incentives if the developing countries were more democratic, allowing their populations a genuine political role. Why then are most of the poor countries so far from being genuinely democratic? This question brings further aspects of the current global institutional order into view.

It is a very central feature of this order that any group controlling a preponderance of the means of coercion within a country is internationally recognised as the legitimate government of this country's territory and people – regardless of how this group came to power, of how it exercises power, and of the extent to which it may be supported or opposed by the population it rules. That such a group exercising effective power receives international recognition means not merely that we engage it in negotiations. It means also that we accept this group's right to act for the people it rules, that we, most significantly, confer upon it the privileges freely to borrow in the country's name (international borrowing privilege) and freely to dispose of the country's natural resources (international resource privilege).

## The role of international borrowing privilege

The international borrowing privilege includes the power[32] to impose internationally valid legal obligations upon the country at large. Any successor government that refuses to honour debts incurred by an undemocratic, unconstitutional, repressive, unpopular predecessor will be severely punished by the banks and governments of other countries; at minimum it will lose its own borrowing privilege by being excluded from the international financial markets. Such refusals are therefore quite rare, as governments, even when newly elected after a dramatic break with the past, are compelled to pay the debts of their predecessors.

The international borrowing privilege has three important negative effects on the corruption and poverty problems in the developing world. First, this privilege facilitates borrowing by destructive governments. Such governments can borrow more money and can do so more cheaply than they could do if they alone, rather than the entire country, were obliged to repay. In this way, the borrowing privilege helps such governments to maintain themselves in power even against near-universal popular discontent and opposition. Second, the international borrowing privilege imposes upon democratic successor regimes the often huge debts of their corrupt predecessors. It thereby saps the capacity of such democratic governments to implement structural reforms and other political programmes, thus rendering such governments less successful and less stable than they would otherwise be. (It is small consolation that authoritarian regimes are sometimes weakened by being held liable for the debts of their democratic predecessors.) Third, the international borrowing privilege further strengthens the incentives toward coup attempts: whoever succeeds in bringing a preponderance of the means of coercion under his control gets the borrowing privilege as an additional reward.[33]

The resource privilege we confer upon a group in power is much more than our mere acquiescence in its effective control over the natural resources of the country in question. This privilege includes the power to effect legally valid transfers of ownership rights in such resources. Thus a corporation that has purchased resources from the Saudis or Suharto, or from Mobuto or Sani Abacha, has thereby become entitled to be – and actually *is* – recognized anywhere in the world as the legitimate owner of these resources. This is a remarkable feature of our global institutional order. A group that overpowers the guards and takes control of a warehouse may be able to give some of the merchandise to others, accepting money in exchange. But the fence who pays them becomes merely the possessor, not the owner, of the loot. Contrast this with a group that overpowers an elected government and takes control of a country. Such a group, too, can give away some of the country's natural resources, accepting money in exchange. In this case, however, the purchaser acquires not merely possession, but all the rights and liberties of ownership, which are supposed to be – and actually *are* – protected and enforced by all other states' courts and police forces. The international resource privilege, then, is the legal power to confer globally valid ownership rights in the country's resources.

This international resource privilege has disastrous effects in many poor countries, whose resource sector often constitutes a large segment of the national economy. Whoever can take power in such a country by whatever means can maintain his rule, even against widespread popular opposition, by buying the arms and soldiers he needs with revenues from the export of natural resources (and funds borrowed abroad in the country's name). Take Nigeria as an example. The value of Nigeria's oil exports has averaged about $20 million a day, roughly one quarter of that country's gross domestic product. Whoever controls this revenue stream can afford enough weapons and soldiers to keep himself in power regardless of what the population may think of him.[34] And so long as he succeeds in doing so, his purse will be continuously replenished with new funds with which he can cement his rule and finance a luxurious lifestyle.

This fact in turn provides a strong incentive toward the undemocratic acquisition and unresponsive exercise of political power in such countries.[35] The international resource privilege also gives foreigners strong incentives to corrupt the officials of such countries who, no matter how badly they rule, continue to have resources to sell and money to spend. These incentives go a long way toward explaining the so-called Dutch Disease,[36] the long-observed negative correlation between resource wealth (defined as the size of the natural resource sector as a percentage of GNP) and economic progress: severe poverty is more persistent in resource-rich countries, because the special incentives arising from the international resource privilege make them more prone to corrupt government, coup attempts, and civil wars. Indeed, a recent regression analysis by two Yale economists confirms that the causal connection between resource wealth and poor economic growth is mediated through reduced chances for democracy.[37] The economists fail to note, however, that it is only because of the international resource privilege that resource wealth has so pernicious effects.

By discussing several global systemic factors in some detail, I hope to have undermined a proposition that, sustained by right-wing and left-wing economists alike, most citizens in the developed countries are all too eager to believe: the causes of severe poverty are indigenous to the countries in which it occurs, and the affluent societies and their governments do not substantially contribute to the persistence of severe poverty world-wide. This view is dramatically mistaken. The non-indigenous factors I have discussed are absolutely crucial for explaining the inability and especially the unwillingness of the poor countries' leaders to pursue more effective strategies of poverty eradication. They are absolutely crucial, therefore, for explaining why global inequality is increasing dramatically, so that income poverty and malnutrition have not declined in the last 14 years,[38] despite substantial technological progress, despite substantial global economic growth, despite a huge poverty reduction in China, despite the post-Cold War 'peace dividend,' and despite a 32 per cent drop in real food prices since 1985.[39] An adequate explanation of the persistence of severe poverty requires analysis of these non-indigenous factors. And effective reduction of such poverty requires modifications in these factors, which, in turn, requires a better understanding in the developed countries of how the social causes of the persistence of severe poverty lie by no means in the poor countries alone.

To recapitulate. What I have tried to substantiate here is a point not of morality, but of causal explanation. One can put this point negatively, as a critique of the conventional wisdom, or rather ideology. Observing much political oppression and severe poverty in the developing countries, and noting that these evils are not evenly distributed among them, experts and laypersons alike are drawn to explanations invoking national factors (history, culture, climate, natural environment, leadership personalities, etc.) and international differences in such domestic factors. But these local explanations are importantly incomplete in two respects.

First, an explanation in terms of domestic factors leaves open why these domestic factors are the way they are in the first place. It is quite possible that global factors significantly affect national institutions and policies, especially in the poorer and weaker countries, and that, in a different global environment, domestic factors that tend to generate oppression, corruption and poverty would occur much less frequently or not at all.

Second, local explanations can show at best how *in the prevailing global context* specific domestic factors are causally connected with oppression, corruption, and poverty. Such explanations leave wide open the possibility that, in a different global environment, the same domestic factors, or the same international differences, would have quite a different impact.

It may be objected that, even if our global institutional order plays an important part in the reproduction of oppression, corruption and poverty in the developing world, there are no feasible institutional alternatives that would lead to substantial improvements. I have tried elsewhere to meet this objection by presenting such an institutional alternative in some detail.[40] Summarizing briefly, the main idea is that the international resource and borrowing privileges are to be assigned only to governments that either came to power pursuant to democratic procedures or have legitimated themselves *ex post* through free and open elections. Governments fulfilling neither condition are not entitled to impose internationally valid repayment obligations upon their country or to effect internationally valid transfers of ownership rights in their country's natural resources.

## Proposal for a Democracy Panel

Internationally authoritative decisions about the democratic legitimacy of a particular government are to be made by a standing Democracy Panel – composed of reputable, independent jurists and affiliated with the UN – which should have at its disposal specially trained personnel for the observation and (in special cases) implementation of elections. This commission should, as far as possible, apply the particular rules of democratic legitimization which each country has imposed on itself in a generally democratic way.[41] By incorporating such rules into written constitutions (which should also lay down precisely how such rules may legitimately be amended), democratic governments would ensure that the Panel will make its decision pursuant to standards approved (in advance) by the country's own population and would also facilitate the work of the commission in a way that helps stabilize that country's democratic institutions. It should nevertheless be possible, in special cases, for governments that came to power by force to legitimate themselves through a newly designed democratic procedure accepted by the commission as satisfying internationally recognized general principles of democratic governance.

The modified borrowing privilege should not have a destabilizing effect on existing democratic governments. Such an effect might come about as follows. If an officially illegitimate government cannot, in any case, borrow abroad in the name of the entire country, it may see no reason to service debts incurred by democratic predecessors. This fact might make borrowing abroad more difficult for democratic governments perceived to be in danger of being overthrown – which would not, of course, be in the spirit of my proposal.[42] This difficulty could be neutralized through an International Democratic Loan Guarantee Fund (IDLGF) that temporarily services the debts of countries with broadly democratic constitutions, as recognized by the Democracy Panel, in the event (and *only* in the event) that unconstitutional rulers of such countries refuse to do so. The existence of the IDLGF does not alter the fact that authoritarian rulers – no matter how illegal and illegitimate their acquisition and exercise of political power may be domestically – are obligated under international law to service their country's public debts abroad and should be sanctioned if they fail to do so. Its sole point is to neutralize precisely the risk that the institutional reform under discussion might otherwise add to the ordinary risks of lending money to countries with fledgling democratic governments.

The modified resource privilege must accommodate the fact

that natural resources located within an illegitimately governed country may belong to private (domestic or foreign, individual or corporate) owners. In this case, revenues from resource sales are generally divided – one part goes to the government (as taxes and other fees) while the remainder goes to the private owners. The modified rules should, in such cases, be sensitive to three considerations. They should be sensitive to the origin of the property right in question and, in particular, to whether this right was acquired at a time when the country was governed democratically. They should be sensitive to the proportions in which the revenues are being divided and, in particular, to how much of these revenues would be diverted to the undemocratic government now in power. And these modified rules should also be sensitive to the degree of illegitimacy of this present government, which depends also on how it is affecting the fulfilment of human rights as well as the incidence of domination, corruption and poverty. To achieve optimal incentive effects, the scheme should be both graduated (responsive to how illegitimate a government is) and rigid (not circumventable through bilateral deals with this or that powerful state).

Clearly, a reform along these lines is feasible in the sense that, with the support of the established affluent democracies, it could be effectively implemented. No less clearly, such a reform is unfeasible in the sense that it will not in fact be supported by the established affluent democracies. We would sustain some minor opportunity costs if our banks could not make safe and profitable loans to autocrats and corrupt élites in the developing world. By contrast, the opportunity costs of not recognizing the power of authoritarian rulers to confer legally valid ownership rights in their country's natural resources are potentially enormous.[43] The international resource privilege brings vast benefits not only to autocratic rulers, but also to us. It guarantees us a reliable and steady supply of resources because we can acquire ownership of them from anyone who happens to exercise effective power, without regard to whether the country's population either approves the sale or benefits from the proceeds. And it greatly reduces the price we pay for these resources because no supplier is excluded (e.g. for lack of democratic authorization) and also because corrupt supplier governments, made more frequent by the international resource privilege, will tend to maximize sales in the short term in order to serve their own personal interests (whereas supplier governments serving the needs of a country's present and future people are more inclined to budget its resources for maximum long-term benefit).[44] Just imagine what the price of globally traded natural resources – crude oil, for instance – would be if internationally valid ownership rights in them could not be procured from rulers who gained power unconstitutionally and exercise it undemocratically.[45]

Clearly, then, the governments and citizens of the developed countries will not agree to any meaningful restriction of the international legal powers of authoritarian and unconstitutional rulers. But this political unfeasibility does not undermine my explanatory thesis. By coercively imposing the international borrowing and resource privileges upon the rest of the world, the developed states make a major causal contribution to the persistence of oppression, corruption and poverty in the developing world. Our refusal to allow meaningful institutional reforms does not alter the fact that we *could* allow them and are thus causally responsible for the misery such reforms would avoid.

This point has important implications for our understanding of moral responsibilities. We tend to blame persistent oppression, corruption and poverty in so many developing countries on their social institutions and élites. In this assessment we are correct: if those social institutions and élites were more reasonable, those problems would rapidly decline. We conclude from this that oppression, corruption and poverty in the developing countries cannot be blamed upon external (foreign or global) factors. But this judgement, encouraged perhaps by faulty additive conceptions of causality and moral responsibility, is in error – we, too, are causally and morally responsible, because we uphold a global order in which persons and groups, if only they can seize effective power within a national territory by whatever means, may count on international recognition and support (exemplified by the international resource and borrowing privileges). This global order foreseeably contributes to the persistence of oppression, corruption and poverty in four main ways. It crucially affects what sorts of people shape national policy in the developing countries, what incentives these people face, what options they have, and

what impact their decisions about these options would have on
the lives of their compatriots.

The flaw in the moral understanding dominant in the developed countries is closely related to a faulty interpunctuation of
the situation. We see two morally significant relations: our relation to any developing country and its government's relation to
its population. The former relation involves us, but it is fair – we
lend money or purchase resources at going world market prices.
The latter relation may be quite unjust, but we, not party to it,
bear no responsibility for this injustice. The foregoing causal
analysis shows how this interpunctuation, which sharply separates
*us* in the developed countries from *them* in the developing
countries, is deeply flawed. The morally relevant interpunctuation separates a larger *us* from the disenfranchised populations
of the developing world. The morally relevant question is, what
entitles us – the governments and citizens of the developed
countries *and* the ruling élites of the developing ones – to
enforce a global order under which we can unilaterally, on mutually agreeable terms, dispossess the majority of humankind of the
world's natural resources and burden them with the servicing of
debts which they do not approve and from which they do not
benefit? How can consent bought from a military strongman –
someone like Sani Abacha of Nigeria – insulate Shell and its
customers from the charge of having stolen the oil they took
from the Nigerians? In fact, was it not worse than theft? Not only
have we taken resources from them and done much environmental damage without their consent, but we have also propped up
their hated dictator with funds he could spend on arms and
soldiers to cement his rule. What is more, we are offering a prize
to every would-be autocrat or junta anywhere – whoever can gain
effective power by whatever means will have the legal power to
incur debts in the country's name and to confer internationally
valid ownership rights in the country's resources. And having
done all this, we lavish condescending pity on impoverished populations for their notorious 'failure to govern themselves
democratically'!

I hope that this essay, though it had to be brief, has lent some
initial plausibility to the claims that a considerable part of the
oppression, corruption and poverty so prevalent in the developing
world is foreseeably and avoidably caused by the current design

of our global institutional order and that we, insofar as we co-operate in upholding this order, share moral responsibility for those foreseeable and avoidable effects. If so, further empirical exploration of the explanatory significance of central features of our global institutional order, such as the resource and borrowing privileges in particular, would seem warranted.

## Notes

1. The paper had previously been presented at conferences in Frankfurt (December 1998), Bielefeld (February 1999), and Stanford (April 1999). I am grateful to my audiences there for valuable comments and criticisms. I am grateful also for a grant from the Research and Writing Initiative of the Program on Global Security and Sustainability of the John D. and Catherine T. MacArthur Foundation, which supported my work of bringing the lecture into publishable form.

2. World Bank, *World Bank Development Report 2002*, New York 2001, p. 233.

3. UNDP (United Nations Development Programme), *Human Development Report 1997*, New York 1997, p. 195.

4. World Bank, *World Bank Development Report 2002*, p. 233.

5. The $-sign stands for the US currency throughout. The figure of $5,149 results from straightforward division: $31,171 billion by 6,054 million. The figure of $2,714 is inflated to reflect the lower value of the dollar in the year 2000. It is estimated from data provided in UNDP (United Nations Development Programme), *Human Development Report 1998*, New York 1998, p. 142; World Bank, *World Development Report 2002*, p. 237, and www.census.gov/ipc/www/worldpop.html

6. UNDP, *Human Development Report 1998*, p. 197.

7. UNDP, *Human Development Report 1999*, New York 1999, p. 191.

8. UNDP, *Human Development Report 1996*, New York 1996, p. 222. For this figure and further explication of the international poverty line, see World Bank, *World Development Report 2000/2001*, New York 2000, pp. 17, 23.

9. Shaohua Chen and Martin Ravallion, 'How Did the World's Poorest Fare in the 1990s?', *Review of Income and Wealth*, vol. 47, no. 3, 2001, p. 286.

10. See http://stats.bls.gov/cpi/home.htm

11. UNDP, *Human Development Report 2001*, New York 2001, pp. 22 and 9. www.undp.org/hdr2001

12. UNDP, *Human Development Report 1999*, p. 22.

13. UNDP, *Human Development Report 1998*, p. 49.

14. FAO (United Nations Food and Agricultural Organization), *The State of Food Insecurity in the World 1999*, Rome 1999, p. 11. www.fao.org/news/1999/img/sofi99-e.pdf

15. World Bank, *World Development Report 1999/2000*, New York 1999, p. 62. www.worldbank.org/wdr/2000/fullreport.html. According to the International Labor Organization 'some 250 million children between the ages of

5 and 14 are working in developing countries – 120 million full time, 130 million part time'. (www.ilo.org/public/english/standards/ipec/simpoc/stats/4stt.htm).

16. Among these causes are (with the number of daily deaths in parentheses): diarrhoea (5819) and malnutrition (1219), perinatal (6682) and maternal conditions (1356), childhood diseases (3795, mainly measles), acute respiratory infections (10,797, mainly pneumonia), sexually transmitted diseases (8658, mainly HIV), chronic obstructive pulmonary disease (6912), tuberculosis (4548), and malaria (2959). See WHO (World Health Organisation), *The World Health Report 2001*, Geneva 2001, Annex Table 2. www.who.int/whr/2001

17. World Bank, *World Development Report 2002*, p. 233.

18. Ibid.

19. Shaohua Chen and Martin Ravallion, 'How Did the World's Poorest Fare in the 1990s?', *Review of Income and Wealth*, Tables 2 and 4, dividing the poverty gap index by the headcount index.

20. Thus the World Bank equates India's *per capita* gross national income of $460 to $2,390 PPP, China's $840 to $3,940 PPP, Nigeria's $260 to $790 PPP, Pakistan's $470 to $1,960 PPP, Bangladesh's $380 to $1,650 PPP, Ethiopia's $100 to $660 PPP, Vietnam's $390 to $2,030 PPP, and so on, World Bank, *World Development Bank Report 2002*, pp. 232–3; I have listed these countries by the number of poor people they contain.

21. These are the poorest of the poor. The World Bank provides statistics also for a more generous poverty line that is twice as high: $786 PPP 1993 ($965 PPP or roughly $241 in the year 2001) per person per year. Over 2,800 million people are said to live below this higher poverty line, falling 43 per cent below it on average, Shaohua Chen and Martin Ravallion, 'How Did the World's Poorest Fare in the 1990s?', *Review of Income and Wealth*, Tables 3 and 4, again dividing the poverty gap index by the headcount index. This much larger group of people can then, on average, buy as much per person per year as we can buy with $550 in a rich country or with $134 in a poor one. And the collective annual income of this group – nearly half of humankind – is then approximately $385 billion or 1.25 per cent of global aggregate income.

22. UNDP, *Human Development Report 1999*, p. 3.

23. Branko Milanovik, 'True World Income Distribution, 1988 and 1993: First Calculation Based on Household Surveys Alone', *Economic Journal*, Vol. 112, 2002, p. 88.

24. UNDP, *Human Development Report 1999*, p. 3.

25. UNDP, *Human Development Report 1998*, p. 30.

26. This has not stopped them from soundly defeating the leftist political coalition responsible for those policies in the last assembly elections, 10 May 2001. The coalition won only 40 seats out of 140.

27. John Rawls' latest book relies heavily on the assumption that people are masters of their own fate, that the causes of international inequality are purely domestic: 'The causes of the wealth of a people and the forms it takes lie in their political culture and in the religious, philosophical, and moral traditions that support the basic structure of their political and social institutions, as well as in the industriousness and co-operative talents of its members, all supported by their political virtues ... Crucial also is the

country's population policy' (Rawls, *The Law of Peoples*, Cambridge, MA 1999, p. 108). If a society does not want to be poor, it can curb its population growth or industrialise (ibid., p. 117f.) and, in any case, 'if it is not satisfied, it can continue to increase savings, or, if this is not feasible, borrow from other members of the Society of Peoples' (ibid., p. 114). With the right culture and policies, even resource-poor countries like Japan can do very well. With the wrong culture and policies, resource-rich countries like Argentina may do very poorly (ibid., p. 108). Everyone can succeed on their own – except only, perhaps, the Arctic Eskimos (ibid., p. 108, n. 34).

28. Here is one notorious example: 'It is not the sign for some collective derangement or radical incapacity for a political community to produce an authoritarian regime. Indeed, the history, culture, and religion of the community may be such that authoritarian regimes are, as it were, naturally, reflecting a widely shared world view or way of life', Michael Walzer, 'The Moral Standing of States', *Philosophy and Public Affairs*, vol. 9, 1980, pp. 209–29, 224f. See also David Landes, *The Wealth and Poverty of Nations*, New York 1998 and the essays collected in Lawrence E. Harrison and Samuel P. Huntington, eds, *Culture Matters: How Values Shape Progress*, New York 2001.

29. This point is well documented in the more sober reportage parts of *The Economist* (e.g., 25 September 1999, p. 89, whose editors have outdone all others in their defence of the WTO and in their vilification of the protesters of Seattle and Washington as enemies of the poor).

30. In the United States, the post-Watergate Congress tried to prevent the bribing of foreign officials through its 1977 Foreign Corrupt Practices Act, passed after the Lockheed Corporation was found to have paid – not a modest sum to some third-world official, but rather – a US$2 million bribe to Prime Minister Kakuei Tanaka of powerful and democratic Japan.

31. The convention went into effect in February 1999 and as of November 2001 has been ratified by 34 states (www.oecd.org/EN/about/0,,EN-about-883-no-no-no-88,00.html). This success was facilitated by public pressure generated by the innovative non-governmental organization Transparency International (www.transparency.de) and by steady support from the US, which understandably did not want its firms to be at a disadvantage vis-à-vis their foreign rivals.

32. As understood by Wesley N. Hohfeld, *Fundamental Legal Conceptions*, New Haven 1919, a power involves the legally recognized authority to alter the distribution of first-order liberty rights, claim rights, and duties. Having *a* power or power*s* in this sense is distinct from having power (i.e., control over physical force and/or means of coercion).

33. The rulers of resource-rich developing countries have been especially adept at mortgaging their countries' future for their own benefit. As of 1998, Nigeria's foreign debt, run up by its succession of military dictatorships, stood at $30 billion or 79% of GNP. The 1998 ratios of foreign debt to GNP for other large resource-rich countries are as follows: Kenya 61%, Angola 297%, Mozambique 223%, Brazil 31%, Venezuela 40%, Indonesia 176%, the Philippines 70%, UNDP, *Human Development Report 2001*, 2001, pp. 219–21. The 1997 ratio for the Congo/Zaire is 232%, UNDP, *Human Development Report 1999*, 1999, p. 195. Needless to say, little of the borrowed funds were channelled into productive investments, e.g. in education and infrastructure, which would augment economic growth and thus tax

revenues that could help meet interest and repayment obligations. Much was taken for personal use or used for military and 'internal security' expenditures.

34. For some background, see 'Going on down,' *The Economist*, 8 June 1996, pp. 46–8. A later update says: 'Oil revenues [are] paid directly to the government at the highest level . . . The head of state has supreme power and control of all the cash. He depends on nobody and nothing but oil. Patronage and corruption spread downwards from the top', *The Economist*, 12 December 1998, p. 19.

35. To be sure, oppression, coups and civil wars may be encouraged by the prospect of mere possession of resources. (As I have learned from Josiah Ober, this is elegantly observed already in Thucydides, *The History of the Peloponnesian War*, Harmondsworth 1986, Book 1, Chapter 1). But without the legal power to confer internationally valid ownership rights, the value of the resources, and the corresponding incentive, would obviously be much diminished.

36. This name alludes to a period in Dutch history which began in 1959 with the discovery of huge natural gas reserves that, by the 1970s, produced revenues and import savings of about $5–$6 billion annually. Despite this windfall (enhanced by the 'oil-shock' increases in energy prices), the Dutch economy suffered stagnation, high unemployment, and finally recession – doing considerably worse than its peers throughout the 1970s and early 1980s. The Dutch Disease is exemplified by many developing countries which, despite great natural wealth, have achieved little economic growth and poverty reduction over the last decades. Here are the more important resource-rich developing countries with their average annual rates of change in real GDP *per capita* from 1975 to 1998: Nigeria −0.8 per cent, Congo/Zaire −4.7* per cent, Kenya 0.4 per cent, Angola −2.1* per cent, Mozambique 1.3* per cent, Brazil 0.8 per cent, Venezuela −1.0 per cent, Saudi Arabia −2.2 per cent, United Arab Emirates −3.7* per cent, Oman 2.8* per cent, Kuwait −1.5* per cent, Bahrain −0.5* per cent, Brunei −2.1* per cent, Indonesia 4.6 per cent, the Philippines 0.1 per cent, UNDP, *Human Development Report 2001*, pp. 178–81; asterisks indicate that a somewhat different period was used due to insufficient data. Thus, with the notable exception of Indonesia, the resource-rich developing countries fell far below the 2.2 per cent annual rate in real *per capita* growth of the developed countries – even while the developing countries on the whole did slightly better (2.3 per cent) than the developed countries, thanks to rapid growth in China and the rest of East and South-East Asia (ibid., p. 181).

37. 'All petrostates or resource-dependent countries in Africa fail to initiate meaningful political reforms . . . besides South Africa, transition to democracy has been successful only in resource-poor countries', Ricky Lam and Leonard Wantchekon, 'Dictatorships as a Political Dutch Disease', Working Paper, Yale University 1999, p. 31; 'Our cross-country regression confirms our theoretical insights. We find that a one percentage increase in the size of the natural resource sector [relative to GDP] generates a decrease by half a percentage point in the probability of survival of democratic regimes' (ibid., p. 35). See also Leonard Wantchekon, 'Why do Resource Dependent Countries Have Authoritarian Governments?', Working Paper, Yale University 1999. www.yale.wdu/leitner/pdf/1999–11.pdf

38. World Bank, *World Development Report 2000/2001*, p. 23. www.worldbank. org/poverty/wdrpoverty/report/index.htm.

39. The World Bank Food Index fell from 124 in 1985 to 84.5 in 2000. These statistics are updated in 'Global Commodity Markets' published by the World Bank's Development Prospects Group.

40. Thomas Pogge, 'Achieving Democracy', in *World Poverty and Human Rights*, Cambridge 2002, chapter 6.

41. The Democracy Panel would obviously work only in the interest of *democratic* constitutions, broadly defined. Its findings would not merely determine whether a government enjoys resource and borrowing privileges, but would also have consequences for its reputation and standing at home and abroad. A government that has been officially declared illegitimate would be encumbered in many ways (trade, diplomacy, foreign investment, etc.). In these ways, the proposed reform would tend further to reduce the incentives toward undemocratic rule, thus also further reducing the frequency of coup attempts.

42. I want to thank Ronald Dworkin for seeing this difficulty and for articulating it forcefully.

43. Still, these opportunity costs are diminished by the fact that the proposed modification of the international resource privilege would reduce the incidence of authoritarian rule in the developing world.

44. It is likely that we also benefit in terms of more lucrative business opportunities as a third dubious benefit from the international resource privilege. Corrupt supplier governments, made more frequent by the international resource privilege, tend to send much of their resource revenues right back to us, to pay for high-margin weaponry and military advisors, advanced luxury products, as well as real estate and financial investments; democratically responsive supplier governments, by contrast, tend to spend more of their resource revenues domestically (stimulating the country's economy) and tend to get better value for what they spend on imports.

45. We should remember this point whenever we hear it said that natural resources are no longer an important part of the global economy. Once we understand why this is true (relating the dollar value of resource sales to that of aggregate global income or of aggregate international trade), we also understand why it is, in a deeper sense, false. Natural resources are of small significance only *modulo current price vectors*, which are heavily influenced by the international resource privilege and by the extreme global income inequality it helps cause. (I am grateful to Kenneth Arrow for pointing out that, with regard to some resources, consumption has a roughly linear correlation with household income so that income distribution among households has little effect on aggregate demand for these resources.) So the small fraction of their GNP that rich countries spend on imported natural resources does not reflect the extent to which their economic prosperity depends on these resources – just as the small fraction of my income spent on water does not reflect the extent of my dependence on it. If we appraise depletable natural resources by their use value for all human beings, present and future, we must judge them grossly undervalued by current market prices. This undervaluation reflects a negative externality that the corrupt élites of

resource-rich developing countries and the heavy consumers of resources together manage to impose upon the populations of those developing countries as well as on future generations, for whom such resources will be considerably less plentiful and more expensive.

# 9

# The Imperial Presidency and the Revolutions of Modernity

*Robin Blackburn*

It is inherent in the concept of a terrorist act that it aims at an effect very much larger than the direct physical destruction it causes. Proponents of what used to be called the 'propaganda of the deed' also believed that in the illuminating glare of terror the vulnerability of a corrupt order would be starkly revealed. Once corruption and oppression were stripped away, a sacred or natural order – the nation, the religious community, the people – would come into its own. The instigators of September 11 brought off a far more spectacular coup than any exponent of the propaganda of the deed, and threaten more than a dozen of the world's most autocratic and corrupt rulers and aim to summon to arms a religious community of well over a billion people. The resources disposed of by this network transcend those traditionally associated with terrorism and are closer to those of a small state, but a state without boundaries whose headquarters hops from country to country.

Given the extent of the destruction wrought by the September 11 attack it is sobering to realize that the effect aimed at was qualitatively larger, namely that of reordering world politics around a 'clash of fundamentalisms', urging the Islamic world to free itself of all infidel trammels.[1] Whether the strategic director of the al Qaeda network was Osama bin Laden, Ayman al-Zawahiri, or someone else, their aim from the outset was not only to provoke the US into a reaction that would alienate Muslim opinion, but also to expose the hereditary and autocratic rulers of the Muslim world and create conditions in which Islamic jihad could seize or manipulate power in one or another of the larger or more significant Muslim states. The new Caliphate at which they aim might appear a medieval fantasy, but are to be equipped with the military and financial power resources of modernity. They ask believers to consider the awesome power of Muslim leaders equipped with Islamic virtue, oil and nuclear weapons. Given the frustrated or desperate condition of much of the Muslim world, this is a message that has great resonance even among Muslims who are uneasy at, or repelled by, terror actions. The message targets the military actions and dispositions of the US and Israel, especially as they are deemed to encroach on Muslim holy places, but it is also aimed at the existing governments of the Islamic world, easily portrayed as pawns of the West. Since Islamic jihad is indeed a network, the overthrow of the Taliban and the dispersal of al Qaeda's bases will not end the threat it poses.

The US president responded to September 11 by proclaiming a global, US-led 'war on terrorism'. Washington sought every conceivable ally or partner but insisted on retaining complete control of its 'war'. The UN and the Security Council were asked to support the US effort, and each of their members to help in whatever way they could, but there was to be no formal anti-terrorism coalition and no supranational organization to embody it. On one side of this new war there is the world's most powerful state, with its awesome fire power and a global system of alliances. On the other there is a makeshift terror network of perhaps no more than a few thousand men acting as a self-proclaimed 'Muslim vanguard', but occasionally able to reflect the resentments and frustrations of tens or even hundreds of millions in the Islamic world. Al Qaeda had the economic and military resources of a small state and aimed to shape the thinking of a civilization. Its members were drawn from many nationalities and have been active in Central Asia, the Balkans, Europe, North America, Kashmir, China, Indonesia and the Philippines as well as the Middle East and Africa. Its ideology appeals to a sense of injury and wounded pride rather than material aspiration. It is virulently anti-infidel and misogynist, anti-secular without being at all anti-capitalist, and egalitarian without being democratic. The neo-fundamentalism of the eighties and nineties, forged in a battle with godless Communism and in reaction to royalist bureaucracy and corruption, accentuated this legacy by basing itself on strong and responsible Islamic business and faith-based charity. While prepared to work with a variety of Islamic political authorities, the project of al Qaeda transcends such boundaries, aiming to unite the faithful against the infidels who have insulted and oppressed Islam. But its weapon of choice – spectacular terror – positively discourages and disables mass mobilization or organization.

In the postwar period the West feared a loss of control in the Middle East and so it allied with the most conservative forces in the Islamic world. The Saudi and Iranian monarchies were chosen as the strategic allies needed to protect vital Middle Eastern oil resources while secular nationalists like Mossadegh in Iran or Kassem in Iraq were destabilized and replaced. In fact the Western system of alliances is not simply a relic of the Cold War but rather a palimpsest that reflects, layer on layer, a longer history and a colonialism that mummified an extraordinary collection of archaic or pseudo-archaic regimes.[2] This embraces Saudi Arabia with its teeming, 30,000-strong Royal Family, the Shaikh of Bahrein and Kuwait, the Sultan of Oman, and the Emirates – boasting the world's longest-serving head of state, Shaikh Sakir al-Qasimi of Ras al-Khaimah, who has been lolling on his throne since 1948. When we add to those the Sultan of Brunei in the South China Sea, it is as if oil is a pickling fluid akin to formaldehyde projecting into the twenty-first century simulacra of the *anciens régimes* of former times. Pakistan, with its notorious 'feudals', does not have oil but enjoys an intimate pact with the oil sheikhdoms. The paradox here for liberal, bourgeois and nationalist forces in the Middle East was that the power that should have been their great ally, the US, actually blocked them at every turn and preferred to do business with pliant royal absolutists.[3]

The US-sponsored Arabian and Gulf regime associates the West with corruption, autocracy and stagnation at a time when there is a yearning for a new start in the Arab world. The dilemma of US policy is that it understandably wishes to avoid a 'clash of civilizations' while being fearful of renewal within the Muslim world. It was a tribute to Washington's diplomacy that its assault on Afghanistan aroused so little official censure in the Muslim world, but an indication of the fragility of this success that no Muslim state was willing to play an active and public role. When the United States proceeded to impose a new government in Afghanistan based on Hamid Karzai, scion of a noble house but with little independent following, it assumed a new risk. Mercenary tribal elders, power-hungry warlords, Taliban turncoats, and even the King, could be bludgeoned into agreement but the result lacked credibility or legitimacy. So far as the wider Islamic world is concerned, such a strategy simultaneously offends the Islamists and those who yearn for more democracy, autonomy and self-respect. Religious fanatics and bourgeois or petty-bourgeois democrats are not natural allies – in Iran they are at loggerheads – but in the territories where the US has allied itself with feudal and autocratic reaction these two currents find a common antagonist. The White House may genuinely believe that the interests of global capitalism are best promoted by its pact with the petrol dynasties and their Pakistani and Egyptian hangers-on, but this is not true. The pact may deliver slightly cheaper oil and privileges to Western oil corporations, but it stifles the growth of an autonomous business culture and circuit of accumulation in the region itself. The resulting frustrations create conditions which politicize religious fanaticism, especially in those countries where it is one of the few officially-tolerated species of public activity.

Washington strives not to inflame Muslim opinion, or to allow the conflict to be defined as a war of religions. It hopes that the danger can be avoided by allowing its Muslim allies to adopt a low profile, or even to stand aside. The UN will be handed responsibility for occupied areas of Afghanistan but Iranian and Egyptian proposals that the UN should take charge of the anti-terrorism campaign were rejected. Given the UN's long history of giving cover to US military campaigns from Korea onwards, entrusting it with nominal responsibility post facto, as in Kosovo, will be of limited value in averting the danger of a 'clash of civilizations'. The UN could sponsor an accord against terrorism and the creation of a supranational force to police it. But such an approach would have little legitimacy if credible governments from the Muslim world are excluded. An international and supranational approach would be far more effective at tackling terrorism than a US-led and -defined 'war', but will not easily be accepted in Washington since it would challenge imperial ideology and control. The Bush team see themselves as champions of the American people and US capitalism, but in fact neither require direct US control of Middle Eastern or Caspian oil, as we will see below.

The most difficult thing for the strategists of empire to perceive, or explain to the American people, is that the best and perhaps only effective coalition against al Qaeda and kindred terrorist networks would be one that they do not lead and do not control. Likewise the only legitimate and effective way of minimizing the much greater threat of weapons of mass destruction will be comprehensive disarmament, embracing all today's nuclear powers, and policed by international agreement and an independent world authority. The food drops in Afghanistan were accompanied by leaflets in English and Pushtu with the heading 'The Partnership of Nations' – a hollow rubric which could not conceal that this was a US and British action. Ejecting the Taliban was not difficult, but there may be continuing resistance. Prior to their withdrawal in 1989, the Soviet forces controlled most of the country and all the main towns and cities. Najibulla's Communist regime survived for a further three years. So the real test of any military accomplishments and political changes will be in the long term and will concern the legitimacy of the new arrangements, and the human cost of achieving and sustaining them. The overthrow of the Taliban is not the same as the destruction of al Qaeda and affiliated forces of Islamic jihad elsewhere in the Muslim world. Isolating and defeating al Qaeda and Islamic jihad will require a political strategy that is willing to disengage from the forces of reaction in the Islamic world and favours the forces of enlightenment, reform and democracy.

While I will focus on Washington's sins of omission and commission, I believe it would be wrong to slight the ability of the Bush administration to impose its own definitions on domestic opponents, and on allies and even enemies abroad. The US president has sometimes been presented as a figure of fun but this has not stopped him having the last laugh on those who ridiculed him. Unlike more brilliant leaders, he surrounds himself with a capable and experienced team, and sometimes heeds words of caution. The secret of his strength – and his fatal flaw – may be the instinctive rapport he enjoys with those gripped by US national messianism, the idea that only the US can tackle the really big global threats and that whatever the US does is ipso facto favourable to freedom. These sentiments are often accompanied by depreciation of international organizations, an unwillingness to consider global complexities, or to contemplate any sacrifice of US sovereignty.

The imperial role is justified on the grounds that the US has a special destiny as world leader and champion of freedom. These roles, it is believed, require Washington to meet the threat of rogue states acquiring weapons of mass destruction, to pre-empt 'global competitors', to secure sources of scarce raw materials (especially oil), and to guarantee the personal security of ordinary Americans. Yet the truth is that the empire does not secure these goals, and actually makes 'blowback' more likely, as Chalmers Johnson so presciently argued.[4] A healthier US polity could dispense with the cumbersome and expensive apparatus of empire, set the scene for a broader, more pluralistic global capitalism, and promote the competence and authority of supranational agencies in the fields of disarmament, anti-terrorism and peacekeeping. But the vested interests which stand in the way of these goals are those of a bloated military-industrial complex and supercharged presidency.

## The imperial presidency

The extraordinary terrorist coup of September 11 set the scene for the resurgence of an imperial presidency. This was initially concealed by Bush's dithering on the day itself. Yet his first words insisted that the nation was at war and that reprisals would be visited not only on the perpetrators but on the states which had backed them. It soon became clear that the Bush White House was taking advantage of the shock at what had happened to demand global 'war powers' and the financial and constitutional means to employ them. In less than 48 hours NATO was persuaded to invoke, for the first time ever, Article 5 and consequently to give the US commander in chief huge scope to act in its name. The Senate took only a little longer unanimously to back the president's declaration of war against an unnamed enemy and for Congress to place a $40 billion war chest at his disposal. When the Senate and House of Representatives passed the anti-terrorism legislation requested by the administration in October many legislators complained that they had had no opportunity even to read the complex legislation they were voting on.[5] The exact wording of the Congressional resolution of September 15 made clear the latitude extended to Bush:

> the president is authorized to use all necessary and appropriate force against those nations, organizations, or persons he determines planned, authorized, committed, or aided the terrorist attacks that occurred on Sept. 11, 2001, or harbored such organizations or persons, in order to prevent any future acts of international terrorism against the United States by such nations, organizations or persons.

Bush was to decide who to fight and how to fight. The only hints at restraint were those words 'necessary and appropriate' and the residual implication that it was only those implicated in September 11 who should be targeted. For the moment these qualifications carried little weight though later, when Iraq was targeted, critics sought to argue that the president had exceeded his remit. On the day after this resolution Bush vowed to 'rid the world of evil-doers' and cautioned: 'This crusade, this war on terrorism, is going to take a while.' In the truncated discussion that followed the speech no member of Congress queried the extraordinary new mandate.

So the presidency came to enjoy almost complete freedom of action and was able to give shape and direction to the widespread sense of shock, anger and alarm. Moreover, Bush repeatedly insisted that the campaign against international terrorism would be a long one, presumably requiring indefinite extension of his special powers. The power of the president had been raised by a quantum leap. The presidency had an imperial potency equal to – or even exceeding – that of Reagan or Nixon at their high point. Bush's authority and freedom of action was suddenly far greater than that enjoyed by his father on the eve of the Gulf War.

The imperial presidency has been struggling to be born for some time. In a book published in September 2001, Daniel Lazare anticipated this state of affairs when he warned of the extraordinary power of a US president compared with counterparts in other democratic states. In European democracies the head of government has greater domestic power than a US president. But

in external affairs, Lazare argues, matters stand the other way
around:

> [A] US president is a good deal more powerful. Surrounded by
> courtiers, intelligence agencies, and military units at his beck and call,
> he is free to launch invasions or order covert operations any time, day
> or night, without fear of contradiction from his cabinet or any of his
> subordinates. Indeed he is *expected* to engage in such unilateral
> displays . . .[6]

Lazare was here drawing attention to a powerful war- and Cold
War-related trend in US government, which witnessed a twentieth-
century aggrandizement of the presidency that would have aston-
ished the framers of the Constitution. But this trend was at least
partly checked by resistance to the Vietnam War, by the impeach-
ment of Nixon and by the considerable public controversy over
Iran–Contra, or even the Gulf War or Kosovo bombardment.
Moreover, the post-Vietnam refusal to accept casualties also hob-
bled the US president and the war machine at his command. The
opinion polls and talk shows now suggest that this restraint has
weakened. Finally, US allies also constrained the White House
during those episodes. Today matters are different and Lazare is
simply stating the bare truth when he writes: 'Short of total war,
the US president has *carte blanche* to attack whom he pleases
virtually anywhere in the world.'[7]

If the imperial presidency legitimated by the resolution might
astound the Founders, it is not thereby unconstitutional. As
Lazare argues, the Constitution was forged for another age and
with the purpose of rendering public power as circumscribed and
divided as possible. The presidency has escaped these bounds
because no state could respect them in modern conditions.
Invoking the archaic features of the Constitution will not restrain
the presidency. Once war powers have been conferred on the
president the executive's already large competence is both
increased and formally sanctioned. The White House later
explained that this will extend to military tribunals which will
dispense summary justice to those who are not US citizens.[8] And
it will encompass bilateral treaty-like agreements with Russia,
which will not be submitted to Congressional scrutiny or
approval.[9]

When Americans say they want action against 'those responsible' for the attacks the sentiment is easy to understand. To expect the mass of US citizens simply to accept that they should be the target of such attacks would be ridiculous. Bush's address to Congress on September 20 outlining his campaign against terrorism addressed these anxieties. Unfortunately it also harnessed them to a boundless and unilateral, US-defined and US-led war against terrorism (the word 'crusade' was avoided this time). For many reasons any repetition of September 11 is most unlikely but the approach outlined by Bush, if adhered to, gets in the way of the strategies that are needed to inflict political defeats on al Qaeda.

## National messianism and recharged unilateralism

In a controlled and polished performance on September 20, Bush underlined the limitless scope and long duration of the new mission which he would undertake on behalf of his wounded but unbowed country. 'Our enemy is a radical network of terrorists and every government that supports them. Our war on terror begins with al Qaeda, but it does not end there. It will not end until every terrorist group of global reach has been found, stopped and defeated . . .' This new war against terror forced a choice upon every nation: 'Every nation in every region of the world now has a decision to make. Either you are with us or you are with the terrorists.' So the president not only commandeered US foreign policy but sought to impose his definitions on every state in the world.

The Clinton administration also claimed and exercised a right of unilateral action against a variety of enemies. Madeleine Albright explained: 'If we have to use force it is because we are America. We are the indispensable nation. We stand tall. We see farther into the future.'[10] Yet the record of the indispensable nation in the nineties was not a good one. The issue of nuclear disarmament was neglected. The Russians were not engaged in this or any other positive way, and instead NATO was enlarged to encircle it. In the absence of an agreement between Moscow and Washington, the secondary nuclear powers did nothing and India and Pakistan tested nuclear devices. Repeated bombardment of Iraq did more to weaken the US in the region than to weaken the regime of Saddam Hussein. Rwanda bled. The break up of

Yugoslavia dragged on for many years and cost many lives.[11] The failure to use Moscow and the OSCE structure to secure Serb withdrawal from Kosovo at Rambouillet led to massive bombing of Serbia and Kosovo, but eventually the European allies insisted that Russian mediation to this end be obtained – and it was this rather than the bombing which secured a result.[12] While Washington might ask the UN to rubber-stamp its own initiatives, it did not even bother to pay its quota. There were very few gains for the US go-it-alone method in the nineties (Haiti?), but an alternative was glimpsed when the UN successfully orchestrated, with the help of regional powers, the Indonesian military withdrawal from East Timor.

When Bush arrived in the White House, its allies were unhappy to discover that the new president, despite his own criticisms of the Clinton–Albright interventions, had an even more vigorous notion of America's special destiny. He regarded international treaties as scraps of paper (ABM or Kyoto), spurned agreements on landmines, biological warfare, and terrorism, slighted international conclaves on racism and sustainable development, and insisted that US soldiers and officials should be exempted from the remit of the International Criminal Court (ICC). Secretary of State Powell seems to have cautioned against some of these decisions, but without any success. Sustaining these positions was a determination not to yield an iota of US sovereignty while often expecting this sacrifice of other states.

Because the US was manifestly the injured party on September 11, the situation itself conspired to reinforce Washington's habitual conduct and assumptions. Washington always insists on running the show, but this time virtually no one objected. Such was the shock at the events of September 11 that the European allies announced their prior willingness to back almost any action the US might launch, even before learning what it would be. Perhaps they thought that their swift support would earn them some influence at a later stage and that in its hour of need the Bush presidency might jettison the unilateral approach. In a way it has, but in the direction of a proliferation of bilateralism as the US Secretary of State and Defense Secretary engage in an unceasing round of consultations across several continents, not a new emphasis on NATO and the European allies.

In the weeks following September 11 both Powell and Rumsfeld undertook a wide-ranging diplomatic effort directed at key regional players, like Pakistan, Saudi Arabia, Uzbekistan, Russia and China. If one wishes this could be called a multilateral approach, especially since US policy evidently took note of reservations and problems raised by the governments of these states. But the choice of whom to approach, and what advice to accept, still lay with Washington. No attempt was being made to mount a collective operation using the UN or some other body. Thus, it is not so much Bush's personality which should be scrutinized as the president's new programme and mandate, the situation and character of his machine, and the facilities it now enjoys, both domestically and abroad. Behind Bush stand more considerable figures like Cheney and Rumsfeld and behind them a military-industrial complex, which begins to see its prayers being answered.[13]

The laying down of the law to other states combined with the refusal to yield up a particle of US sovereignty establishes the principle of the new empire.[14] The obsessively reiterated discourse of war directed attention away from what could have been an international police action. And its definition as a 'new kind of war' allowed unilateralism to be raised to a new pitch. This was the unilateralism of imperial leadership, not that of isolationism or withdrawal. The attack had demonstrated 'global reach', yet had been aimed this time exclusively at targets on US soil. The fact that both attackers and victims were of many nations, and the worldwide revulsion at its devastating consequences, could have been used to mount a multilateral response. But that would have been contrary to the administration's every instinct and inclination. That such an approach might be more effective in tracking down and punishing the network responsible for the attack would appear a crazy notion not only to the Bush White House but to the powerful jingoistic reflex often articulated by liberal commentators, such as Thomas Friedman, as much as conservative commentators like William Safire.

When Bush declared that states implicated in terrorism would be treated as enemies he was announcing a new, and in some ways welcome, policy since too many such states have in the past been close friends of the US. The US president showed no awareness, for example, that the US had aligned itself with states that unleashed death-squads in Central and South America. In

the days following September 11 the Senate ratified Bush's nomi-
nee as Ambassador to the UN, John Negroponte, a man notorious
for his failure to report large-scale violations of human rights by
US-linked contra forces when he was ambassador in Honduras in
the eighties. Thus the man who will represent the US case against
terrorism to the major world forum will himself be someone who
at best turned a blind eye to the slaughter of many thousands,
and whose complicity may well have been worse than that.[15]

After the terrible events of September 11 any US president, it
might be urged, would have reacted in much the same way. But
some might have avoided the continued and strident unilateralism. They might have seen that the international revulsion already
evident, and willingly given, made it clear the UN, and its Security
Council, could play a crucial role in combating terrorism. In the
aftermath of the two world wars US presidents did advocate
supranational organization, in the shape of the League of Nations
and UN. The aftermath of September 11 was a good moment to
work out with other governments what was justified and effective
in a campaign against terrorism, and what would merely feed it.

The unilateralist conclusions drawn by Bush were superficially
at odds with one theme of his speech on September 20: 'This is
not, however, just America's fight. And what is at stake is not just
America's freedom. This is the world's fight. This is civilization's
fight.' Given this claim, it might seem strange that a world body,
such as the UN, was not entrusted with conducting the fight. The
explanation, of course, was the doctrine of national messianism.
The US is the leader and representative of humanity and civilization, acting in their name.

## The US alliance with militant Islam

In the weeks following September 11 an astonishing picture
emerged of the extent to which Osama bin Laden, al Qaeda and
the Taliban had been enjoying crucial support from supposed US
friends and client states. It became clear that a steady stream of
financial contributions from Saudi Arabia and the Emirates had
furnished al Qaeda and the Taliban with their lifeblood in the
days, months and years leading up to September 11. The US
government itself tilted to the Taliban in 1996, notwithstanding
their determination to impose on the whole of Afghanistan a

direly repressive regime. Later in 2000, when no further doubt could exist, they paid the Taliban $42 million in the 'war against drugs'.[16] US courts had already established both al Qaeda's role in the East African embassy bombings in 1998 and the presence of the al Qaeda training camps in Afghanistan.

The US military and intelligence community has the most intimate relationship with the security services of Saudi Arabia and Pakistan. These states, as we know them today, would not exist without US support. Saudi oil and Pakistani proximity to Afghanistan led Washington to confer great importance on these states. And it was only Saudi and Pakistani support for the Taliban – including military units as well as lavish amounts of money, arms and training – which allowed them to seize power in Afghanistan in 1996, displacing the fractious alliance of mujahedeen and military men which ruled the country from 1992. The Taliban movement received help from bin Laden and subsequently allowed his al Qaeda network to set up training camps there. It was Prince Turki al Feisal, the then head of Saudi intelligence, who first recruited bin Laden to organize resistance in Afghanistan, with US approval. (He was removed from his post without explanation two months before the attack.) For its part, the Pakistani military intelligence, the ISI, sponsors of the Taliban, welcomed the Saudi money which bin Laden continued to attract.

The US charge against the bin Laden network was plausible partly because the ramifications of this claim were bound to be so awkward and embarrassing for the US authorities themselves. In an affair like this, the focus of so much attention, pinning the blame immediately on a convenient but false target – say Castro, Chavez, Saddam or Ghaddafi – would have been too risky. But when the overthrow of the Taliban failed to lead to the capture of the top leaders of al Qaeda then Bush dramatically widened the 'war on terrorism' to include 'regime change' in Iraq, offering only the most perfunctory evidence of any link to September 11. The option for unilateralism thus grows on what it feeds on, with setbacks prompting further lurches and adventures.

While the execution of the September 11 attacks required comparatively modest sums the extensive operational network and training camps of al Qaeda certainly demands deep pockets. This is where bin Laden's supporters in Saudi Arabia and the Emirates come in. An editorial in the *New Republic* on September

24 hinted at this when it referred to Saudi Arabia's 'filthy secrets'. In an article in the same issue Martin Peretz explained that Saudi money has been flowing into the coffers of the bin Laden network: 'Many Saudis – maybe even the monarchy itself – finance it, if only to keep it engaged and out of Riyadh.' Further details were vouchsafed by Seymour Hirsh in the *New Yorker* in an article based in part on US intelligence transcripts of conversations among members of the Saudi Royal Family:

> When the Saudis were confronted by press reports that some of the substantial funds that the monarchy routinely gives to Islamic charities may actually have gone to Al Qaeda and other terrorist networks, they denied any knowledge of such transfers. The intercepts, however, have led many in the intelligence community to think otherwise. The Bush administration has chosen not to confront the Saudi leadership over its financial support of terror organizations and its refusal to help in the investigation [of September 11].[17]

Saudi Arabia maintains sixty Islamic Centers spread through the world which proselytize the unforgiving doctrines of the militant Wahabi sect. The supposedly charitable and educational trusts supported by huge amounts of Saudi cash have been used to fund *madrassas*, or religious schools, where the basic needs of poor students are met but nothing is taught except the Wahabi interpretation of the Koran and the need for jihad. Inside Saudi Arabia itself hatred of the infidel is also inculcated by the Wahabi-dominated educational system despite the fact that only a tenth of the population belong to the Wahabi sect. A *New York Times* report from Riyadh observes the paradox:

> [E]xtremism, born of the local, puritanical Wahabi brand of Islam, constrains life here, shaping the way people live and the way Saudi Arabia greets the world. The United States seeks to build a coalition against terror with the kingdom, long a Western business and military ally, and yet the country has revealed itself as the source of the very ideology confronting America in the battle against terrorism.[18]

Despite its prodigious oil wealth the Saudi kingdom has failed to achieve rounded economic or social development – indeed its economy has recently been less buoyant than that of Iraq.[19] As a result there are many frustrated and unemployed youths who aspire to a middle-class existence but are unlikely to obtain it. And there are upper-class youths who despise their parents' complicity in a corrupt and arbitrary order. As an educational force the Saudi autocracy not only diffuses Wahabibism but also seeks to instill terror by judicial maiming and execution. Against this background the fact that fifteen of the September 11 hijackers came from Saudi Arabia is not surprising. Other hijackers came from the Emirates and from the fundamentalist milieu in Egypt where a stagnant and corrupt autocracy has also helped to make middle-class frustration and *ressentiment* a powerful force.

While Saudi and Pakistani authorities were scared of al Qaeda and only dealt with it at arm's length via 'charitable' intermediaries, they were closely involved in the rise of the Taliban. Their support for this organization, itself linked to al Qaeda, was given quite voluntarily and cannot be explained away as an attempt to buy off the militants. The Saudi security services supplied money and arms, the Pakistani ISI, training, officers and military experts. The Saudis appreciated the Taliban's narrow Deobandi theology, while their seizure of power was one of the very few successes that could be claimed by Pakistani state policy.[20] Without Pakistani and Saudi help, the Taliban would never have seized power and the bin Laden network would have had no haven for its training camps. Mullah Muhammad Omar, the Taliban leader, formed an alliance with al Qaeda because it also could supply money and men, and because this somewhat reduced reliance on Pakistan and Saudi Arabia. No doubt the latter were not unhappy to see al Qaeda drawn off to Afghanistan but they also identified with the Taliban project. A later report revealed that the ISI was also in league with al Qaeda: 'The intelligence service of Pakistan . . . has had an indirect but longstanding relationship with al Qaeda, turning a blind eye for years to the growing ties between Osama bin Laden and the Taliban, according to American officials. The intelligence service even used al Qaeda camps to train covert operatives for use in a war of terror against India.'[21] The US was aware of such connections. Following the embassy bombings in 1998 a State Department official, Michael Sheenan, urged that the US should make isolating al Qaeda its priority:

> Mr Sheenan's memo outlined a series of actions the United States could take toward Pakistan, Afghanistan, Saudi Arabia, the United Arab Emirates and Yemen to persuade them to help isolate Al Qaeda. The document called Pakistan the key, and it suggested that the

administration make terrorism the central issue in the relations between Washington and Islamabad. The document also urged the administration to find ways to curb terrorist money-laundering . . . Mr Sheenan's plan 'landed with a resounding thud,' one former official recalled. 'He couldn't get anyone interested.'[22]

Washington cannot have been unaware of the pitiless Taliban theology but had long grown used to the idea that Muslim fanatics were convenient and easily manipulated allies and that the real enemy was secular authorities who don't truckle to the US. Historically the US security establishment did not see the Islamic jihad and bin Laden terror networks as a negative phenomenon. In the eighties such networks were financed, trained and armed so long as they were fighting against the Russian-supported regime in Afghanistan.[23] Al Qaeda was established in 1989 at the high point of this effort. But in addition, and subsequent to this, Muslim jihad networks were often still seen as an ally or tool in former Soviet lands and in parts of the Middle East. Elements of the al Qaeda network were active in Chechnya and former Soviet central Asia. They were also active in Bosnia and Kosovo. The Western press did not like to make much of it, but some of the Bosnian and KLA units resorted to terror tactics. Indeed, as a legacy of this, gangs of ethno-religious thugs still terrorize the populations of the Balkan statelets set up by NATO and act as a prime conduit for the thriving drug trade from Afghanistan to Western Europe.[24]

Free market ideology combined with anti-Communism and suspicion of Russia helped to produce an extraordinary laxness when it came to US invigilation of the bin Laden network, even long after the 1993 World Trade Center bomb and the African embassy bombings. Clinton sought Congressional approval for checks on capital movements to make sure that they were not helping to finance terrorist activity. They were blocked by the Texas Republican Phil Gramm, who was then the chairman of the Senate's Banking Committee, as well as by the banking industry. Gramm was reported after September 11, 2001 standing by his previous opposition to any type of capital movement monitoring: ' "I was right then and I am right now" in opposing the bill, Mr Gramm said yesterday. He called the bill "totalitarian" and added: "The way to deal with terrorists is to hunt them down and kill them." '[25] The religious authorities in Saudi Arabia also uphold

the absolute rights of property-owners and the secular authorities
allow unlimited cross-border cash transfers. This is a country
without capital gains tax, inheritance tax, or income tax. As
*Business Week* explains: 'While Saudi Arabia may seem like a tightly
controlled society, its Hanbali system of Islamic jurisprudence
puts great emphasis on the sanctity of private property. "What you
do with your money is utterly up to you," says Michael Field, a
London-based author of several books on business in the Gulf.'[26]

In his important study, *Islam and Capitalism,* the French scholar
Maxine Rodinson explained Islam's compatibility with mercantile
and financial accumulation.[27] The first years of the Iranian revolution saw the state given some importance in Islamic economics
but, as Olivier Roy explains, this unusual feature was to be
explained by the tradition of Shi'ite Islam in Iran, which was
originally state-sponsored, and by Khomeini's need to compete
with nationalist and leftist ideologies. It was eventually to be
'supplanted by a less state oriented and more liberal image, at
least with respect to the economy, in Iran as in the rest of the
Muslim world'.[28] This author adds: 'This evolution goes hand in
hand with Islamism's shift towards neo-fundamentalism and with
the diffusion of the Islamist message to a wider audience (businessmen, students of economics, and others).'[29] In the summer
of 2001 the Bank-e-Eqtesadi Novine became the first private bank
to be set up in Iran since the revolution, with many likely to
follow. Saudi Arabia and the Gulf states are well supplied not just
with financial institutions but with proudly Islamic banks. While
Islamic investors have to be careful not to enjoy the fruits of
'usury', they are able to claim quarterly or annual 'bonuses' and
they can invest in stocks and shares because such instruments
allow them to share profits and losses. As Roy explains, the type
of mercantile and financial capitalism endorsed by Islamic ideology in Saudi Arabia, taking mainly parasitic and rentier forms,
has failed to stimulate or diversify its economy. Straddling the
latter are giant 'state-owned' corporations, notably Sabic, Saudi
Airlines, and Saudi Aramco, the last with revenues of some $80
billion annually. The Islamist view that these instruments of
princely patronage should be broken up and turned over to
honest Islamic businesses is gaining ground.

The al Qaeda group has had access to the most sophisticated
banking services but it combines this with the ability to use an

informal network of paperless cash transfers, constituted by the facilities of *hawala* or trust brokers. These brokers regularly transfer large sums from the Middle East or the Indian sub-continent to North America or Europe leaving only the most cryptic records (a telephone remark or an e-mail saying 'Abdullah to receive twelve crates of mangoes'). Bin Laden himself has specialized in finance and banking, and in commissioning and monitoring large-scale construction projects. Even in his Afghan cave, Bin Laden was accompanied by mobile generators, computers, and communications equipment. A visiting Arab journalist explained: 'The mujahideen around the man belong to most Arab states, and are of different ages, but most of them are young. They hold high scientific degrees: doctors, engineers, teachers.'[30] While it is likely that major Gulf state businesses do not speak with one voice, and spread their bets, some of them contributed to al Qaeda and its campaign against a petrified social order. Jane Mayer in a study of the Bin Laden family for the *New Yorker* reports that several people close to the family believe that Osama continued to receive help from this quarter long after he was formally stripped of Saudi citizenship in 1994. She also points out that the Bin Laden Family Group had stakes in such US investment concerns as the Carlyle Bank and the Fremont Group, and that the family had played host in Jedda to such representatives of these companies as Frank Carlucci, George H. W. Bush, James Baker and George Shultz.[31]

The bond between Washington and Saudi Arabia has obviously been based on oil though sometimes this has been reinforced by a shared commitment to anti-Communism and free market ideology. The treatment of women in Saudi Arabia is bad enough but in the case of the Taliban it reached a pitch of oppression that makes it curious that the movement and regime were not branded as pariahs long before 2001. If an ethnic group had been treated as women were by the Taliban they would surely have attracted censure more swiftly. For several years Pakistan, Saudi Arabia and Washington's foreign policy lobbies protected them.

Now that the Taliban have been reassessed it will be interesting to see whether there will be a strategic review of the value of the Saudi link. Washington needs credible partners in the Islamic world if it is to head off the danger of a 'clash of civilizations'. And that is what it lacks.

## Coming to terms with the revolution in the Islamic world

Before addressing alternatives to the Bush approach, it is necessary to assess the capacity of the governments of the region to meet the aspirations of their peoples. The Middle East and the Muslim world are caught up in the maelstrom of modernity and democracy, as are all parts of the world. Their peoples crave a better life, a degree of respect, and a say in how their countries are run, and have done for a long time past. Autocratic, monarchical and traditionalist regimes were often set up to bar the road to the sort of secular progress that was promised by Arab nationalism or by such figures as prime minister Mossadegh in Iran, until his overthrow in 1953, and President Kassem in Iraq, until his overthrow in 1963, or prime minister Bhutto in Pakistan until his overthrow in 1977. The progress promised, still less achieved, by these leaders was, of course, in various ways incomplete and uneven. But compared to their rivals and successors they offered hope and a way forward. Generally the West accommodated, or actually sponsored, the forces of reaction, counter-revolution and military overthrow, with their dismal train of corrupt, wasteful and vicious dictators, sheikhs, kings and princelings. It should not therefore surprise that, as Said Aburish flatly asserts: 'There are no legitimate regimes in the Arab Middle East.'[32] Often the nearer a regime is to the West the more discredited it is, and the more hostile to the US its population. Saudi dependence on the US military and Mubarak's dependence on US aid are powerful agents of delegitimization. Washington's countenancing of Israeli settlement and repression in the occupied areas, its support for the blatantly unfair Oslo accords, and the televised images of Palestinians being beaten and killed further discredited all pro-Western governments.

In a context where secular politics failed to generate progress, political Islam became an increasing force. Compared to secular nationalists and the left, the Islamists had the considerable advantage that their activity could for a time proceed in the shadow of the mosques and seminaries. And even once they faced repression, Islam gave them communication with a large following. In some countries, notably Iran at the time of the overthrow of the Shah, the Islamist movement became, for better or worse, intimately associated with a popular upheaval against autocracy. The

Iran of Ayatollah Khomeini might appear, and in some respects be, a throwback to the past. But the constitution of the 'Islamic republic' was in fact a novel confection, quite unlike the autocracy of a Caliph.

While the analogy is no doubt a limited one, we should consider the outlook of Puritan revolutionaries in the early modern period when assessing developments in Iran. Michael Walzer, in his book *The Revolution of the Saints*, explains how Puritanism, with its fixation on the need to fight a this-worldly Satan, gave rise to new ways of waging war.[33] Puritan militancy and organization had an egalitarian appeal in a decaying feudal order and laid the basis for secular citizenship. Such an outlook led some English Puritan soldiers to rid themselves of monarchy – and some to massacre the Irish or persecute witches. The overthrow of the Shah and the rise of the Islamic republic, both sponsored by an alliance of clerics and bazaar merchants, witnessed similar contradictory tendencies.[34] Women kept the vote but were still policed and subordinated. The war with Iraq led to a horrendous loss of life and elements of a war economy. But gradually a more vigorous civil society emerged. The hardline clerics lost ground from 1990, opposed by bazaar merchants who had tired of their populist experiments. A more pragmatic leadership resorted to a programme of privatization.[35] In the 1997 presidential election the more moderate and tolerant, but cautious, cleric Khatami won, to be re-elected with even more support in 2001. This whole process resumes the trajectory of the interrupted bourgeois revolution in Iran.

Today political Islam still has an egalitarian resonance in feudal societies like those of Pakistan and the Arabian Peninsula. The first bourgeois revolutions came into the world animated by Puritan righteousness, hatred of Satan, and a belief that the Elect must prove themselves in purifying and terrifying deeds. The Enlightenment and the French Revolution, the defeat of fascism, decolonization, and the Russia and Chinese revolutions opened up different paths to modernity in succeeding centuries. But apparently, because of the defeat of secular revolutionary forces in the Islamic world, we now witness a throwback to the dawn of the bourgeois epoch.[36]

If the Puritans represented a kind of progress in the seventeenth century could the same be said of today's hardline Islamic clerics? The answer is no. The secular spaces of the modern world create other possibilities (and weapons of mass destruction create other dangers). Indeed, even in the seventeenth century there were proto-secular currents, like the Levellers, to which Walzer gives too little attention. Anyway it would be wrong to exalt the Puritans above such counter-currents as humanism and the baroque, as reflected in, say, Montaigne and Shakespeare, which also made a contribution to modernity and civility. However, where radical Islam has become a mass force, as it did in Iran, its evolution may bear comparison with that of the Puritans. Those Iranian clerics who wish to keep a theological straitjacket on Iranian society, and who mystify political realities with pseudo-religious categories like the Great Satan, are losing ground. Over two decades after the overthrow of the Shah some of the processes noted by Walzer seem to be at work in Iranian society, with student revolts, the assertion of women's civic rights, a flourishing Iranian cinema, and the tussle between elected officials and hardline clerics. In these we see some rays of light in a darkening landscape. Iranian developments are closely followed by the Al Jazeera TV station, which projects them to the Arab world. The fact that the Iranians are Shi'ite and the Taliban are Sunni apparently does not lend the latter greater authority in the eyes of the Sunni majority in the Muslim world, because of the manifest excesses and failures of Taliban rule.

With the proclamation of the need for 'regime change' in Iraq and for 'reform' in the Palestinian authority, it might seem that in 2002 the Bush administration hoped to be seen as the spear-head of democracy in the Arab and Muslim world. But with all its failings Arafat's authority was the only elected body in the Arab world. While it certainly needs democratic reform, if this happened it would make it more resistant to the sort of puppet status envisaged by the Israeli government. The US probably has the military strength for a quick victory in Iraq and war could well trigger popular upheaval not only in parts of Iraq but also in Jordan and the Arabian peninsula. But, sadly, there is absolutely no reason to suppose that the United States under President Bush would use its enhanced position to encourage or permit really democratic revolutions since the latter would sooner or later threaten the oil companies and/or bring to power political forces abominated by Bush. If the record of the last half century is anything to go by, 'regime change' will lead to more of the same, as the US finds more pliant military strong men and mercenary politicians. In this respect the US conduct in post-Taliban Afghanistan was instructive.

## Overthrowing the Taliban

The Taliban were not a deep-rooted, popular force. They were young men brought up abroad and indoctrinated in *madrassas*, or religious colleges, sponsored by the ISI. Their movement would not have prevailed without foreign backing. Their rule was baneful for most of the population. The Taliban were highly vulnerable by September 2001 even though some Afghans supported them because of tribal or family ties. This is why an indigenous force, supported by regional powers, was best placed to replace them. The US commanders understood this and left the fighting to the Northern Alliance. But after the Taliban had collapsed they introduced about 10,000 US troops, imposed the presidency of Karzai and proceeded to treat swathes of the country as a free fire zone. US allies were allowed to furnish peace keeping troops, but Iran was first kept at arm's length and then denounced in January 2002 in President Bush's State of the Union speech as a part of the 'axis of evil'.

Allowing Iran to play a leading role within a genuinely international anti-terrorist coalition would have offered many advantages and would have dramatized that no assault on Islam was intended. If it wished, Washington could regard such a course as embodying a Kissingeresque realism – like the recognition of 'Red China', but without the cynicism and in a better cause. The Iranian government and state, whatever its divisions, has far greater legitimacy than most others in the Islamic world. Over the last decade there has been a real, if still incomplete, democratization of Iranian society. All Iranian groupings were strongly opposed to the Taliban. There are some two million Afghan refugees within its borders, most of whom would like to return. Iran had supported some elements in the Northern Alliance and its ties with Afghanistan make it a force there. With a population of 70 million Iran is a key power in the region.

Unfortunately, far from normalizing relations with Iran, the administration chose to cast it into outer darkness. *The Economist* informs us that the US State Department cold-shouldered Iranian overtures from the outset: 'On September 16 a State department official said that Iran's help in the campaign against terrorism would be welcomed only if it withdrew support from Hizbullah – hardly a realistic demand, not least because few countries, apart from America and Israel, consider Hizbullah to be a terrorist organization.'[37] On September 30 the Iranian assistant foreign minister gave an interview to the *New York Times* in which he explained the critical failings of US diplomacy and strategy:

'No single nation can take up this fight,' Mr. Zarif said . . . 'This is a global fight. And a cold warrior mentality against the global menace of terrorism is not going to produce the results necessary to eradicate terrorism.' He said the coalition must both be inclusive and authorized by the United Nations. 'Everybody has to be in,' he said, 'you can't pick and choose the members.' Mr. Zarif extended his condolences to the American people. 'The magnitude of this attack has been unprecedented,' he said, 'it is difficult for the world to comprehend that in a few seconds so many people have been lost. Certainly in Iran we understand the trauma that the American people are suffering and will continue to suffer for many years to come.' . . . While expressing sympathy for the victims of the attacks, Mr Zarif criticized statements by Secretary of State Colin L. Powell about Iran's possible inclusion in an American led coalition. . .' The notion that you are either with the US or with the terrorists is problematic. People are not in line to join the coalition. There is no queue. In the Iranian psyche the United States is not the center of the world,' he said, 'so it would be advisable if the American people look at themselves from the perspective of others.'[38]

While the US refused a role to Iran, it did take advantage of its hostility to the Taliban to forward its Afghan campaign. Unlike the governments of most other large Muslim states, the government of Iran is not financially or militarily dependent on the US. It has a long border with Afghanistan and many ties with its population. The overthrow of Taliban rule in Western Afghanistan, especially around Herat, was the direct result of forces entering from Iran and backed by Iran.

Indeed if the Northern Alliance had not been kept going by Iran, Tajikistan and Uzbekistan, the US would have been deprived of the ground forces which actually defeated the Taliban. Iran alone has standing within the Muslim world and was manifestly better placed than they were to appeal for a broader internal government to replace the Taliban. The best that can be said about the regimes in Tajikistan and Uzbekistan is that they have a broadly secular character, and could allow secular Afghan refugees to return to their homeland. Because of their autocratic character, brutal treatment of opposition, past subservience to Moscow, and ethnic links, the support of the Uzbek and Tajik governments does not strengthen the appeal of any Afghan regime they support. The Northern Alliance itself was an uneasy alliance of warlords and of political and religious leaders who had responsibility for the misrule of 1992–96. The US opted for a new regime to be led by Hamid Karzai, a leading member of the royal clan, and successfully pressured the loya jirga to endorse their man. But while dollars will buy seeming compliance, and US special forces guard the new president, the future will remain uncertain. Significant secular and civilian forces, such as the RAWA (association of Afghan women), were allowed no part. The US had successfully leant on the Pakistan military help in order to turn the Taliban but the effect of this is that former Taliban and those close to them still have power in much of the country. Pakistan's influence in Afghanistan would be more healthy if it was itself democratized.

The formation of a government in Pakistan committed to holding elections, and incorporating the main political parties on an interim basis, would help to weaken the Islamic jihad network and prevent backsliding in Afghanistan. Pakistan's civilian forces were not committed to the Taliban though they failed to prevent the ISI from sponsoring them. Islamist parties have never been able to demonstrate electoral support in Pakistan. Notwithstanding the main parties' hostility to the Taliban, they will see good reasons to make sure that a post-Taliban government has friendly relations with Pakistan. The ISI remains strongly attached to its 'ex-Taliban' Afghan protégés and the problem this poses is increased by the fact that, like other intelligence services, it has sources of revenue stemming from the drug trade that are not controlled by its government.[39] Pakistan's previous civilian governments had little or no control over the intelligence network and they have been scared to challenge it. But public opinion and the aspiration to be free of military misrule also count for something in the country. As Robert Fisk explains: 'Corrupt, drug-ridden, and inherently unstable Pakistan may be, but General Musharraf allows a kind of freedom of speech to continue.' The public opinion to which this allows expression is not favourable to the ISI or the Taliban, but neither does it like the US and Musharraf. Fisk notes: 'Aqil Shah put it very well when he wrote in Lahore's *Friday Times* last week that, by allying himself with America's "War on Terror", General Musharraf had secured de facto international acceptance for his 1999 coup.'[40] Musharraf has offered elections but also introduced a new constitution that will make their outcome of little consequence. He reserves all real power for himself. Because of its reliance on him, Washington can do little to restrain the Pakistani dictator. And the example of US unilateralism encourages the Pakistani, Indian and Israeli governments to pursue their own projects by resort to military violence and war.

The future of Afghanistan will not be secure until there is a wide regional solution supported by Iran, Pakistan and Uzbekistan, and linked to the prospects for democratization in those countries. Outside powers can mainly help by offering a really large aid package to reward cooperation between them. The West expended huge sums in prosecuting a proxy war in Afghanistan and the US and Britain are currently engaged in costly military operations. If similar sums were available for reconstruction and development in the region, this would powerfully assist the chances of a joint approach in Teheran, Tashkent and Islamabad. And only such an approach will offer the hope of an Afghan settlement that does not store up new conflicts by enshrining the rule of an ethno-religious faction or giving a new lease to discredited and oppressive Islamist practices.

Ideally the UN should have had a crucial role to play in the future of Afghanistan, as the Iranian Foreign Minister observed, and as the Northern League itself requested. But, as presently constituted, the UN has neither the will nor the ability to act independently of the United States. The Security Council adopted a strong resolution against terrorism on September 28 but no UN police body was set up to enforce it. Instead each member state was asked to take its own measures and to report back within 90 days on its success in identifying and stamping out terrorist support networks. While seemingly multilateralist, this approach allows Washington to retain control of all cross-border initiatives – and to act as judge in 90 days of the adequacy of the measures reported. Under UN auspices a so-called 'two plus six' group comprising the US and Russia (the 'two') and Afghanistan's neighbours (Iran, Turkmenistan, Uzbekistan, Tajikistan, China and Pakistan) did in fact help to furnish crucial support for the onslaught on the Taliban but the grouping was not given any formal responsibilities. Instead of fostering a regional UN body, Washington took care to retain all the initiative.

The US approach was clear from the explanations of the Secretary of Defense. In an article entitled 'A New Kind of War', Rumsfeld explained, that this 'will not be waged by a grand alliance united for the single purpose of defeating an axis of hostile powers'. Instead of such an alliance, in which the US would have to compromise with allies, there will be 'floating coalitions' adopted or discarded at will by the directing centre: 'Countries will have different roles and contribute in different ways. . . In this war the mission will determine the coalition, not the other way round.'[41] And the mission was set by Washington. This is how it turned out in Afghanistan and as a methodology it allowed the 'war against terrorism' to become transformed into a war against the 'axis of evil' and for 'regime change' in Iraq in 2002.

The US is compromised by the fact that its cause is still yoked to Saudi Arabia, the Emirates and Egypt, as well as Israel. For Bush to imagine that the US stands for liberty and justice in the Middle East is a strange delusion. It could only ever be seen in this light if it broke with the Saudi monarchy and obliged Israel to withdraw completely from the occupied territories, something that would obviously require a complete revolution in its policy and priorities in the region. But Washington, which happily bullies governments in Europe, followed tamely in the wake of the aggressive policy of Israel's prime minister, Ariel Sharon, as he sent in tanks to terrorize the Palestinian enclaves. In an answer to an Iranian journalist the British Foreign Secretary observed: 'I understand that one of the factors that helps to breed terrorism is the anger which many people feel at the events over the years in Palestine.'[42] But the year that followed September 11 witnessed further reckless Israeli armed incursions and bloody bombardments.

The need for Arab and Muslim allies might have led the Bush administration to offer concessions to Arab opinion. But in the event, the belligerence of the Israeli government, and the inability of Bush to curb it, neutralized the paltry concessions on offer. Alliance with the 'moderate' Arab states – and the sort of token sops that might satisfy them – does not help since these are autocratic, repressive and discredited. So a replay of the Gulf War coalition could not work even on its own terms. An attempt simply to re-start the flawed and discredited 'peace process' would not be convincing even to most 'moderate' Arabs. The minimum would have to be compliance with UN Resolution 242 and willingness to discuss a territorial settlement that gives both Israelis and Palestinians contiguous land and reasonably defensible borders.[43]

The militants of al Qaeda and Islamic jihad have some very unattractive, indeed repellent, beliefs and there is no need to respect or compromise on any of these. Islamic jihad believes in a draconian subordination of women and the drastic curtailment of cultural and intellectual life. They are willing to pitilessly destroy believers and non-believers alike since the believers will go to paradise and the infidels deserve to die anyway. This was already evident before September 11: the East African embassy bombings wounded and maimed 4,000 people. But al Qaeda and its allies also try to gain support by appearing to champion causes which are popular and justified. Al Qaeda is manifestly a threat to the cause of democracy and progress. But to oppose measures simply because they are supported by al Qaeda plays into their hands.

While apparently secular objectives are proclaimed in its videos, these are wrapped up in a religious worldview. The ability of al Qaeda to attract sympathy and support in the Islamic world can certainly be undercut by initiatives favourable to democracy, economic development, self-determination, and respect for the peaceful exercise of religious rites (and rights). Although, in current circumstances, it is dangerous to underestimate al Qaeda's appeal, it is not a mass force anywhere in the Muslim world. It is a network of several thousands, not millions or even hundreds of thousands. There is evidence of bickering, factionalism and disorganization within it. Without continuing subventions its finances would be strained. Its addiction to terrorism itself, while claiming to express Muslim anger, in fact offers it an empty symbolic satisfaction which builds nothing. So for all these reasons the network could shrivel if the peoples of the Muslim world saw real opportunities to achieve recognition, justice and progress.

Islamic jihad has a political logic which feeds off the need for revolutionary transformations in the Islamic world and the failures of existing regimes, whether conservative or nationalist. As a way of mobilizing the 'Arab street' it has not proved at all effective. But the excessive and 'symbolic' dimensions of the September 11 action could still have furthered its political objectives if it drives Washington mad, if it makes the custodians of global capital forget how much they have to lose and if it plays to the Manichean phobias still evident in US political culture. Basking in the glow of a flawed 'victory' in Afghanistan, Bush could seek to distract attention from this, and the woes of the US economy, by an escalation of perilous military exploits.

The Belgian Marxist Ernest Mandel used to say that the hugely prosperous American bourgeoisie had no rational interest in blowing up the world in a nuclear conflagration. Once again bourgeois America is in a like situation and does not have an interest in, say, promoting the fundamentalist network in the Pakistani armed forces. But this does not mean that American political leadership can find within itself the wisdom, imagination and patience to see that, however powerful it is, the United States is no substitute for a new, more representative and democratic, global order. The Islamic warriors who immolated themselves in the World Trade Center and the Pentagon were armed only with knives and cardboard cutters. They turned their opponent's civilian airliners into devastating instruments of destruction. They are also ready to turn American belligerence into their ally.

Even 'rational' capitalists, however, may favour belligerent action – say against Iraq or to shore up the Saudi monarchy – if they come to believe that this could secure future control of Middle Eastern oil. The US way of life owes much to cheap oil and gasoline, but the real interests at stake are easy to over-pitch. In recent years the Middle East has been supplying only about fifteen per cent of total US oil imports. Even if the US government and oil companies lost all privileged leverage in the Middle East, they would still be able to buy some supplies from the region. The advocates of radical Islam urge that better prices should be obtained for oil and that Islamic banks and corporations would make better use of oil revenues than the hereditary states: they speak of raising prices or using oil revenues differently, not keeping the oil to themselves. The prices which eventually prevail will before long reflect supply and demand in what is an internationally competitive market.[44] Mercantile activity, as we have pointed out, has always been compatible with Islam. It could be that average prices would be a little higher, but this would scarcely be a disaster for the US. Indeed, if it encouraged greater efficiency and economy in the use of fossil fuels, it would be a good thing. On the other hand, the risks entailed by unending US military adventures are of a quite different description and Mandel's argument applies.

## Cosmopolitics versus terror

The flaw in the US proclamation of itself as the arbiter of global terror and regime acceptability is not only its past record, but also its continuing imperial disposition and the readiness of US leaders to discount political and social considerations in favour of a stark opposition of good and evil. The British government has, in my view, been far too subservient to Washington. But as an ex-colonial power it knows that terrorist movements can be undercut by political initiatives. It knows that the irreconcilables can be isolated by acts of decolonization and negotiations with those formerly regarded as terrorists like Jomo Kenyatta, Archbishop Makarios and Gerry Adams. It is true that the White House has many times welcomed Yasser Arafat and was at one time willing to turn a blind eye to Saudi support for terrorists. But such pragmatism is no good unless informed by a willingness to accept structural change. The British did eventually accept decolonization, but it is less clear that the US understands that the time has come for a new type of empire, a network empire of many centres.

Instead of decolonization, the Palestinians were offered besieged and fragmented enclaves. In Saudi Arabia and the Gulf, decolonization would mean the withdrawal of US and UK troops. A campaign against terror in the region would have to base itself on dismantling regimes that are based on terror rather than popular consent, whether in the occupied territories or in the motley retinue of monarchies and sheikdoms that have been the buttress of empire. The species of bourgeois revolution now stalking the Islamic world threatens to sweep all these regimes into the dustbin of history. In the Gulf a large immigrant work-force could assert its presence. If the US and Britain insist on ringing the changes on the old order, it will ensure that this process is more bloody and dangerous than would otherwise be the case – and less likely to find a relatively more democratic, secular and pacific outcome.

'Regime change' accomplished by the citizens of each state or territory will be more durable and democratic than solutions imposed from the outside. On the other hand a campaign against terrorism will be far more likely to succeed if it is genuinely international in character, if implementation is entrusted to a supranational agency, if it is even-handed and consistent, if it is equally intolerant of state terror, if political and social injustices are resolutely addressed, and if it pays attention to all the destructive potentials that have appeared as by-products of modernity.

President Bush's inclinations today are as anachronistic as were those of President McKinley when he led the US to victory over Spain in 1898 but then did not know what to do with it. His instinct was to use Spain's defeat to acquire pieces of imperial real estate (the Philippines, Guam, Cuba and Puerto Rico). He did not realize that territorial empires had peaked and that it was America's mission to embody the non-territorial variety that was to count in the twentieth century. Under pressure from an impressive anti-imperialist movement Cuba was given its independence in 1902, but with a Platt amendment that was long to rankle: it enshrined a US right of intervention in the island. Today Bush aspires to be a second McKinley exercising a sort of global Platt amendment in the war against terrorism and the 'axis of evil'. But the time for this type of imperial governance is over and a more plural capitalist world requires supranational agencies that do not only reflect the 'Washington consensus'.

Terror networks with 'global reach' will not be suppressed or minimized without a new and more authoritative network of institutions at a global and supranational level. This means abating US national messianism together with the willingness of its allies to defer to Washington on a string of crucial issues for global governance. The US is tempted to play the role of global gendarme because everyone knows that the UN, as it is, lacks the resources and capacity to fill this role. The weakness of the UN was cited by Richard Falk in *The Nation* as the reason for supporting Bush's go-it-alone strategy.[45] But the same argument could be deployed to argue for the international body to be given specified supranational powers and for its decision-making powers to be enhanced. Obviously those would have to be accompanied by juridical restraints and democratic accountability such as have anyway been urged by writers like Daniele Archibugi.[46] The situation created by September 11 created conditions where such issues could be urgently addressed and an anti-terrorist task force quickly assembled. Indeed even prior to September 11 Saul Mendlovitz and John Fousek had already urged the need for such a force to combat crimes against humanity.[47]

Of course the UN could be far more effective if it was not continually by-passed and slighted by the US. But it also needs, as it has since its inception, new authority and resources. Already in 1944 some argued for the UN to have its own armed force (World Guard) with its own budget and commanders (i.e., one not formed by contributions from existing national armies). This is still a distant prospect today. But a supranational agency to deal with 'global terrorism' is another matter, requiring fewer resources and implying a smaller derogation of sovereignty. And if the principle can be won in this area this could be of great help in tackling nuclear and germ-war disarmament and inspection.

The fact that there is no Islamic country as a permanent member of the Security Council while there are two European states deprives it of much legitimacy in the Arab world. The inclusion of, say, Indonesia might help to boost the standing of the UN in the Islamic world. It is interesting to reflect that when William Penn and Abbé de St Pierre first proposed an international league to suppress war and piracy they urged that the Ottoman Empire should be bound into it from the outset.[48] Three centuries later we still haven't caught up with these bold thinkers.

An international accord against terrorism could be positive so long as there was the opportunity for each state's self-interested approach to be qualified by the need for a genuine international consensus. The latter would itself not be perfect, of course, but it would be better than encouraging each state to prosecute its own war against global terrorism. There are already international agreements which it could have invoked and which the Security Council of the UN could see were more vigorously enforced.

The succession of treaties and agreements aimed at suppressing first piracy and then the Atlantic slave trade, with the latter often seen as legally equivalent to the former, furnish interesting precedents. At the Congress of Vienna in 1815 there was an international accord to equate slaving with piracy. But Washington would not agree. The US government had suppressed legal slave imports in 1808 but rejected effective international action against the Atlantic slave trade since this required a mutual right of inspection, which was deemed to be an infringement on US sovereignty. As a result the Atlantic slave trade to Cuba continued and the building of ships destined for the slave trade was a major New York industry in the 1850s. It was only in 1862 that Lincoln and Seward accepted the need for the US to cooperate in suppressing the Atlantic traffic – and it was only then that the bans on Atlantic slaving became effective.[49]

Other than the US, the permanent members of the UN Security Council are ready for joint police action against terrorism, even the establishment of a supranational agency. The Chinese and Russian governments may use terror themselves but are sincerely opposed to the freelance variety, especially when connected to Islamic fundamentalism. At one point in Bush's September 20 speech when he was listing the failed twentieth-century doctrines comparable to al Qaeda's fundamentalism, he mentioned fascism, Nazism and totalitarianism but left out, in deference to China and Russia, a specific mention of Communism. Perhaps someone in the Bush entourage was already aiming at an entente with Beijing and Moscow.

While President Bush's onslaught on the 'axis of evil' represented a perilous further ratcheting up of imperial ambitions its focus on the dangers posed by 'weapons of mass destruction' was not itself wrong. When wielded by a state these weapons, especially nuclear weapons, do pose a dreadful threat to humanity, one which is qualitatively greater than the danger posed by any terrorist movement. Naturally the greatest threat is posed by powers which have not only nuclear weapons but also the means to deliver them. If we wish to rid the world of the nightmare of nuclear conflict then we must address ourselves, in the first instance, to the destruction of the stockpiles, submarines and missiles held by the United States, Britain, France, Russia, China, India, Pakistan and Israel. If these weapons systems were dismantled, so would be the spectre of nuclear doomsday.

It is just possible that an international accord against terrorism, a comparatively small-scale threat, could pave the way to international agreements which remove the far greater – but now not entirely unrelated – terror of nuclear war. It could furnish a positive precedent. In the aftermath of September 11 Bush and Putin did agree to some missile reductions but this was not a formal treaty, did not allow for international inspections and leaves each with enough warheads to destroy the world several times over. The pre-September 11 international order was based on the effective exclusion of Russia and China from any real role in global governance. That was the logic of Clinton's NATO expansion policy and of Bush's characterization of China as a 'global competitor'. Russia and China not only have nuclear weapons but they also have the means to deliver them. Washington's policy of maintaining its own nuclear arsenal and blocking supranational inspection also made it very difficult to tackle the most dangerous type of proliferation, as seen in the nuclear tests conducted by India and Pakistan. New Delhi and Islamabad were censured for developing their nuclear capability but nobody could suppose that these powers would renounce such weapons so long as others possessed them. The US, Britain and France are theoretically committed to eventual nuclear disarmament, but nobody takes this seriously since the governments concerned evidently do not do so themselves.

Nuclear disarmament would only be acceptable to existing nuclear powers if carried out as part of *a common agreement entered into by all* and backed up by international inspection. Willingness to accept any such sacrifice of national sovereignty was very remote on September 11. During the Cold War nuclear dispositions were at least inserted into an overall strategy of control. But the anarchic dispositions that now reign constitute the terrifying legacy of that 'unfinished twentieth century' about which Jonathan Schell has written.[50] It may be that international nuclear disarmament will not be achieved until after a nuclear weapon has been used, but that terrible possibility should not stop us from identifying its necessity.

It will be easier to get an accord against the vastly lesser danger of terrorism because the major powers would perceive this as less of a derogation of their sovereignty. However unless there is some concession of sovereignty even this accord will be nugatory. A UN secretariat against terrorism should have its own professional staff and should be able to prompt and require compliance from the police in any member state. Anything less than this would not be serious. A UN convention against terrorism could be based on its existing articles and protocols. Inevitably governments would try to invoke it to suppress legitimate opposition, but in such cases they might find it difficult to get a quorum to support them and would have to work through an agency, and submit to a court, they did not control. There should be habeas corpus and judicial safeguards against wrongful arrest, with the opportunity for representations to be made by social movements as well as states. The sanctions available to the international court should include imprisonment but not capital punishment (as is the case with the ICC).

Israel and its friends will no doubt claim that al Fatah and the PLO are terrorist organizations. The Russian government will claim that the entire Chechen movement is terrorist. The Indian government likes to brand as terrorist any aspiration to Kashmiri independence. The Chinese government will brand Tibetan aspirations as terrorist. The US, France and Britain might seek to indict organizations at work in Puerto Rico, Northern Ireland or Corsica. Indeed the British 'anti-terrorist' legislation is framed broadly enough to target non-violent direct action by 'eco-warriors.' For these reasons progressives and liberals, and anybody who cherishes civil liberties and rights of national determination, will argue strongly against accepting accusations at face value or the setting up of an organization responsible to individual governments.

What should count as terrorism? Obviously actions aimed at sowing terror by killing civilians, or seriously harming them, or threatening them with death or disfigurement. Such actions are supposedly illegal everywhere. Similar attacks or threats directed only against military personnel in times of peace are a more awkward case. If the government served by those personnel is autocratic and oppressive, this could justify armed resistance rather than terrorism. According to circumstances such armed resistance might be ill-advised or wrong, but it would not be terrorism. We should bear in mind that the US would not exist if its Founding Fathers had not taken up arms. There will, of course, be dispute about whether such and such a regime is repressive or autocratic, or whether an act really harmed civilians, but in practice it is often not so difficult to reach agreement. The aim of an anti-terrorist accord would be to identify and suppress clear cases of terrorism. It might even make sense to confine the competence of the agency to terrorist activity that crossed borders. Where the anti-terrorist agency could not decide, governments would formulate their own response. The attempt to reach agreement, and the supranational character of an anti-terrorist agency, would be quite different from bilateral deals whereby the US forgets about the Chechens in return for Russia accepting NATO expansion.

The existence of such a supranational agency would hopefully tend to pre-empt and contain terrorist activity. But governments would still retain the ability to deal with terrorist threats as they saw best within their own borders. Likewise, political or religious movements would no doubt still contrive to evade the reach of the agency. There would have to be sanctions for governments which flouted the accord or sabotaged the agency. Much would depend on the quality and authority of those in charge of investigations and operations; hopefully it would be possible to attract men like the Italian prosecutor Di Pietro and the Spanish judge Garzon.

The US has insisted that state-backed terrorism should be outlawed. Distinguishing between state-backed terror and state-backed acts of war will not be easy, but the challenge is a good one. Since state-backed terror often causes greater loss of life, it is eminently worth identifying and opposing. Once again independent investigators and jurists, with their own staff and budget, will be needed if such identifications are to be made with any credibility. The resources misspent on suppressing drug trafficking could be used to coordinate police action against terrorism. Indeed, the link between drug trafficking and terrorism means that a policy of de-criminalizing drugs would fit well with a strategy for minimizing terrorism. In the nature of any anti-terrorism agreement, it should not be possible for one state to impose its criteria of terrorism on another. And states which themselves practised or condoned terror will destroy their own legitimacy. Realists may say that Washington and Moscow will covertly support terrorist groups in the future as they have in the past. Perhaps this is true. But in this case they will risk being arraigned before a supranational body and further arousing world public opinion. If the supranational body refuses to arraign powerful states, as may well happen, then this itself will prompt further protests and campaigns. Stopping powerful states from colluding with terror is not going to be easy but that is not a reason for not making the effort and for making sure that there are supranational guarantees.

So moves to an accord against terrorism would furnish opportunities to combat false accusations with the international secretariat developing its own criteria and tests. There remains the uncomfortable fact that not all such accusations will be false. Obviously good causes can be championed by bad methods. But when that happens it usually weakens those causes.

The term 'terror' entered the political lexicon with the guillotine when the French revolution was hurling itself against the counter-revolutionary offensive of the European *ancien régime*. Much of the legislation of this time – freeing the slaves, establishing secular education, and proclaiming universal social rights – represented a huge step forward for humanity. But the terror weakened the Jacobin republic and hastened its overthrow. Stalin's much more extensive terror in the thirties weakened the Soviet Union at a critical time, contributing to early Nazi advances. Likewise, the Western allies' 'terror bombing' in 1944 had negligible impact on German output while actually boosting civilian morale.[51]

If all movements of political or social liberation were induced to abandon terrorist methods, there would be a gain and more space would be created for mass opposition to injustice. The tactics of guerrilla war, as elaborated by Guevara, Mao and Ho Chi Minh, aimed at cultivating civilian support, winning over enemy soldiers, and isolating the opposing governments, not terrorizing the population. In the early labour movement, Marxists, social democrats and most syndicalists opposed terroristic methods, and it was those movements that clung to this restraint which generally survived and flourished. The practice of terror by the early Soviet republic during the civil war was defended on the grounds that it helped to win more time but was probably a factor of demoralization both then and subsequently.[52] In any military conflict violence is deployed in ways that aim to destroy, immobilize or capture the opponent, but it is usually much better to surprise than to terrify. Recently in Lebanon some observers detected a shift in the policy of Hizbullah when it moved away from indiscriminate attacks against all Israelis and concentrated instead on attacking occupying military personnel in southern Lebanon – a move to a political focus which led to Israeli withdrawal. If there was an international agreement against terrorism, some Palestinians organizations might feel the need to abandon terror tactics that do them no good anyway – in the process they could isolate the Israeli state and throw into proper relief the ethnic cleansing which it continues to practise.

So long as there is oppression in the world there will be resistance, and where political systems are autocratic or alien this will often produce violent resistance. But progressives have learned to distinguish between resistance which uses just and effective means to challenge and overthrow intolerable conditions, on the one hand, and acts of indiscriminate and exemplary violence, targeted against civilians and whole communities, on the other. Sometimes it may seem instrumentally effective to countenance torture or terror, but movements that employ such methods begin to stultify, deaden and demoralize themselves and to poison the cause for which they are fighting. Some nationalist movements have made gains as a consequence of using terrorist campaigns (Algeria, Israel) but at a dire cost to their own political culture.

President Bush's notion of a 'war on terrorism' does have one advantage over the alternative notion that bringing terrorists to book is just a matter of law enforcement against criminals. As noted above, the British discovered in India, Cyprus, Kenya, Malaya, Palestine and Ireland that it was better to treat resistance, even terrorist resistance, as political since this was a way of controlling it. Sometimes British withdrawal was seen as completing the military effort (e.g., Malaya) while, in other cases, there were direct negotiations with political leaders linked to terrorist movements, leading to a hand over of power to them. If there was an international accord against terrorism, it would be necessary and advisable that it should try to bring out into the open any genuine political and social injustices that might motivate, or lend credibility to, the terrorist group. A moralistic refusal to negotiate with terrorists in such a situation is rarely effective and merely serves to perpetuate hatred and injustice.

While the critique of terrorism should not be skipped simply because of the misdeeds, including complicity in terrorism, of the US, the number and extent of the misdeeds should induce a more chastened American approach to the question. US presidents have sanctioned the assassination of foreign leaders like Lumumba, Allende and Castro. They have connived at death squads, carpet-bombed Iraq and fostered the terror sown by RENAMO and UNITA in Southern Africa. So some contrition on their part is in order. Even in the current campaign there are voices urging the brutal assertion of US power, willingness to inflict large-scale civilian casualties and to work with 'unsavory allies' (as if that was unprecedented). Consider Senator John McCain's bluster:

> Only the complete destruction of international terrorism and the regimes that sponsor it will spare America from future attack ... American military power is the most important part. When it is brought to bear in great and terrible measure, it is a thing to strike terror in the heart of anyone who opposes it. No mountain is big enough, no cave deep enough to hide from the full fury of American power.[53]

But if Washington allows itself to be swayed by such overwrought counsel then the resulting firestorms will only encourage further 'blowback'.

There are those in the Muslim world who find something positive in the democratic aspects of US culture. But if they see the US President propping up autocracy and monarchy in their lands, the influence of US culture will undermine US state policy. The terror network has already shown the autonomy of these far-flung exile chains and of the new alliances they make possible. Democratic, radical and secular nationalist currents are also present in this milieu, including in the Saudi, Afghan and Pakistani diaspora, and their mobilization could help to head off the 'clash of civilizations' danger. But these people will not be rallying behind generals, sheiks and kings, even comparatively decent ones like the ex-monarch of Afghanistan.

If the US does not commit itself to a genuinely democratic solution, under UN auspices and supported by credible Muslim states, it risks strengthening al Qaeda and, as has been starkly clear from the outset, could help them to seize power in a nuclear state – a country as unstable as former Yugoslavia and with a deep grudge against India, another nuclear state. The transnational structures so far proposed by the US are even more dangerous and deficient than those of the Cold War era. It would also involve spurning the opportunity to make a reality of the UN Security Council and to bring in Russia and China from the diplomatic limbo to which they are periodically assigned. Since these two powers are also armed with nuclear weapons, the potential gain from an internationalist approach is genuinely epochal. But international nuclear disarmament – and parallel agreements covering other weapons of mass destruction – will require that the major powers are also covered and that they will permit international inspection and verification. Only this would make it impossible for medium and smaller states to stand apart from the process. A genuine campaign against terrorism could thus actually help the world to face up to the much worse threat of the tens of thousands of nuclear warheads which still menace our species and planet. Terror weapons cannot be kept in sealed and self-contained compartments. If terrorism itself proliferates and escalates it will be more difficult to insulate weapons of mass destruction – biological as well as nuclear – from terrorist appropriation.

Since 1945 no nuclear bomb has exploded in a populated area. The destruction of Lower Manhattan on and after September 11 was terrible enough but only a fraction of the devastation that a single nuclear weapon would cause if dropped on a city in the Indian subcontinent. But because it has happened, September 11 could help us to grasp the importance of the still greater – if less palpable – calamities that current global arrangements still menace.

## Notes

1. See Tariq Ali, *The Clash of Fundamentalisms*, London and New York 2001.
2. For an excellent survey see Fred Halliday, *Arabia Without Sultans*, London 1978.
3. For a spirited account see Said Aburish, *Brutal Friendship: The West and the Arab Elite*, London 1997. For Iran see Lucien Rey, 'Persia in Perspective', parts I and II, *New Left Review*, nos 19 and 20, 1963, and Fred Halliday, *Iran: Dictatorship and Development*, London 1979.

180     DEBATING COSMOPOLITICS

4. Johnson, *Blowback*, pp. 9–11.
5. In her October 8 interview with *The Nation*, Rep. Barbara Lee (D-CA) tells us many legislators shared her fears. They just lacked the courage of their convictions.
6. Daniel Lazare, *The Velvet Coup*, London and New York 2001, pp. 100–101. But see also Perry Anderson, 'Testing Formula Two', *New Left Review*, no. 8, March–April 2001.
7. Ibid., p. 101.
8. Elizabeth Bumiller and David Johnston, 'Bush Sets Option of Military Trials in Terrorist Cases', *New York Times*, 14 November 2001.
9. Michael R. Gordon, 'U.S. Arsenal: Treaties vs. Nontreaties', *New York Times*, 14 November 2001.
10. Chalmers Johnson, *Blowback: The Costs and Consequences of American Empire*, New York 2000, p. 217.
11. For an incisive critique of Western policy towards Yugoslavia see Elizabeth Woodward, *The Break-up of Yugoslavia*, Washington 1996, and Tariq Ali, ed., *Masters of the Universe*, London 1999.
12. Washington squelched Russian mediation at Rambouillet because, if successful, it would have given Russia an ongoing role in former Yugoslavia. In the end Russia had to be given a minor role anyway. Russia had great leverage in Belgrade because Yugoslav forces were highly dependent on Russian oil and military supplies. Washington regarded the Primakov government as a throwback to the Soviet era. In fact his fall and eventual replacement by Putin led to bloody Russian aggression in Chechnya, with only token Western protests. The unspoken agreement was that if you let us bomb Serbia, we'll let you bomb Chechnya. Also note that mass opposition to Milošević, including street demonstrations by hundreds of thousands of citizens maintained for months took place in 1996–97 and in 2000 but not in the period of Western bombardment. On all this see my 'The War of NATO Expansion', in Ali, *Masters of the Universe*.
13. It is astonishing to recollect that on 2 September 2001 the *New York Times* ran a headline: 'Dogfight for Dollars on Capitol Hill: The Winnowing Begins on Contracts for Planes, Ships and All Things Military.'
14. The US response to the challenge is, as explained by Hardt and Negri, to evoke the false universality of the US as the ultimate custodian and guarantor of all that is valuable in human civilization. But these authors are wrong to equate 'imperial sovereignty' with an imperial network, as they define it, since the latter would tolerate and encourage a multiplicity of centres within a capitalist world. Instead the US sees itself as the sole centre. See Michael Hardt and Antonio Negri, *Empire*, London 2000.
15. See Stephen Kinzer, 'Our Man in Honduras', *New York Review of Books*, 20 September 2001.
16. Barry Meier, 'Most Afghan Opium Grown in Rebel-Controlled Areas', *New York Times*, 5 October 2001. On the US tilt towards the Taliban see Ahmed Rashid, *Taliban: Militant Islam, Oil and Fundamentalism in Central Asia*, London and New Haven, CT 2000, pp. 159–69. He believes that Unocal lobbying helps to explain the tilt.
17. Seymour Hirsh, 'King's Ransom', *New Yorker*, 22 October 2001. Cf., Thomas Friedman, 'Hama Rules', *New York Times*, 21 September 2001.

18. Neil MacFarquhar, 'Anti-Western and Extremist Views Pervade Saudi Schools', *New York Times*, 19 October 2001.

19. Raad Alkadiri writes: 'Today it is not Israel but Iraq that is emerging as a regional trade hub', Radd Alkadiri, 'The Iraqi Klondike', *Middle East Report*, 220, Fall 2001.

20. 'Pakistan's Inter-Services Intelligence directorate, or ISI [was] responsible for channeling large amounts of military and financial aid to the Taliban. Until the attacks in New York and Washington, that support had been quietly tolerated by the United States, despite the bitter opposition to the repressive forms of Islamic rule imposed by the Taliban'. John Burns, *New York Times*, 18 September 2001. See also Tariq Ali, 'Muslim Coup in Pakistan?', *Independent*, 14 September 2001.

21. James Risen and Judith Miller, 'Pakistani Intelligence Had Ties To Al Qaeda, U.S. Officials Say', *New York Times*, 29 October 2001.

22. Ibid.

23. For good accounts see John Cooley, *Unholy Warriors: Afghanistan, America and International Terrorism*, London 1999, Ahmed Rashid, *Taliban*, and Tariq Ali, 'Between Hammer and Anvil', *New Left Review*, no. 2, March–April 2000.

24. 'When police in Oslo made Norway's largest-ever heroin seizure, they discovered that former fighters from the Kosovo Liberation Army controlled the distribution chain.' 'War and Drugs', *The Economist*, 20 October 2001. Of course neither the terrorism nor the drug running of some KLA justifies Milošević's repression of the Kosovan people which was of long standing. See Branka Magas, 'Yugoslavia: The Spectre of Balkanisation', *New Left Review*, no. 174, March–April 1989. At this time the US State Department had a soft spot for Milošević and did nothing to avert the disintegration of a country that was seen as a 'neutral' and 'socialist' power by many in the West. Because of the demands of Western creditors the Yugoslav government swept aside by Milošević was unable to pay the salaries of its soldiers, a circumstance which greatly increased its vulnerability.

25. Tim Weiner and David Cay Johnston. 'Roadblocks Cited in Efforts to Trace Bin Laden's Money', *New York Times*, 20 September 2001.

26. 'Following the Money', *Business Week*, 1 October 2001. In Washington it has fallen to Grover Nordquist, the neo-conservative and free market advocate, to give radical Islam access to the Republicans and the Bush administration; for some time the Muslim Institute has operated out of the offices of his Institute for Tax Reform. Franklin Foer, 'Grover Norquist's Strange Alliance with radical Islam', *New Republic*, 12 November 2001.

27. Rodinson, *Islam and Capitalism*, New York 1974.

28. Oliver Roy, *The Failure of Political Islam*, Cambridge, MA, 1996.

29. Ibid.

30. Yossef Bodansky, *Bin Laden: The Man Who Declared War on America*, New York 2001, p. 198. For Bin Laden's financial operations and construction work see pp. 40–47, 307–36. The interpretations offered by this author should be treated with caution. He rarely supplies references even to secondary sources and is inclined to postulate a seamless conspiracy linking Middle Eastern political and religious currents that are often at odds with one another. Bodansky in the director of a Congressional task force on terrorism.

His account of Osama bin Laden's financial and commercial undertakings seems plausible. But he does not draw attention to the Saudi Bin Laden Group's stake in the Carlyle Group (see next note). See Kurt Eichenwald, 'Bin Laden Family Liquidates Holding with Carlyle Group', *New York Times*, 26 October 2001.

31. Jane Mayer, 'The House of Bin Laden', *The New Yorker*, 12 November 2001. See also Kurt Eichenwald, 'Bin Laden Family Liquidates Holding with Carlyle Group'.

32. Aburish, *Brutal Friendship*, p. 13.

33. Michael Walzer, *The Revolution of the Saints*, New York 1965. Walzer's argument can be seen as developing an aspect of Max Weber's famous argument concerning the Protestant ethic and the rise of capitalism. The broadly Marxist account of the role of the Puritans in the English Civil War – as advanced by Christopher Hill and Robert Brenner (*Merchants and Revolution*, Princeton 1993) – is compelling. But the logic and passion of Puritanism as a religious current contributed to the momentous secular outcome. It is here that some parallel with Islamic radicalism today may be worth exploring. As in the seventeenth century these Islamic radicals are often dealing with the problems of traditional tribal or feudal social relations in societies where capitalist modernization has taken hold but is very incomplete.

34. See Roy, *The Failure of Political Islam*, pp. 168–82. The Shah's regime did not repudiate all Mossadegh's reforms and appeared to some as a modernizing dictatorship, but its bureaucratic and mercantilist character failed to stimulate capitalist transformation. While some Westernizing compradors, technocrats and professionals supported the Shah, the bazaar merchants, linked to the internal market, played an important part in sustaining the opposition. See Misagh Parsa, *Social Origins of the Iranian Revolution*, New Brunswick 1989, pp. 91–125, 299–315.

35. Sohrab Behdad, 'The Post-Revolutionary Economic Crisis', in Saeed Rahnema and Sohrab Behdad, eds, *Iran and the Revolution: Crisis of an Islamic State*, London 1995, pp. 97–128.

36. The path of 'bourgeois democratic revolution' has always been complex and uneven, yoking together new freedoms with new and old slaveries. Perry Anderson's essay on 'Bourgeois Revolution' in *English Questions*, London 1992, insists on the variety of social forces which have historically sponsored the revolutions that constitute capitalist modernity. The actuality of the bourgeois or bourgeois-democratic revolution in world history used to be a Marxist theme but is now also encountered in non-Marxist authors, as witness work in the last decade by Gordon Wood, John Markoff and Francis Fukuyama. The classical notion of capitalism and democracy advancing in lockstep certainly needs to be revised, but the conceptual field remains indispensable. See Eric Hobsbawm's *Age of Revolution*, London 1964, Barrington Moore's *Social Origins of Dictatorship and Democracy*, New York 1974 and George Novack's stimulating primer, *Democracy and Revolution*, New York 1972.

37. *The Economist*, 22 September, 2001.

38. Elaine Sciolino, 'Tehran Aide Assails Terror But Opposes Bush Attack', *New York Times*, 1 October 2001.

39. According to *The Economist*, 'the one country that all drug traffickers try to avoid is Iran. Some 204 tonnes of opium and 29 tonnes of heroin

and morphine were seized in Iran in 1999 by a combination of army battalions and police units ... (In Turkey by contrast, only one third of a tonne of opium was confiscated in the same year).' *The Economist*, 20 October 2001.

40. Robert Fisk, 'Farewell to Democracy in Pakistan', *Independent*, 26 October 2001.

41. Donald Rumsfeld, 'A New Kind of War', *New York Times*, 27 September 2001.

42. James Bennett, 'Muddle Over Arafat–Peres Meeting Is Frustrating for Bush', *New York Times*, 25 September 2001. Challenged to withdraw these remarks by the Israeli government Straw explained: 'There is never any excuse for terrorism. At the same time, there is an obvious need to understand the environment which breeds terrorism. That is why the whole of the international community is so concerned to see lasting peace in the Middle East.'

43. See 'Scurrying Towards Bethlehem' by Perry Anderson on the background, and 'Redividing Palestine?' by the French General Guy Mondron, who details proposals for one possibility, both articles in *New Left Review*, no. 10, 2001.

44. On the significance of oil and other strategic raw materials, see Michael Klare, 'The New Geography of Conflict', *Foreign Affairs*, May/June 2001.

45. Richard Falk, 'Ends and Means: Defining a Just War', *The Nation*, 29 October 2001.

46. See Daniele Archibugi, 'Cosmopolitical Democracy' and the replies by Geoffrey Hawthorne, Timothy Brennan and others originally published in *New Left Review* and now reprinted in this book.

47. See the contribution by Saul Mendlovitz and John Fousek to Neal Reimer, ed., *Protection Against Genocide: Mission Impossible?*, Westport, CT 2000.

48. William Penn, 'An Essay Towards the Peace of Europe', in *The Peace of Europe and other essays*, London 1993, pp. 5–22. For Abbé de saint-Pierre see Denis de Rougmont, *The Idea of Empire*, London 1964, pp. 112–20.

49. David Murray, *Odious Commerce*, Cambridge 1980, p. 304–307.

50. Jonathan Schell, *The Unfinished Twentieth Century*, New York 2001.

51. For a good discussion of the history of bombing see Trevor Corson's review of a book on the topic by Sven Lundquist, *The Nation*, 29 October 2001. He makes the point that bombing has rarely been effective unless closely tied into the action of ground troops.

52. Samuel Farber, *Before Stalinism*, New York 1992.

53. John McCain, 'Hit Them Harder', *Guardian*, 30 October 2001.

# Violence, Law and Justice
# in a Global Age

*David Held*

On Sunday, 23 September 2001, the novelist Barbara Kingsolver wrote in *The Los Angeles Times*:

> It's the worst thing that's happened, but only this week. Two years ago, an earthquake in Turkey killed 17,000 people in a day, babies and mothers and businessmen . . . The November before that, a hurricane hit Honduras and Nicaragua and killed even more . . . Which end of the world shall we talk about? Sixty years ago, Japanese airplanes bombed Navy boys who were sleeping on ships in gentle Pacific waters. Three and a half years later, American planes bombed a plaza in Japan where men and women were going to work, where schoolchildren were playing, and more humans died at once than anyone thought possible. Seventy thousand in a minute. Imagine . . .
>
> There are no worst days, it seems. Ten years ago, early on a January morning, bombs rained down from the sky and caused great buildings in the city of Baghdad to fall down – hotels, hospitals, palaces, buildings with mothers and soldiers inside – and here in the place I want to love best, I had to watch people cheering about it. In Baghdad, survivors shook their fists at the sky and said the word 'evil'. When many lives are lost all at once, people gather together and say words like 'heinous' and 'honor' and 'revenge' . . . They raise up their compatriots' lives to a sacred place – we do this, all of us who are human – thinking our own citizens to be more worthy of grief and less willingly risked than lives on other soil.[1]

This is an unsettling and challenging passage. When I first read it, I felt angered and unsympathetic to its call to think systematically about September 11 in the context of other disasters, acts of aggression and wars. A few days later I found it helpful to connect its sentiments to my own strong cosmopolitan orientations.

Immanuel Kant wrote over two hundred years ago that we are 'unavoidably side by side'. A violent challenge to law and justice in one place has consequences for many other places and can be experienced everywhere.[2] While he dwelt on these matters and their implications at length, he could not have known how profound and immediate his concerns would become.

Since Kant, our mutual interconnectedness and vulnerability have grown rapidly. We no longer live, if we ever did, in a world of discrete national communities. Instead, we live in a world of what I like to call 'overlapping communities of fate' where the trajectories of countries are heavily enmeshed with each other. In our world, it is not only the violent exception that links people together across borders; the very nature of everyday problems and processes joins people in multiple ways. From the movement of ideas and cultural artefacts to the fundamental issues raised by genetic engineering, from the conditions of financial stability to environmental degradation, the fate and fortunes of each of us are thoroughly intertwined.

The story of our increasingly global order – 'globalization' – is not a singular one. Globalization is not a one-dimensional phenomena. For example, there has been an expansion of global markets which has altered the political terrain, increasing exit options for capital of all kinds, and putting pressure on polities everywhere.[3] But the story of globalization is not just economic: it is also one of growing aspirations for international law and justice. From the UN system to the EU, from changes to the laws of war to the entrenchment of human rights, from the emergence of international environmental regimes to the foundation of the International Criminal Court, there is also another narrative being told – a narrative which seeks to reframe human activity and entrench it in law, rights and responsibilities. In the first section of this essay, I would like to reflect on this second narrative and highlight some of its strengths and limitations. Once this background is sketched, elements of the legal and political context of September 11 can be better grasped.

## Reframing human activity: international law, rights and responsibilities

The process of the gradual delimitation of political power, and the increasing significance of international law and justice, can be illustrated by reflecting on a strand in international legal thinking which has overturned the exclusive position of the state in international law, and buttressed the role of the individual, in relation to, and with responsibility for, systematic violence against others.

In the first instance, by recognizing the legal status of conscientious objection, many states – particularly Western states (I shall return to the significance of this later) – have acknowledged there are clear occasions when an individual has a moral obligation beyond that of his or her obligation as a citizen of a state.[4] The refusal to serve in national armies triggers a claim to a 'higher moral court' of rights and duties. Such claims are exemplified as well in the changing legal position of those who are willing to go to war. The recognition in international law of the offences of war crimes, genocide and crimes against humanity make clear that acquiescence to the commands of national leaders will not be considered sufficient grounds for absolving individual guilt in these cases. A turning point in this regard was the judgment of the International Tribunal at Nuremberg (and the parallel tribunal in Tokyo). The Tribunal laid down, for the first time in history, that when *international rules* that protect basic humanitarian values are in conflict with *state laws*, every individual must transgress the state laws (except where there is no room for 'moral choice', e.g. when a gun is being held to someone's head).[5] Modern international law has generally endorsed the position taken by the Tribunal, and has affirmed its rejection of the defence of obedience to superior orders in matters of responsibility for crimes against peace and humanity. As one commentator has noted: 'Since the Nuremberg Trials, it has been acknowledged that war criminals cannot relieve themselves of criminal responsibility by citing official position or superior orders. Even obedience to explicit national legislation provides no protection against international law.'[6]

The most notable recent extension of the application of the Nuremberg principles has been the establishment of the war crimes tribunals for the former Yugoslavia (established by the UN

Security Council in 1993) and for Rwanda (set up in 1994).[7] The Yugoslav tribunal has issued indictments against people from all three ethnic groups in Bosnia, and is investigating crimes in Kosovo, although it has encountered serious difficulty in obtaining custody of the key accused. (Significantly, of course, ex-President Slobodan Milošević has recently been arrested and brought before The Hague War Crimes Tribunal). Although neither the tribunal for Rwanda nor the Yugoslav tribunal have had the ability to detain and try more than a small fraction of those engaged in atrocities, both have taken important steps toward implementing the law governing war crimes and, thereby, reducing the credibility gap between the promises of such law, on the one hand, and the weakness of its application, on the other.

Most recently, the proposals put forward for the establishment of a permanent International Criminal Court are designed to help close this gap in the longer term.[8] Several major hurdles remain to its successful entrenchment, including the continuing opposition from the United States (which fears its soldiers will be the target of politically motivated prosecutions) and dependency upon individual state consent for its effectiveness.[9] However, it is likely that the Court will be formally established (with or without the USA) and will mark another significant step away from the classic regime of state sovereignty – sovereignty, that is, as effective power – toward the firm entrenchment of the 'liberal regime of international sovereignty' as I refer to it – sovereignty shaped and delimited by new broader frameworks of governance and law (see Held, 2002, for a fuller account).[10]

The ground now being staked out in international legal agreements suggests something of particular importance: that the containment of armed aggression and abuses of power can only be achieved through both the control of warfare and the prevention of the abuse of human rights. For it is only too apparent that many forms of violence perpetrated against individuals, and many forms of abuse of power, do not take place during declared acts of war. In fact, it can be argued that the distinctions between war and peace, and between aggression and repression, are eroded by changing patterns of violence.[11] The kinds of violence witnessed in Bosnia and Kosovo highlight the role of paramilitaries and of organized crime, and the use of parts of national armies which may no longer be under the direct control of a state. What these kinds of violence signal is that there is a very fine line between explicit formal crimes committed during acts of national war, and major attacks on the welfare and physical integrity of citizens in situations that may not involve a declaration of war by states. While many of the new forms of warfare do not fall directly under the classic rules of war, they are massive violations of international human rights. Accordingly, the rules of war and human rights law can be seen as two complementary forms of international rules which aim to circumscribe the proper form, scope and use of coercive power.[12] For all the limitations of its enforcement, these are significant changes which, when taken together, amount to the rejection of the doctrine of legitimate power as effective control, and its replacement by international rules which entrench basic humanitarian values as the criteria for legitimate government.

How do the terrorist attacks on the World Trade Center and the Pentagon fit into this pattern of legal change? A wide variety of legal instruments, dating back to 1963 (the Convention on Offences and Certain Other Acts Committed on Board Aircraft), enable the international community to take action against terrorism, and bring those responsible to justice. If the persons responsible for the September 11 attacks can be identified and apprehended, they could face prosecution in virtually any country that obtains custody of them. In particular, the widely ratified Hague Convention for the Suppression of Unlawful Seizure of Aircraft (1970) makes the highjacking of aircraft an international criminal offence. The offence is regarded as extraditable under any extradition treaty in force between contracting states, and applies to accomplices as well as to the hijackers. In addition, the use of hijacked aircraft as lethal weapons can be interpreted as a crime against humanity under international law (although there is some legal argument about this). Frederic Kirgis has noted that the statute of the International Criminal Court 'defines a crime against humanity as any of several listed acts "when committed as part of a widespread or systematic attack directed against any civilian population . . ." The acts include murder and "other inhumane acts of a similar character intentionally causing great suffering, or serious injury to body or to mental or physical health." '[13]

Changes in the law of war, human rights law and in other legal domains have placed individuals, governments and non-governmental organizations under new systems of legal regulation – regulation which, in principle, recasts the legal significance of state boundaries. The regime of liberal international sovereignty entrenches powers and constraints, and rights and duties in international law which – albeit ultimately formulated by states – go beyond the traditional conception of the proper scope and boundaries of states, and can come into conflict, and sometimes contradiction, with national laws. Within this framework, states may forfeit claims to sovereignty, and individuals their right to sovereign protection, if they violate the standards and values embedded in the liberal international order; and such violations no longer become a matter of morality alone. Rather, they become a breach of a legal code, a breach that may call forth the means to challenge, prosecute and rectify it.[14] To this end, a bridge is created between morality and law where, at best, only stepping stones existed before in the era of classic sovereignty. These are transformative changes which alter the form and content of politics, nationally, regionally and globally. They signify the enlarging normative reach, extending scope and growing institutionalization of international legal rules and practices – the beginnings of a 'universal constitutional order' in which the state is no longer the only layer of legal competence to which people have transferred public powers.[15]

In short, boundaries between states are of decreasing legal and moral significance. States are no longer regarded as discrete political worlds. International standards breach boundaries in numerous ways. Within Europe the European Convention for the Protection of Human Rights and Fundamental Freedoms and the EU create new institutions and layers of law and governance which have divided political authority; any assumption that sovereignty is an indivisible, illimitable, exclusive and perpetual form of public power – entrenched within an individual state – is now defunct.[16] Within the wider international community, rules governing war, weapon systems, terrorism, human rights and the environment, among other areas, have transformed and delimited the order of states, embedding national polities in new forms and layers of accountability and governance (from particular regimes such as the Nuclear Non-Proliferation Treaty to wider frameworks of regulation laid down by the UN Charter and a host of specialized agencies).[17] Accordingly, the boundaries between states, nations and societies can no longer claim the deep legal and moral significance they once had; they can be judged, along with the communities they embody, by general, if not universal, standards. That is to say, they can be scrutinized and appraised in relation to standards which, in principle, apply to each person, each individual, who is held to be equally worthy of concern and respect. Concomitantly, shared membership in a political community, or spatial proximity, is not regarded as a sufficient source of moral privilege.[18]

The political and legal transformations of the last fifty years or so have gone some way toward circumscribing and delimiting political power on a regional and global basis. Several major difficulties remain, nonetheless, at the core of the liberal international regime of sovereignty which create tensions, if not fault-lines, at its centre.[19] I shall dwell on just one aspect of these here.

Serious deficiencies can, of course, be documented in the implementation and enforcement of democratic and human rights, and of international law more generally. Despite the development and consolidation of the regime of liberal international sovereignty, massive inequalities of power and economic resources continue to grow. There is an accelerating gap between rich and poor states as well as between peoples in the global economy.[20] The development of regional trade and investment blocs, particularly the Triad (NAFTA, the EU and Japan), has concentrated economic transactions within and between these three areas.[21] The Triad accounts for two-thirds to three-quarters of world economic activity, with shifting patterns of resources across each region. However, one further element of inequality is particularly apparent: a significant proportion of the world's population remains marginal to these networks.[22]

Does this growing gulf in the circumstances and opportunities of the world's population highlight intrinsic limits to the liberal international order or should this disparity be traced to other phenomena? The particularization of nation-states and the inequalities of regions with their own distinctive cultural, religious and political problems contribute to the disparity between the universal claims of the human rights regime and its often tragically limited impact.[23] But one of the key causes of the gulf lies, in my judgment, elsewhere – in the tangential impact of the liberal international order on the regulation of economic power and market mechanisms. The focus of the liberal international order is on the curtailment of the abuse of political power, not economic power. It has few, if any, systematic means to address sources of power other than the political.[24] Its conceptual resources and leading ideas do not suggest or push toward the pursuit of self-determination and autonomy in the economic domain; they do not seek the entrenchment of democratic rights and obligations outside of the sphere of the political. Hence, it is hardly a surprise that liberal democracy and flourishing economic inequalities exist side by side.

Thus, the complex and differentiated narratives of globalization point in stark and often contradictory directions. On the one side, there is the dominant tendency of economic globalization over the last three decades toward a pattern set by the deregulatory, neo-liberal model; an increase in the exit options of corporate and finance capital relative to labour and the state, and an increase in the volatility of market responses, which has exacerbated a growing sense of political uncertainty and risk; and the marked polarization of global relative economic inequalities (as well as serious doubt as to whether there has been a 'trickle down' effect to the world's poorest at all). On the other side, there is the significant entrenchment of cosmopolitan values concerning the equal dignity and worth of all human beings; the reconnection of international law and morality; the establishment of regional and global systems of governance; and growing recognition that the public good – whether conceived as financial stability, environmental protection, or global egalitarianism – requires coordinated multilateral action if it is to be achieved in the long term.

## September 11, war and justice

If September 11 was not a defining moment in human history, it certainly was for today's generations. The terrorist violence was an atrocity of extraordinary proportions. It was a crime against America and against humanity; a massive breach of many of the core codes of international law; and an attack on the fundamental principles of freedom, democracy, justice and humanity itself, i.e.

those principles which affirm the sanctity of life, the importance of self-determination and of equal rights and liberty.

These principles are not just Western principles – they are the basis of a fair, humane and decent society, of whatever religion or cultural tradition. To paraphrase the legal theorist Bruce Ackerman, there is no nation without a woman who yearns for equal rights, no society without a man who denies the need for deference and no developing country without a person who does not wish for the minimum means of subsistence so that they may go about their everyday lives.[25] The principles of freedom, democracy and justice are the basis for articulating and entrenching the equal liberty of all human beings. They are the basis of underwriting the liberty of others, not of obliterating it. Their concern is with the irreducible moral status of each and every person – the acknowledgement of which links directly to the possibility of self-determination and the capacity to make independent choices.[26]

The intensity of the range of responses to the atrocities of September 11 is understandable. There cannot be many people in the world who did not experience shock, revulsion, horror, anger and a desire for vengeance, as the Kingsolver passage acknowledges. This emotional range is perfectly natural within the context of the immediate events. But it cannot be the basis for a more considered and wise response.

The founding principles of our society dictate that we do not overgeneralize our response from one moment and one set of events; that we do not jump to conclusions based on concerns that emerge in one particular country at one moment; and that we do not re-write and re-work international law and governance arrangements from one place – in other words, that we do not think and act over-hastily and take the law into our hands. Clearly, the fight against terror must be put on a new footing. Terrorists must be brought to heel and those who protect and nurture them must be brought to account. Zero tolerance is fully justified in these circumstances. Terrorism does negate our most elementary and cherished principles and values. But any defensible, justifiable and sustainable response to September 11 must be consistent with our founding principles and the aspirations of international society for security, law, and the impartial administration of justice – aspirations painfully articulated after the Holocaust and the Second World War – and embedded, albeit imperfectly, in regional and global law and the institutions of global governance. If the means deployed to fight terrorism contradict these principles and achievements, then the emotion of the moment might be satisfied, but our mutual vulnerability will be deepened.

War and bombing were and are one option. President Bush described the attacks of September 11, and the US-led coalition response, as a 'new kind of war'; and, indeed, the attacks of September 11 can be viewed as a more dramatic version of patterns of violence witnessed during the last decade, in the wars in the Balkans, the Middle East and Africa. These wars are quite different from, for example, the Second World War. They are wars which are difficult to end and difficult to contain and where, typically, there have been no clear victories. There is much that can be learned from these experiences that is relevant to the situation now unfolding.

The contours of these 'new wars' are distinctive in many respects because the range of social and political groups involved no longer fit the pattern of a classical inter-state war; the type of violence deployed by the terrorist aggressors is no longer carried out by the agents of a state (although states, or parts of states, may have a supporting role); violence is dispersed, fragmented and directed against citizens; and political aims are combined with the deliberate commission of atrocities which are a massive violation of human rights. Such a war is not typically triggered by a state interest, but by religious identity, zeal and fanaticism. The aim is not to acquire territory, as was the case in 'old wars', but to gain political power through generating fear and hatred. War itself becomes a form of political mobilization in which the pursuit of violence promotes extremist causes.

In Western security policy, there is a dangerous gulf between the dominant thinking about security based on 'old wars' – like the Second World War and the Cold War – and the reality in the field. The so-called Revolution in Military Affairs, the development of 'smart' weaponry to fight wars at long distance, the proposals for the National Missile Defense programme, were all predicated on out-dated assumptions about the nature of war – the idea that it is possible to protect territory from attacks by outsiders. The language of President Bush, with its emphasis on the defence of America and of dividing the world between those 'who are with us or against us', tends to reproduce the illusion, drawn from the experience of the Second World War, that this is a war between simply 'good' states led by the United States and 'bad' states. Such an approach is regrettable and, potentially, very dangerous.

Today, a clear-cut military victory is very difficult to achieve because the advantages of supposed superior technology have been eroded in many contexts. As the Russians discovered in Afghanistan and Chechnya, the Americans in Vietnam, and the Israelis in the current period, conquering people and territory by military means has become an increasingly problematic form of warfare. These military campaigns have all been lost or suffered serious and continuous setbacks as a result of the stubborn refusal of movements for independence or autonomy to be suppressed; the refusal to meet the deployment of the conventional means of inter-state warfare with similar forces which play by the same set of rules; and by the constantly shifting use of irregular or guerrilla forces which sporadically but steadily inflict major casualties on states (whose domestic populations become increasingly anxious and weary). And the risks of using high-tech weapon systems, carpet bombing and other very destructive means of inter-state warfare are very high, to say the least.

The risks of concentrating military action against states like Afghanistan are the risks of ratcheting up fear and hatred, of actually creating a 'new war' between the West and Islam, a war which is not only between states but within every community in the West as well as in the Middle East. No doubt, the terrorists always hoped for air strikes, which would rally more supporters to their cause. No doubt they are now actively hoping for a global division between those states who side with America and those who do not. The fanatical Islamic networks that were probably responsible for the attacks have groups and cells in many places including Britain and the United States. The effect of the US-led war might very well be to expand the networks of fanatics, who may gain access to even more horrendous weapons, to increase racist and xenophobic feelings of all kinds, and to increase repressive powers everywhere, justified in the name of fighting terrorism.

An alternative approach existed, and might even be salvaged in some respects. An alternative approach is one which counters the strategy of 'fear and hate'. What is needed, as Mary Kaldor and I have argued,[27] is a movement for global, not American, justice and legitimacy, aimed at establishing and extending the rule of law in place of war and at fostering understanding between communities in place of terror. Such a movement must press upon governments and international institutions the importance of three things.

First, there must be a commitment to the rule of law not the prosecution of war. Civilians of all faiths and nationalities need protection, wherever they live, and terrorists must be captured and brought before an international criminal court, which could be either permanent or modelled on the Nuremberg or Yugoslav war crimes tribunals. The terrorists must be treated as criminals, and not glamorized as military adversaries. This does not preclude internationally sanctioned military action under the auspices of the United Nations both to arrest suspects and to dismantle terrorist networks – not at all. But such action should always be understood as a robust form of policing, above all as a way of protecting civilians and bringing criminals to trial. Moreover, this type of action must scrupulously preserve both the laws of war and human rights law. Imran Khan put a similar point forcefully in a recent article:

> The only way to deal with global terrorism is through justice. We need international institutions such as a fully empowered and credible world criminal court to define terrorism and dispense justice with impartiality. . . The world is heading towards disaster if the sole superpower behaves as judge, jury and executioner when dealing with global terrorism.[28]

The news (in October 2001 and later in 2002) of an increasingly intense pattern of extra-judicial, outlaw killings (organized, targeted murders) on both sides of the Israeli–Palestine conflict compounds anxieties about the breakdown of the rule of law, nationally and internationally. This only leads one way; that is, toward Hobbes' state of nature: the 'warre of every one against every one' – life as 'solitary, poore, nasty, brutish, and short'.

Second, a massive effort has to be undertaken to create a new form of global political legitimacy, one which must confront the reasons why the West is so often seen as self-interested, partial, one-sided and insensitive. This must involve condemnation of all human rights violations wherever they occur, renewed peace efforts in the Middle East, talks between Israel and Palestine, and rethinking policy towards Iraq, Iran, Afghanistan, and elsewhere. This cannot be equated with an occasional or one-off effort to create a new momentum for peace and the protection of human rights. It has to be part of a continuous emphasis in foreign policy, year-in, year-out. Many parts of the world will need convincing that the West's interest in security and human rights for all regions and peoples is not just a product of short-term geo-political or geo-economic interests.

And, third, there must be a head-on acknowledgement that the ethical and justice issues posed by the global polarization of wealth, income and power, and with them the huge asymmetries of life chances, cannot be left to markets to resolve. Those who are poorest and most vulnerable, locked into geo-political situations which have neglected their economic and political claims for generations, will always provide fertile ground for terrorist recruiters. The project of economic globalization has to be connected to manifest principles of social justice; the latter need to reframe global market activity.

To date the US-led coalition, in pursuing, first and foremost, a military response to September 11, has chosen *not* to prioritize the development of international law and UN institutional arrangements (point one above); and *not* to emphasize the urgency of building institutional bridges between the priorities of social justice and processes of economic globalization (point three above), although one or two coalition politicians have made speeches acknowledging the importance of this question. Peace in the Middle East has been singled out as a priority by some coalition leaders, but there is little sign as yet that this is part of a broader rethinking of foreign policy in the Middle East, and of the role of the West in international affairs more generally (point two above). These are political choices and, like all such choices, they carry a heavy burden of possibility and lost opportunity.

Of course, terrorist crimes of the kind we witnessed on September 11 may often be the work of the simply deranged and the fanatic and so there can be no guarantee that a more just world would quell this danger. But if we turn our back on this challenge, there is no hope of ameliorating the social basis of disadvantage often experienced in the poorest and most dislocated countries. Gross injustices, linked to a sense of hopelessness born of generations of neglect, feed anger and hostility. Popular support against terrorism depends upon convincing people that there is a legal and pacific way of addressing their grievances. Without this sense of confidence in public institutions and processes, the defeat of terrorism becomes a hugely difficult task, if it can be achieved at all.

Kant was right; the violent abrogation of law and justice in one place ricochets across the world. We cannot accept the burden of putting justice right in one dimension of life – security – without at the same time seeking to put it right everywhere. A socio-economic order in which whole regions and peoples suffer serious harm and disadvantage independently of their will or consent, will not command widespread support and legitimacy. If the political, social and economic dimensions of justice are separated in the long term – as is the tendency in the global order today – the prospects of a peaceful and civil society will be bleak indeed.

## Islam, the Kantian heritage and double standards

The responsibility for the pursuit of justice does not just fall on the West as some commentators believe. It is not simply the US and Europe who must look critically at themselves in the after-math of September 11; there is a chronic need for self-examin-ation in parts of Islam as well. The Muslim writer Ziauddin Sardar wrote recently:

> To Muslims everywhere I issue this fatwa: any Muslim involved in the planning, financing, training, recruiting, support or harbouring of those who commit acts of indiscriminate violence against persons . . . is guilty of terror and no part of the *ummah*. It is the duty of every Muslim to spare no effort in hunting down, apprehending and bringing such criminals to justice.
>
> If you see something reprehensible, said the Prophet Muhammad, then change it with your hand; if you are not capable of that then use your tongue (speak out against it); and if you are not capable of that then detest it in your heart. The silent Muslim majority must now become vocal.[29]

Iman Hamza, a noted Islamic teacher, has spoken recently of the 'deep denial' many Muslims seem to be in. He is concerned that 'Islam has been hijacked by a discourse of anger and a rhetoric of rage'.[30] The attacks of September 11 appear to have been perpetrated in the name of Islam, albeit a particular version of Islam. It is this version of Islam which must be repudiated by the wider Islamic community, who need to re-affirm the compatibility of Islam with the universal, cosmopolitan principles that put life, and the free development of all human beings, at their centre.

Hugo Young made the same point rather bluntly in the *Guardian* recently: 'The September terrorists who left messages and testaments described their actions as being in the name of Allah. They made this their explicit appeal and defence. Bin Laden himself, no longer disclaiming culpability for their actions, clothes their murders and their suicides in religious glory. A version of Islam – not typical, a minority fragment, but undeniably Islamic – endorses the foaming hatred for America that uniquely emanates, with supplementary texts, from a variety of mullahs.[31]

Accordingly, it is not enough for the West to look critically at itself in the shadow of September 11. Muslim countries need to confront their own ideological extremists, and reject without qualification any doctrine or action which encourages or condones the slaughter of innocent human beings. In addition, they need to reflect on their own failings to ensure minimum standards of living, and a decent, free and democratic life, for all their citizens. As Bhikhu Parekh, Chair of the Commission on the Future of Multi-ethnic Britain, put it, Muslims must 'stop blaming the West for all their ills' and must grapple with the temptation to locate all the main sources of their problems elsewhere.[32]

September 11 can be linked to a new, integrated political crisis developing in west Asia. The crisis has been well analysed by Fred Halliday:

> in several countries, there has been a weakening, if not collapse, of the state – in the 1970s and 1980s in Lebanon, more recently in Afghanistan and Yemen. . . It is in these countries, where significant areas are free of government control, or where the government seeks to humour autonomous armed groups, like al-Qaeda, that a culture of violence and religious demagogy has thrived. . . This is compounded by the way in which the historically distinct conflicts of Afghanistan, Iraq and Palestine have, in recent years, come to be more and more connected. Militants in each – secular nationalist (Saddam) as well as Islamist (Osama bin Laden) – see the cause of resistance to the West and its regional allies as one.[33]

Hence, Osama bin Laden's first target was the government of Saudi Arabia, to which he later added the governments of Egypt and Jordan (and the Shi'ite Republic of Iran). Only later did he formally connect (via a declared fatwa in 1998) his war against these governments to the United States, which he came to see as the key source of, and support for, the corruption of Islamic sovereignty in the Middle East.[34]

The fundamental fissure in the Muslim world is between those who want to uphold universal standards, including the standards of democracy and human rights, and want to reform their societies, dislodging the deep connection between religion, culture and politics, and those who are threatened by this and wish to retain and/or restore power to those who represent 'fundamentalist' ideals. The political, economic and cultural challenges posed by the globalization of (for want of a better shorthand) 'modernity' now face the counterforce of the globalization of radical Islam. This poses many big questions, but one in particular should be stressed; that is, how far and to what extent Islam – and not just the West – has the capacity to confront its own ideologies, double standards, and limitations. Clearly, the escape from dogma and unvindicated authority – the removal of constraints on the public use of reason – has a long way to go, East and West. The Kantian heritage should be accepted across Islam as well.

It's a mistake to think that this is simply an outsider's challenge to Islam. Islam, like the other great world religions, has incorporated a diverse body of thought and practice. In addition, it has contributed, and accommodated itself, to ideas of religious tolerance, secular political power and human rights. It is particularly in the contemporary period that radical Islamic movements have turned their back on these important historical developments and sought to deny Islam's contribution both to the Enlightenment and the formulation of universal ethical codes. There are many good reasons for doubting the often expressed Western belief that thoughts about justice and democracy have only flourished in the West.[35] Islam is not a unitary or explanatory category (see Halliday, 1996).[36] Hence, the call for cosmopolitan values speaks to a vital strain within Islam which affirms the importance of rights and justice.

## Concluding reflections

It is useful to return to the passage with which I started this essay. It makes uncomfortable reading because it invites reflection on September 11 in the context of other tragedies and conflict situations, and asks the reader to step outside of the maelstrom of September 11 and put those events in a wider historical and evaluative framework. It is important to affirm the irreducible moral status of each and every person and, concomitantly, reject the view of moral particularists that belonging to a given community limits and determines the moral worth of individuals and the nature of their freedom. At the centre of this kind of thinking is the cosmopolitan view that human well-being is not defined by geographical and cultural locations, that national or ethnic or gendered boundaries should not determine the limits of rights or responsibilities for the satisfaction of basic human needs, and that all human beings require equal moral respect and concern. Cosmopolitanism builds on the basic principles of equal dignity, equal respect, and the priority of vital need in its preoccupation with what is required for the autonomy and development of all human beings.

Cosmopolitan principles are not principles for some remote utopia; for they are at the centre of significant post Second World War legal and political developments, from the 1948 UN Declaration of Human Rights to the 1998 adoption of the Statute of the International Criminal Court. Many of these developments were framed against the background of formidable threats to humankind – above all, Nazism, fascism and the Holocaust. The framers of these initiatives affirmed the importance of universal principles, human rights, and the rule of law when there were strong temptations to simply put up the shutters and defend the position of some nations and countries only. The response to September 11 could follow in the footsteps of these achievements and strengthen our multilateral institutions and international legal arrangements; or, it could take us further away from these fragile gains toward a world of further antagonisms and divisions – a distinctively uncivil society. At the time of writing the signs are not good, but we have not yet run out of choices – history is still with us and can be made.[37]

# Notes

1. B. Kingsolver, 'A Pure, High Note of Anguish', *Los Angeles Times*, 23 September 2001.

2. Immanuel Kant, *Kant's Political Writings*, edited by H. Reiss, Cambridge 1970, pp. 107–108.

3. See D. Held and A. McGrew, D. Goldblatt and J. Perraton, *Global Transformations: Politics, Economics and Culture*, Cambridge 1999, chapters 3–5; and D. Held and A. McGrew, eds, *The Global Transformation Reader*, Cambridge 2000, ch. 25.

4. See J. Vincent, 'Modernity and Universal Human Rights', in A. McGrew and P. Lewis, eds, *Global Politics*, Cambridge 1992, pp. 269–92.

5. A. Cassese, *Violence and Law in the Modern Age*, Cambridge 1988, p. 132.

6. Y. Dinstein, 'Rules of War', in J. Krieger, ed., *The Oxford Companion to Politics of the World*, Oxford 1993, p. 968.

7. Cf. C. Chinkin, 'International Law and Human Rights', in T. Evans, ed., *Human Rights Fifty Years On: A Reappraisal*, Manchester 1998; *The Economist*, 'A Survey of Human Rights', no. 5, December 1998.

8. Cf. J. Crawford, 'Prospects for an International Criminal Court', in M.D.A. Freeman and R. Halson, eds, *Current Legal Problems*, Oxford 1995; J. Dugard, 'Obstacles in the Way of an International Criminal Court', *Cambridge Law Journal*, vol. 56, no. 2, 1997; M. Weller, 'The Reality of the Emerging Universal Constitutional Order: Putting the Pieces Together', *Cambridge Review of International Studies*, Winter–Spring 1997.

9. C. Chinkin, 'International Law and Human Rights', pp. 118–19.

10. D. Held, 'Law of states, law of peoples', *Legal Theory*, vol. 8, no. 2, 2002.

11. See M. Kaldor, 'Reconceptualizing Organized Violence', in D. Archibugi, D. Held and M. Köhler, eds, *Re-imagining Political Community. Studies in Cosmopolitan Democracy*, Cambridge 1998; and M. Kaldor, *New and Old Wars*, Cambridge 1998.

12. See M. Kaldor, *New and Old Wars*, chapters 6 and 7.

13. F. Kirgis, *Terrorist Attacks on the World Trade Center and the Pentagon*, September 2001. www.asil.org/insights/insigh77.htm

14. See J. Habermas, 'Bestialität und Humanität', *Die Zeit*, 18 April 1999.

15. J. Crawford and S. Marks, 'The Global Democracy Deficit: An Essay on International Law and its Limits', in Daniele Archibugi et al., eds, *Re-imagining Political Community. Studies in Cosmopolitan Democracy*, M. Weller, 'The Reality of the Emerging Universal Constitutional Order: Putting the Pieces Together', p. 45.

16. D. Held, *Democracy and the Global Order: From the Modern State to Cosmopolitan Governance*, Cambridge 1995, pp. 107–13.

17. See Held and McGrew, Goldblatt and Perraton, *Global Transformations: Politics, Economics and Culture*, chapters 1 and 2.

18. C. Beitz, 'Philosophy of International Relations', in the *Routledge Encyclopedia of Philosophy*, London 1998; C. Beitz, *Political Theory and International Relations*, Princeton 1979; T. Pogge, *Realizing Rawls*, Ithaca, NY 1989; T. Pogge, 'Cosmopolitanism and sovereignty', in C. Brown, ed., *Political Restructuring in Europe: Ethical Perspectives*, London 1994; T. Pogge, 'An Egali-

tarian Law of Peoples', *Philosophy and Public Affairs*, vol. 23, no. 3, 1994; and B. Barry, 'Statism and Nationalism: a Cosmopolitan Critique', in I. Shapiro and L. Brilmayer, eds, *Global Justice*, New York 1999.

19. See Held, 'Law of State, Law of Peoples', *Legal Theory*.

20. UNDP, *Globalization with a Human face: Human Development Report 1999*, New York 1999.

21. G. Thompson, 'Economic Globalization?', in David Held, ed., *A Globalizing World?*, London 2000.

22. T. Pogge, 'Economic Justice and National Borders', *Revision*, vol. 22, no. 2, 1999, p. 27; see UNDP, *Human Development Report 1997*, New York 1997; UNDP, *Human Development Report 1999*; David Held and A. McGrew, eds, *The Global Transformation Reader*.

23. See T. Pogge, 'Economic Justice and National Borders', A. Leftwich, *States of Development*, Cambridge 2000.

24. See D. Held, *Democracy and the Global Order: From the Modern State to Cosmopolitan Governance*, part 3.

25. B. Ackerman, 'Political Liberalisms', *Journal of Philosophy*, vol. 91, no. 7, 1994; and see A. Sen, *Inequality Reexamined*, Oxford 1992; A. Sen, *Development as Freedom*, Oxford 1999.

26. See M. Nussbaum, 'Kant and Cosmopolitanism', in J. Bohman and M. Lutz-Bachmann, eds, *Perpetual Peace: Essays on Kant's Cosmopolitan Ideal*, Cambridge, MA 1997.

27. D. Held and M. Kaldor, 'What Hope for the Future? Learning the Lessons from the Past', OpenDemocracy.net. 2001.

28. I. Khan, 'Terrorist Should be Tried in Court', *Guardian*, 12 October 2001.

29. Z. Sardar, 'My Fatwa on the Fanatics', *Guardian*, 22 September 2001.

30. H. Young, 'It May not be PC to Say', *Guardian*, 9 October 2001.

31. Ibid.

32. B. Parekh, 'Interview', *Guardian*, 11 October 2001.

33. F. Halliday, 'No Man Is an Island', *Observer*, 16 September 2001.

34. K. Armstrong, 'The War We Should Fight', *Guardian*, 13 October 2001.

35. A. Sen, 'Humanity and Citizenship', in J. Cohen, ed., *For Love of Country*, Boston 1996, p. 118.

36. F. Halliday, *Islam and the Myth of Confrontation*, London 1996.

37. Two sections of this essay have been adapted from my previous writings. The first section draws on some material developed at much greater length in my 'Law of states, law of peoples', *Legal Theory*, vol. 8, no. 2, 2002. The second section draws on my 'Violence and justice in a global age' and, with Mary Kaldor, on 'What hope for the future? Learning the lessons of the past'. Both these pieces were made available initially through OpenDemocracy.net. I would like to thank Mary Kaldor for allowing me to draw on our joint essay and to adapt some of the material for this new piece. Her work on old and new wars has been an especially important influence on me here.

# 11

# The Deeper Challenges of Global Terrorism: A Democratizing Response

*Richard Falk and Andrew Strauss*[1]

## Answering the terrorist challenge

The audacious and gruesome terrorist attacks on the World Trade Center and the Pentagon, along with the military response, have been the defining political events of this new millennium. The most profound challenge directed at the international community, and to all of us, is to choose between two alternative visions. What we call the traditional statist response emphasizes 'national security' as the cornerstone of human security. Centralization of domestic authority, secrecy, militarism, nationalism, and an emphasis on unconditional citizen loyalty, to her or his state as the primary organizing feature of international politics are all attributes of this approach.

We recommend an alternative vision, one that we call democratic transnationalism. Democratic transnationalism attempts to draw on the successes of democratic, particularly multinational democratic, domestic orders as a model for achieving human security in the international sphere. This approach calls for the resolution of political conflict through an open transnational citizen/societal (rather than state or market) centred political process legitimized by fairness, adherence to human rights, the rule of law, and representative community participation. The promotion of security for individuals and groups through international human rights law in general, as reinforced by the incipient international criminal court with its stress on an ethos of individual legal responsibility, assessed within a reliable constitutional setting, is a crucial element of this democratic transnationalist vision, which aspires to achieve a cosmopolitan reach.

Before the events of September 11 we had argued in favour of the establishment of a distinct, global institutional voice for the peoples of the world as a beneficial next step to be taken to carry forward the transnational democratic project. We proposed a GPA, which we have variously identified as a Global Parliamentary Assembly, and interchangeably as a Global Peoples' Assembly.[2] So far we have deliberately refrained from setting forth a detailed blueprint of our proposal, partly to encourage a wide debate about the general idea, partly to generate a sense of democratic participation in the process of establishing such a populist institution. We have expressed a tentative preference for representation on a basis that would to the extent possible incorporate the principle of one person one vote. The eventual goal would be to enfranchise as voting constituents all citizens of the planet above a certain age. We have further taken the position that the GPA should not interfere in matters appropriately defined as within 'the internal affairs of states', although acknowledging that the extent of such deference is bound to shift through time and often be controversial in concrete instances. The main mission of the GPA would be to play a role in democratizing the formulation and implementation of global policy. It is our conviction that such an assembly's powers should always be exercised in conformity with the Universal Declaration of Human Rights, and other widely accepted international human rights instruments.

We believe that carrying out the transnational democratic project, including establishing the GPA, should be treated as part of the political response to the challenges posed by the sort of mega-terrorism associated with the September 11 attacks. Transnational terrorism, which consists of networks of dedicated extremists organized across many borders, of which al Qaeda is exemplary, is so constituted that its grievances, goals, recruitment tactics and membership, as well as its objects of attack, are all wholly transnational. This form of political violence is a new phenomenon. It is the frightfully dark side of an otherwise mostly promising trend toward the transnationalization of politics. This trend, a result of economic and cultural globalization, has manifested itself in a pronounced way since the street demonstrations staged against the 1999 WTO meeting in Seattle.

The state-centric structures of the international system are not adequate to address this new transnational societal activism and, in fact, the arbitrary territorial constraints on the organization of work and life have intensified various forms of frustration, which feed the rise of transnational terrorism. One cause of this frustration is that globalization in all its dimensions is bringing with it changes of great magnitude that often directly impact on the lives of individuals and regions. These changes range from growing income inequality within and between many societies to powerful assaults on cultural traditions that offend non-Western peoples. Adverse impacts of globalization on many adherents of Islam have definitely induced political extremism in recent decades even before September 11, starting with the Iranian Revolution of the late 1970s.

Even in democratic societies there is a growing sense that domestic politics is not capable of responding creatively to long-range challenges of regional and global scope. It is certainly the case that the magnitude of these challenges is well beyond the capacities of even the strongest of states to shape benevolently on their own. At the same time individuals have an ever-greater incentive to influence global decision-making through their use of the technologies of globalization, especially the Internet. Information technology has given individuals an unprecedented ability to increase their leverage on public issues by making common cause with like-minded others without regard to considerations of geography or nationality.

An institutional framework such as that which would be provided by a GPA is a democratic way to begin peacefully to accommodate this new internationalization of civic politics. Individuals and groups could channel their frustrations into efforts to attempt to participate in and influence parliamentary decision-making as they have become accustomed to doing in the more democratic societies of the world. Presently, with trivial exceptions, individuals, groups and their associations are denied an official role in global political institutions where decision-making is dominated by élites who have been officially designated by states. Intergovernmental organizations, such as the United

Nations, the World Trade Organization and the International Monetary Fund are run as exclusive membership organizations, operated by and for states. With the possibility of direct and formalized participation in the international system foreclosed, frustrated individuals and groups (especially when their own governments are viewed as illegitimate or hostile) have been turning to various modes of civic resistance, both peaceful and violent. Global terrorism is at the violent end of this spectrum of transnational protest, and its apparent agenda may be mainly driven by religious, ideological and regional goals rather than by resistance directly linked to globalization. But its extremist alien-ation is partly, at the very least, an indirect result of globalizing impacts that may be transmuted in the political unconscious of those so afflicted into grievances associated with cultural injustices.

In addition to helping provide a non-violent and democratic channel for frustrated individuals and groups to affect meaning-fully global decision-making, a GPA has the potential to provide a way of helping to resolve inter-societal and more recently inter-civilizational conflict and polarization. Presently, the institutions around which citizen politics is formally structured are confined within distinct domestic political systems. This makes a unified human dialogue on issues of shared concern impossible. And transnational remedies for perceived injustices are not available. In a globalizing world it is crucial to encourage debate and discussion of global issues that builds consensus, acknowledges grievances, and identifies cleavages in a manner that is not dominated by the borders of sovereign territorial states, or even by innovative regional frames of reference as in Europe. As a consequence of this existing pattern of fragmentation in the political order, societies and cultures develop their own distinctive and generally self-serving distortions and myths, or perhaps, at the very least, experience exaggerated differences of perception that feed pre-existing patterns of conflict. Most persons within one society have little difficulty identifying the distorted percep-tions of others, but tend to be oblivious to their own biases, an insensitivity nurtured by mainstream media especially in the midst of major crises. The oft heard American response to the Septem-ber 11 attacks, 'Why do they hate us so?' and the seething anger in the Muslim world that has risen to the surface in the aftermath of the attacks starkly demonstrate just how profound and tragic is the perception gap for societies on both sides of this now crucial civilizational and societal divide.

The establishment of a GPA provides one way to address constructively this perception gap. Like all elected assemblies, a GPA would be a forum engendering debate on the main global controversies, especially as they affect the peoples of the world. Because elected delegates would be responsive to their respective constituencies, and because the media would cover proceedings, this debate would likely exert an influence far beyond the parliamentary chambers. Its echoes would be heard on editorial pages, listservs, and TV, in schools and churches, and in assorted discussions at all levels of social interaction around the world. Spokespersons directly connected to aggrieved groups of citizens would have a new transnational public arena to voice their opinions and grievances, as well as to encounter opposed views. Those attacked or criticized would have ample opportunity to defend themselves and express their counter-claims. From such exchanges would come the same pull toward a less confrontational understanding between diverse groups of citizens that we find within the more successful domestic democratic systems of the world. Of course, complete agreement would never be achieved and is not even a worthy goal. Conformity of outlook is never healthy for a political community, but it is especially inappropriate in a global setting, given the unevenness of economic and cultural circumstances that exist in the world. But a GPA process could at least greatly facilitate convergent perceptions of reality, thereby making controversies about problems and solutions more likely to be productive, including a mutual appreciation and acceptance of differences in values, priorities and situations.

In addition to helping reduce the perception gap as an underlying cause of social tensions, a GPA would further promote the peaceful resolution of enduring social tensions by encouraging reliance on procedures for reaching decisions based on compromise and accommodation. Even where mutually acceptable solutions are not immediately achievable, parliamentary systems of lawmaking and communication, if functioning well, at least provide a civil forum where adversaries can peacefully debate and clarify their differences. If such institutions generate community respect and gain legitimacy, then those who do not get their way on a particular issue will be generally far more inclined to accept defeat out of a belief in the fairness of the process and with an understanding that they can continue to press their case in the future.

Of course, the brand of Muslim fundamentalism embraced by Osama bin Laden is illiberal and anti-democratic in the extreme. Given the existence of such extremism, it is appropriate to question the ability of liberal democratic institutions to absorb successfully those who share the worldview of al Qaeda, or adhere to similar orientations. One of the impressive features of liberal parliamentary process, however, is its considerable ability to assimilate many of those who do reject its democratic outlook. Because parliamentary process invites participation and because it has the politically powerful capacity to confer or deny the imprimatur of popular legitimacy upon a political position, experience at the domestic level suggests that even those with radical political agendas will seldom decline the opportunity to participate. In the United States, for example, those on the Christian right who have deep religious doubts about the validity of secular political institutions have not only participated in the parliamentary process, but have done so at times with zeal, tactical ingenuity, and considerable success despite their minority status. In other countries, small political parties at the margins of public opinion often exert disproportionate influence in situations where a majority position is difficult for dominant parties to achieve. By participating in the process they have come to accept, at least in practice, the legitimacy of these institutions and procedures for societal decision-making.

Somewhat analogously, in the Cold War era the orthodox Soviet-inspired critique of the American system nominally accepted by those American Communists represented by the Communist Workers Party included a rejection of 'bourgeois' rights in favour of what was then identified as 'the dictatorship of the proletariat'. Yet, despite their professed rejection of 'bourgeois democracy', their leader Gus Hall ran for President of the United States repeatedly in an attempt to gain a tiny bit of electoral legitimacy for his position of isolation at the outermost reaches of public opinion. The relative domestic openness of the American political process helps explains why the United States has suffered relatively little indigenous political violence in the twentieth century. During the period of heightened political tensions in the 1960s, groups committed to violence such as the Weather Underground, unlike al Qaeda today, could not attract popular support for their radical rejection of the American governing process, and never became more than a nuisance, posing only the most tangential threat to the security, much less the stability, of the country. This lack of societal resonance soon leads to the decay, demoralization and collapse of such extremist groups, a dynamic of rejection that is far more effective in protecting society than law enforcement is even if enhanced by emergency powers as is the case in wartime conditions. To a lesser extent, the same self-destruct process seems to have kept the right-wing militia movement from posing a major threat to civic order, although it was indirectly responsible for inspiring the 1995 Oklahoma City bombing. This phenomenon with variations can be observed within all of the more democratic systems of the world. The Osama bin Ladens of the planet would be highly unlikely themselves to participate in a global parliamentary process, but their likely ability to attract any significant following would be substantially undermined to the extent that such an institution existed and gave the most disadvantaged and aggrieved peoples in the world a sense that their concerns were being meaningfully addressed. Indeed, if such a safety valve existed, it might prevent, or at least discourage, the emergence of the Osama syndrome, that the only way to challenge the existing arrangement of power and influence is by engaging in totalizing violence against its civilian infrastructure.

## Civic activism: setting the stage for a GPA

We believe that the underlying preconditions for a GPA are being created by the way that civic politics is increasingly challenging the autonomy of the state-centric international system. In one of the most significant, if still under-recognized, developments of the last several years, both civic voluntary organizations and business and financial élites are engaged in creating parallel structures that complement and erode the traditionally exclusive role of states as the only legitimate actors in the global political system. Individuals and groups, and their numerous transnational associations, rising up from and challenging the confines of territorial states, are promoting 'globalization-from-below', and have begun to coalesce into what is now recognized as being a rudimentary 'global civil society'. Business and financial élites, on their side, acting largely to facilitate economic globalization, have launched a variety of mechanisms to promote their own preferred global policy initiatives, a process that can be described as 'globalization-from-above'. While these new developments are rendering the territorial sovereignty paradigm partially anachronistic, they are still very far from supplanting the old order, or even providing a design for a coherent democratic system of representation that operates on a truly global scale. Until the international community creates such a representative structure, the ongoing tension between the democratic ideal and the global reality will remain unresolved. And we will continue to be plagued by an incoherent global political structure in which the peoples of the world are not offered the sort of democratic alternative to violence that is increasingly considered the *sine qua non* of legitimate domestic governance.

## The organizations of global civil society

Is this coalescence of personal initiatives with an array of transnational initiatives that we identify as global civil society capable of mounting a transformative challenge to the customary role of states as the representatives of their citizens in the international system? Civil society, roughly defined as the politically organized citizenry, is mostly decentralized, broken down into non-profit organizations and voluntary associations dedicated to a wide variety of mostly liberal, humanitarian and social causes (though some decidedly illiberal and anti-liberal, of which terrorist and criminal networks are the worrisome instance). Transnationally, the largest and most prominent of these organizations bear such respected names as Amnesty International, Greenpeace, Oxfam, and the International Committee of the Red Cross. There are now more than 3,000 civil society organizations either granted consultative status by the United Nations Economic and Social Council or associated with the UN Department of Public Information.

As described by Jessica Mathews in her landmark 1997 article in *Foreign Affairs*,[3] global civil society gained significantly in influence during the second half, and particularly the last quarter, of the twentieth century. The early 1990s, however, was the time when civic transnationalism really came of age. If any single occasion deserves to be identified with the emergence of civil society on the global scene it would probably be the June 1992 UN Conference on the Environment and Development held in Rio de Janeiro. More than 1,500 civil society organizations were accredited to participate and 25,000 individuals from around the world took part in parallel NGO forums and activities. Civic associations and their representatives were for the first time recognized as an important and independent presence at a major world inter-governmental conference. The Rio Conference, partly responsive to this active involvement of global civil society, produced four major policy-making instruments.[4]

After Rio the pattern intensified. In the first half of the 1990s there were several other major global conferences under UN auspices at which civil society participation was an important factor. The most significant of these dealt with human rights (Vienna 1993), population (Cairo 1994), and women (Beijing 1995). The democratizing success of these global events produced a backlash among several major governments, especially the United States. The result in the short term has been the virtual abandonment of such conferences by the United Nations, supposedly for fiscal reasons, but actually because governments were afraid of losing some of their control over global policy-making. With the exception of the racism conference in Durban, South Africa, during 2001, there has been no major conference of this sort in the new millennium. It is important to evaluate this experience in the setting of the quest for global democracy. There is little doubt that these conferences in the 1990s did a great deal to establish the role and presence of civil society as a significant player in the global arena.

When the 1990s came to an end, the decade's balance sheet of accomplishments reflected for the first time in history the impact of global civil society. These transnational forces had been instrumental in promoting treaties to deal with global warming, establish an international criminal court and outlaw anti-personnel landmines. These same actors were also influential during these years in persuading the International Court of Justice to render an Advisory Opinion on the legality of nuclear weapons and in defeating an OECD attempt to gain acceptance for a multilateral investment agreement. This global populist movement at the turn of the millennium gained widespread attention through its advocacy of the cancellation of the foreign debts of the world's poorest countries. While all of these efforts to a greater or lesser extent remain works-in-progress, civil society has clearly been indispensable in achieving current levels of success.

During the formative years of the 1990s the most visible gatherings of civil society organizations took place beneath the shadow of large multilateral conferences of states. As the decade drew to a close, and with these conferences, at least in the near term, mostly foreclosed, something different began to occur. The multitude of global civil society organizations began to act on their own, admittedly in an exploratory and highly uncertain fashion, and yet independently of states and international institutions. For instance, in May 1999 at The Hague Appeal for Peace, 8,000 individuals, mostly representing civil society organizations from around the world, and given heart by the presence of such luminaries as Nobel Peace Laureates Archbishop Desmond Tutu, José Ramos-Horta, and Jody Williams, met to shape a strategy for the future and to agree on a common agenda. Throughout the following year there were similar though smaller meetings in Seoul, Montreal, Germany, and elsewhere.

These meetings were a prelude to the Millennium NGO Forum held at the UN in May 2000 at the initiative of UN Secretary-General Kofi Annan. It was an expression of his 'partnership policy' to reach out to non-state actors of both a civic and a market character. The Secretary-General invited some 1,400 individuals from international civil society to UN Headquarters in New York to present their views on global issues and to debate an organizational structure that might enable the peoples of the world to participate effectively in global decision-making. That UN Millennium Forum agreed to establish a permanently constituted assembly of civil society organizations called the Civil Society Forum that is mandated to meet at least every two to three years, scheduled so as to precede the annual sessions of the UN General Assembly. While progress has been uneven, civil society has been continuing to work in the face of statist resistance and skepticism to bring this forum into fruition.

Many activists within global civil society regard this UN millennial initiative as the first step toward the establishment of a popular assembly that would meet at regular intervals, if not on a continuous basis. The emergence of such a Civil Society Forum might over time come to be recognized as an important barometer of world public opinion, and significantly, from the perspective of this chapter, could be seen as a preliminary, yet significant, step on the path to the establishment of a GPA.

## The global business élite at Davos

Complicating, yet undeniably crucial to the dynamics of global democratization, are the efforts of business and finance to reshape the international order to render the global marketplace more amenable to the expansion of trade and investment. Transnational business and financial élites have so far clearly been more successful than civil society. Through their informal networks and their stature in society, financial and business élites often blend seamlessly with national and international structures of governance. State emissaries to the international system are frequently chosen directly from their ranks, and the acceptance of the neo-liberal economic ideology as tantamount to the official ideology not only of international economic institutions, but of other international organizations and most governments, has given business and banking leaders an extraordinary influence on global policy. Even in formerly exclusive arenas of state action, these private sector actors are flexing their muscles. As an indication of this expanding international influence, by bringing business and banking officials into United Nations policy-making circles for the first time, the UN Secretary-General has made 'partnering' with the business community a major hallmark of his leadership. The United Nations has now established a formal business advisory council that is meant to institutionalize a permanent relationship between the business community and the UN, as well as initiated a 'Global Compact' in which major multinationals sign on to a set of guidelines that commits them to uphold international standards pertaining to environment, human rights and labour practices in exchange for being given what amounts to a UN stamp of approval for their conduct.

As with civic groups, élite business participation in this emerging globalism is in the process of transforming itself into an informal institutional structure that indirectly challenges the statist paradigm. The best example of the ability of élite business networks to extend their influence into the international system has been the World Economic Forum that has been meeting annually in Davos, Switzerland. The WEF was begun modestly three decades ago by the Swiss business visionary, Klaus Schwab. During its early years the WEF concentrated its efforts primarily on rather humdrum management issues. In the early 1980s, however, it succeeded in transforming itself into a political forum. In many ways Davos as we know it today is the legacy of earlier attempts to create transnational networks tasked with joining together international corporate and policy-making élites. Most observers agree that the most prominent of these precursors to the WEF was the highly secretive Bilderberg Conferences. Also important was David Rockefeller's Trilateral Commission (which also began in the 1970s, with an immediate display of influence on the highest levels of governmental decision-making in the industrial countries of the North before largely fading out of sight, in large part because Western governments adopted and acted upon its policy agenda). In terms of sheer concentration of super-élites from around the world, however, there has never been anything approaching the scale and salience that has been achieved by Davos over the course of the late 1990s. Annually, 1,000 of the world's most powerful executives and another 1,000 of the world's senior policy-makers participate in a week of roundtables, discussions, lectures and presentations by world leaders.

But Davos has become much more than an assemblage of the rich and famous, although it is far less menacing and conspiratorial than its most severe critics allege, and it espouses no grandiose project that seeks to rule the world. At the same time, its advocates often make claims that stretch the reality of its considerable influence beyond the point of credibility. The WEF provides flexible arenas for discussion and recommendation that give its membership the ability to shape global policy on a continuous and effective basis. It is notable that the UN Secretary-General's ideas about a partnership with business and civil society have been put forward as proposals during several high-profile appearances by Kofi Annan at Davos. In addition to encouraging the development of its own well-articulated approaches to global problems on the basis of neo-liberal precepts, the WEF conducts and disseminates its own research, which not surprisingly exhibits a consistent economistic outlook that portrays the future as market-driven. The WEF produces an annual index ranking the relative economic competitiveness of all countries in the world, which is given substantial media attention at the time of release each year. There is no objective way to gauge the extent of influence exerted by Davos. Its own claims as a facilitator of conflict resolution are often not convincing. For example, the WEF takes credit for facilitating early meetings between the apartheid regime and the ANC, and for bringing Israeli Prime Minister Shimon Peres and PLO Chairman Yasser Arafat together in 1992, where they purportedly reached a preliminary agreement on Palestinian administration of Gaza and Jericho. The WEF is far more discreet about claiming any direct influence on global social and economic policy, being sensitive to accusations of back channel lobbying on behalf of transnational corporate interests. If the focus is placed on global economic policy then Davos together with other overlapping networks of corporate élites, such as the International Chamber of Commerce, seems to have been remarkably successful up to this time in shaping the global policy setting in directions to its liking. This success is illustrated by the expansion of international trade regimes, trends toward privatization, the maintenance of modest regulation of capital markets, the credibility accorded only to a neo-liberal interpretation of state/market relations, and the supportive collaboration of most governments, especially those in the North.

All in all the WEF has managed to position itself so as to provide a vital arena of inquiry and decision during this early stage of economic globalization. Such positioning has reduced the significance of democratic forces operating within states in relation to foreign economic policy, which in turn strengthens the argument to provide opportunities for civic participation in transnational institutional settings that will offset the impact of the multinational corporate arenas and give more voice to grassroots and populist concerns. Again, the focus on this dynamic is likely to be lost in the short-term aftermath of the September 11 attacks, which has temporarily restored the state as guardian of security to its traditional pre-eminence. Underlying globalizing trends are likely with the passage of time, however, to reassert the significance of establishing the structures of global governance in forms that take into account the goals of both market and transnational civic forces.

## A GPA as the logical outcome of the process of global democratization

Putting aside the backlash against the global conference format, it seems reasonable to suggest that the international system is now exhibiting greater participation by non-state actors than ever before in its history. Without question, global civil society is unable to equal the influence, resources and power linkages of the corporate and banking communities. Nevertheless, relying on imagination and information, many of these civic networks have found ways to carve out a niche within the international order that enables effective pressures to be mounted. At the same time, there are many shortcomings of such an ad hoc and improvised approach to global democracy. This transformation of the international system has been occurring in a largely uncoordinated and uneven fashion that further tends to disadvantage the concerns of the weakest and poorest. This obscures the need to connect these two types of globalizing networks (from above, from below) in a manner that is coherent, fair and efficient from the perspective of global governance.

In effect, what we have at present is a partial transplant from domestic political systems where interest group pluralism flourishes within an overarching representative structure of parliamentary decision-making. At the global level we currently have rudimentary interest group pluralism, but it is deficient in several respects. There is a lack of accountability due to the absence of a representative structure and a low quality of functionality as a result of statist unwillingness to provide institutional capabilities for transnational political life. We believe this to be an inherently unsustainable path to a more evolved global system that is humane and comes to approximate a democratic model. What is notably missing from these intersecting forms of transnationalism is some type of unifying parliamentary body that can represent general as well as special interests.

The prevailing understanding of democracy today rejects the view that organized interest groups can validly claim to represent society as a whole. As global civil society has become more of an international presence, those opposing its agenda and activism have already begun to ask upon what basis are those within it entitled to represent the peoples of the world. Awkward questions are asked: 'Who other than themselves do civil society organizations speak for?' 'Who elected them?' 'To whom are they accountable for their actions?' As global civil society becomes more influential, and as more ideologically diverse and antagonistic groups such as, for example, the American National Rifle Association, or for that matter Islamic fundamentalist organizations, clamour for access to global arenas of decision, this problem of representation can only become more complex and ever more hotly contested.

This illegitimacy charge can be equally levelled at the Davos improvisation, which, unlike civil society, does not even possess that degree of representativeness that comes from having within its ranks large membership organizations. Certainly those citizens who oppose mainstream globalization regard the Davos model of élite politics to be extremely suspect. Such an assessment of these transnational developments suggests that the kinds of opening of the international system that have been occurring do not satisfy the demand for democratic participation. Something more is needed. Some sort of popular assembly capable of more systematically representing the diverse peoples of the world is necessary if the democratic deficit is to be meaningfully reduced. To the extent that the global undertakings are criticized for their failure to measure up to modern democratic standards, then world order seems ever more vulnerable to the charge of being more of an insiders' game than all but the most corrupt and draconian domestic political systems. Even before the events of September 11 it was evident that those whose interests were not being addressed, were unwilling to accept the legitimacy of existing global arrangements. It seems likely that given the continuation of these conditions, that the democratic deficit will grow even larger, leading to the further proliferation of various types of severe instability, which are currently causing such widespread turmoil and suffering in the world system.

The absence of a unifying parliamentary structure also means that there is currently no institutional vessel capable of bringing together the organized groupings of transnational activism that are identified with civil society and the Davos constituencies so as to facilitate dialogue, and the search for compromises and accommodations. As matters now stand, only governments have the institutional capacity to find such common ground and strike deals. As we discussed previously, there is no process for individuals and groups themselves to create a social consensus across borders or to engage formally with those acting on behalf of market forces. To the extent that solutions to global problems can be arrived at within a structure that institutionalizes interaction and allows for direct communication among competing interests, such interests will be much more likely to accept as legitimate, policy outcomes that have been fairly negotiated and agreed upon.

## A GPA as a practical political project

We believe that the establishment of some sort of parliamentary assembly is necessary to begin to deal seriously with the democratic deficit. At the same time we realize that scepticism is rampant: is the creation of such a global assembly politically possible at this stage of history? For a variety of reasons, we believe that it is not Panglossian to believe it possible for the global community to take this vital step in building global democracy. After all, empirically suggesting the viability of such a project is the European Union, which has been making impressive attempts to overcome a purported regional democratic deficit. The EU already possesses a transnationally elected legislative body, the European Parliament. The European Parliament, along with the European Council and the European Commission, is one of three legislative bodies operating within the framework of the European Union. As we would expect to be the case with a globally elected assembly, the Parliament has struggled to establish credibility over time in the face of statist scepticism and media scorn. In recent years, however, the European Parliament has finally begun to gain respect, and has started to exercise significant power. Europe is, of course, far more homogeneous and economically integrated than the world at large, and the establishment of the Parliament was a part of a broader movement toward regional unity. At the same time this European evolution shows that there are no absolute political or logistical barriers to the creation and functioning of such an assembly on a transnational scale, and further, that such a development is fully compatible with the persistence of strong states and robust nationalist sentiments. In fact, on a global level, those with a pronounced interest in global governance – civil society, the corporate élite, and many governments – have an individual as well as collective stake in erecting some type of overarching democratic structure.

## The role of civil society

Certain sectors of civil society in particular could likely be, and in fact are being, mobilized to lead the drive for such an assembly.[5] This is important, because while there is the potential to find some support from corporate and political élites, it is unrealistic to expect the main initiative to come from these sectors. Most of the individuals leading business and governmental organizations tend to be institutionally conservative, as well as often too closely linked to state structures to support such a bold initiative. For these reasons, the primary energy for a global parliament will come from civil society, or nowhere.

It is rather obvious, however, that not even all civil society organizations are in favour of the creation of such an assembly. Some evidently sense that their influence would shrink in an altered world order. Nevertheless, the sentiments throughout global civil society are overwhelmingly in favour of establishing institutions and practices that will enable global democracy to flourish in the years ahead. Within this broader consensus there exists a realization that the creation of a functioning global parliament or assembly is a necessary and desirable step. The appeal of the GPA proposal to advance the agenda of global civil society seems rather obvious. At a general level, a democratically constituted assembly would be likely to address widespread societal concerns about the undemocratic nature of existing international institutions such as the World Trade Organization, the International Monetary Fund and the World Bank. It would almost certainly encourage further democratizing global reforms, as well as provide a setting for debates about the positive and negative effects of globalization. There would for the first time a widely recognized global forum in which such matters of public be concern as environmental quality, labour standards, and economic justice could be discussed from a variety of perspectives, including encounters between civil society representatives from North and South who set forth contrasting concerns embodying differing priorities. The presence of democratic structures does not, of course, guarantee that participants will consistently behave responsibly. We have learned from experience that even the most experienced and respected legislative institutions within states can act in an erratic fashion from time to time that does not reflect the real interests or values of constituents, but such is the cost incurred to sustain democratic processes as the basis of governance.

Even an initially weak and controversial global assembly could at least provide the beginnings of democratic oversight and accountability for the international system. The fact that individuals from many parts of the world would directly participate in elections would likely lead the assembly to have an impressive grassroots profile that would lend a certain populist authenticity to its pronouncements and recommendations. In all probability, at first, most governments would refuse to defer to such an assembly that operated beyond their control, but such rejectionist attitudes would be unlikely to persist very long. After all, we are living at a time when democracy has increasingly become the *sine qua non* of legitimacy around the world and the assembly would be the only institution that could validly claim to represent the peoples of global society *directly*. The comparison of its views with those of governments and market-dominated forums would likely attract media attention before long; becoming a part of public discourse would in turn influence the course of civil-political decision-making.

Besides exercising a democratic influence on the formulation of social policy, such an assembly could also be instrumental in helping to encourage compliance with international norms and standards, especially in the realm of widely supported human rights. Currently, the international system generally lacks reliable mechanisms to implement many of its laws. Civil society organizations such as Amnesty International, and even international organizations such as the International Labor Organization and the UN Human Rights Commission, attempt to address this deficiency and exert significant pressure on states by exposing failures of compliance by states, relying on a process that is often referred to as the 'mobilization of shame'. This pressure is premised on the importance to governments of sustaining their reputation for acting in conformity with normative standards and the reliability of established NGOs in identifying patterns of abusive behaviour. In contributing to such an oversight function, a popularly elected GPA would likely soon become more visible and credible than are existing informal watchdogs that seek to expose corporate and governmental wrongdoing, and in any event, would complement such activism. A GPA would also tend to be less deferential to leading sovereign states than the more official watchdogs that function within the essentially statist framework of the United Nations System.

Perhaps most fundamentally, the mere existence and availability of the assembly would likely be helpful in promoting the peaceful resolution of international conflicts. We have already discussed how a GPA might be useful in undermining wider circles of societal support for international terrorism as a form of non-state violence. It could also in time help to reduce the likelihood of interstate violence as well. Instead of representing states, as in the United Nations and other established international organizations, delegates would directly represent various constituencies with societal roots. This means that, unlike the present system, the assembly would not be designed to reinforce artificially constructed 'national interests' or to promote the special projects of rich and influential élites. Rather, as in multinational societies such as India or Switzerland, or in the European Parliament, most elected delegates do not consistently or mechanically vote along national lines, except possibly in instances where their national origins are directly engaged with the issue in dispute. Coalitions form in these settings on other bases, such as worldview, political orientation, class and racial solidarities, and ethical affinities. The experience of engaging in a democratic process to reach legislative compromises on the part of antagonists that are organized as opposing, but non-militarized and often shifting, coalitions may over time help establish a culture of peace. It is perhaps too optimistic to think that such a learning curve might eventually undermine reliance on the present war system to sustain national and global security. It is difficult to transform the militarist mentalities associated with the pursuit of security in a world that continues to be organized around the prerogatives of sovereign national units that are heavily armed and disposed to destroy one another if the need arises. The hope is that over time the organization of international relations would come more closely to resemble decision-making within the most democratic societies of the world. Not only would an assembly tend to oppose military establishments as the foundation of global security, but it is also likely to build confidence in the perspectives of human security and in the efficacy of peaceful approaches to world order. Only when enough people begin someday to feel that non-violent structures of governance, including law enforcement, can ensure their individual and collective survival will meaningful disarmament become a genuine political option.

Any proposed institution that can credibly claim a potential for advancing causes as central to the agenda of various global civil society organizations as global democratization, labour and environmental regulation, effective global governance, peace, and human rights obviously should possess the capacity to generate broad-based support within civil society. So far, however, the nascent civil society movement that favours the establishment of such an assembly remains separate and distinct. It has not managed to gain significant levels of support, or even interest, from the issue-oriented actors that have so far been the main architects of global civil society. The present movement for an assembly consists mainly of individuals and groups who believe in holistic solutions to global problems, and seek to promote humane global governance for the world. Such proponents of a GPA are culturally influenced by a range of contemporary traditions of thought and modalities of action as varied as ecology, religion, spirituality, humanism and, most recently of all, the Internet. Each of these orientations proceeds from a premise of human solidarity and a belief in the essential unity of planet earth. Significant organizing efforts associated either with building support for the GPA or experimenting with its local enactment are under way in many different places around the world. This is an exciting development. It portends the possibility that from within civil society a truly innovative and visionary politics is beginning to take shape after centuries of dormancy. Such movement is an expression of the increasing robustness of democratic values as the foundation for all forms of political legitimacy regardless of the scale of the unit of social action being appraised. Also relevant are many types of transnational connectivity that manifest the globalizing ethos of our twenty-first-century world.

## The receptivity of the business élite to a GPA

The global outlook of the corporate and financial élites represented at Davos, and elsewhere is also relevant to the prospects for furthering the cause of a GPA. The Davos network has been singularly successful in marshalling support for new international regimes that promote its interests in an open global economy. The World Trade Organization and NAFTA are two obvious examples. Certainly some within its ranks will oppose a new global parliamentary institution because a more open political system would mean a broader decision-making base, a questioning of the distribution of the benefits and burdens of economic growth, and more pressure for transnational regulation of market forces. Such developments would almost certainly be viewed with suspicion, if not hostility, by those who meet regularly at Davos to construct a world economy that is committed to the 'efficient' use of capital, and dubious about any incorporation of social and normative goals into the formation of world economic policy. It would almost certainly be the case that such an assembly, if reflective of grassroots opinion around the world, would be highly critical of current modes of globalization, and hence at odds with the outcomes sought by the Davos leadership. But with transnational corporations having been, and in all likelihood continuing to be, beneficiaries of this globalization-from-above, those in the business world with a more enlightened sense of their long-term interest are already coming to believe that the democratic deficit must be addressed by way of stakeholder accommodations. It is perhaps relevant to recall that although hostile at first, many members of the American managerial class came under the pressure of the Great Depression and its societal unrest to realize that the New Deal was a necessary dynamic of adjustment to the claims of workers and the poor during a crisis time for capitalism. The same kind of dynamic made social democracy acceptable to the business/financial leadership of leading European countries, and helped give capitalism a more human face that enhanced its legitimacy at the level of society. In a similar vein, many of the leading figures in world business seem to find congenial the idea that some sort of democratizing improvisation along the lines we are suggesting is necessary to make globalization politically acceptable to more of the peoples of the world.

As the large street protests of the last few years in various places around the world suggested to many observers, globalization has not yet managed to achieve grassroots acceptance and societal legitimacy. Lori Wallach (the prime organizer of the Seattle anti-WTO demonstrations) said in an interview that her coalition of so many diverse groups, in addition to battling a series of distinct social issues, was held together by the 'notion that the democracy deficit in the global economy is neither necessary nor acceptable'.[6]

In fact, the main basis of popular support for globalization at present is not political, but economic. Globalization has either been able to deliver or to hold out the promise of delivering the economic goods to enough people to keep the anti-globalization forces from gaining sufficient ground to mount an effective challenge against it. Economic legitimacy alone is rarely able to stabilize a political system for long. Market-based economic systems have historically undergone ups and downs, particularly when they are in formation. The emerging-markets financial crisis that almost triggered a world financial meltdown in 1997 will surely not be the last crisis to emerge from the current modalities of globalization. Future economic failures are certain to generate strong and contradictory political responses. We know that standing in the wings, not only in the United States but in several other countries, are politicians, ultra-nationalists, and an array of opportunists on both the left and the right who, if given an opening, would seek to dismantle the system so as to restore territorial sovereignty, and with it, nationalism and protectionism. If the globalizing élite is seeking to find a political base that will allow it to survive economic downturns, particularly in the event that economic and social forces in powerful countries are in the future adversely affected, then it would do well to turn its attention urgently to reducing the global democratic deficit. Global terror plays a diversionary role at present, especially in the United States, but this distraction from the imperatives of global reform are not likely to persist, especially in the face of widespread economic hardship and distress.

There is a lesson to be learned from Suharto's Indonesia that offers some striking parallels to the vulnerabilities of the current global system. Indonesian citizens had come to believe in democratic practices, but the political system remained largely authoritarian, and unresponsive to the concerns of the people. As long as Indonesia was both a Cold War ally of the West and enjoyed the dramatic economic growth rates that had been sustained for nearly 30 years, American support was solid and there were enough benefits for most of the population to control political restiveness in a country with many acute ethnic and regional tensions. The great majority of the Indonesian people seemed either intimidated or willing to tolerate the country's failure to live up to the democratic ideal. But when the economy found itself in serious trouble during the last months of 1997, President Suharto had little to fall back upon internally or externally to maintain the political allegiance of the citizenry and his political edifice, which had seemed so formidable just months earlier. The Jakarta regime rapidly crumbled around him. The latent political illegitimacy of the Java-centric Indonesian government became a destabilizing factor that accompanied and intensified the economic and ethnic tribulations of the country.

## The receptivity of the political élite to a GPA

Portions of the corporate élite might be persuaded that it is in their interest to support a GPA. Would not those who control state power, however, be less likely to go along with such an innovation? Surely any public institution that could reduce the global democratic deficit by claiming to speak directly for global society could eventually become an important counterweight to state and market power. The important word here is eventually. A relatively weak assembly constituted initially mainly with advisory powers would begin to address concerns about the democratic deficit while posing only a long-term threat to the citadels of state power. This being the case national leaders, whose concerns tend to be associated with short-term prerogatives, have little reason to feel significantly challenged by the establishment of such an assembly. Systemic transformation of world order that could affect successors would not to be threatening to, and might in fact appeal to those political leaders who are themselves most inclined to extend democratic ideals to all arenas of authority and decision.

Putting in place a minimally empowered, but politically saleable institutional structure that nonetheless has far-reaching transformative potential is, in fact, an approach often adopted by the most effective advocates of new global institutions. What has become the European Union, for example, began after the Second World War as the European Coal and Steel Community, a modest, skeletal framework for what would decades later evolve into an integrated European political structure that more recently poses some serious challenges to the primacy of the European state. The French Declaration of 9 May 1950 initially proposing the European Coal and Steel Community makes clear that this humble beginning was by design:

> Europe will not be made all at once, or according to a single plan. [The French Government] proposes that Franco-German production of coal and steel as a whole be placed under a common High Authority, within the framework of an organization open to the participation of the other countries of Europe. The pooling of coal and steel production should immediately provide for the setting up of common foundations for economic development as a first step in the federation of Europe, and will change the destinies of those regions which have long been devoted to the manufacture of munitions of war, of which they have been the most constant of victims.[7]

Within the European Union, by far the best model for a globally representative assembly, the European Parliament started life as an institutional vessel largely devoid of formal powers. Through time, as the sole direct representative of the European citizenry, the Parliament began to acquire an important institutional role that has given vitality to the undertaking, as well as increasingly reinforcing the European will to carry on with their bold experiment in regional governance.

One source of optimism that many national leaders can be persuaded to support this assembly project arises from the recent experience of building a coalition to push for the establishment of a permanent International Criminal Court. A large number of civil society organizations, working in collaboration with governments, have been very effective, at least so far,[8] in building widespread cooperation among political élites around the world on behalf of a project that only a decade earlier had been dismissed as utopian. The willingness of political leaders to support the creation of such a tribunal is quite surprising. It also lends indirect encouragement to efforts to establish a GPA because the criminal court compromises traditional sovereign prerogatives far more than would be the case initially if a global parliament comes into existence. The court has the substantive power to prosecute individuals for their failure to comply with international criminal law, which means that states have lost exclusive control over the application of penal law, which had been regarded as one of the traditional and fundamental attributes of sovereignty. Government leaders have lost their immunity to some extent in relation to international standards. By comparison a parliament with largely advisory powers would appear to be a relatively modest concession to the growing demand for a more democratic and legitimate global order, and would initially not significantly impinge upon the exercise of sovereign powers of a state. Of course, the idea of a parallel international law-making body, even if advisory, does raise the possibility in the moral and political imagination, that more centralization of authority is necessary and desirable, and this possibility, however remote, is likely to be threatening to governments administering nation-states.

## Realizing the vision

While the rationale for establishing such an assembly definitely exists, this is, of course, not enough. There needs to be some viable way for this potential to be realized. We believe the formula with the best ability to take advantage of the political promise we have identified can be found in what is being called the 'New Diplomacy'. Unlike traditional diplomacy, which is solely conducted among states, the New Diplomacy is based on the collaboration of civil society with whatever states are receptive, allowing the formation of flexible and innovative coalitions that shift from issue to issue and over time. The major success stories of global civil society in the 1990s were produced in this manner including the Global Warming Treaty, the Landmines Convention and the International Criminal Court.

This New Diplomacy (if it is to continue into this new century) is well adapted to meeting the challenge of creating a globally elected assembly. Nevertheless, the seemingly most natural way to bring a new international regime into being, a large-scale multilateral conference, does not appear well suited to this project. Despite the receptivity of some political élites, there is unlikely to be a critical mass of states in the UN General Assembly or outside its confines that would be willing to call for the convocation of such a conference. We believe that the momentum that would lead to significant state support for the assembly would undoubtedly have to be developed indirectly and gradually. Two other possible approaches seem worth considering in relation to bringing the GPA into being.

One approach that we discuss in more detail in the Summer 2000 edition of the *Stanford Journal of International Law*[9] would be for civil society with the help of receptive states to proceed to create the assembly without resorting to a formal treaty process. Under this approach the assembly would not be formally sanctioned by the collectivity of states and hence its legitimacy would probably be contested by governments at the outset unless they chose to ignore its existence altogether. This opposition could be neutralized to some extent by widespread grassroots and media endorsement, and by the citizenry as expressed through popular elections that were taken seriously by large numbers of people and were fairly administered.

The other approach is to rely on a treaty, but to utilize what is often called the Single Negotiating Text Method as the process for coming to an agreement on the specifics of an assembly among supportive states. Pursuant to this approach after extensive consultations with sympathetic parties from civil society, business and nation-states, an organizing committee would generate the text of a treaty establishing an assembly that could serve as the basis for negotiations. Momentum could be generated as civil society organized a public relations campaign and some states were persuaded (sometimes as a result of agreed upon modifications in the draft) to accede to the treaty one at a time. As in the Ottawa Process that ultimately led to the Landmines Convention, a small core group of supportive states could lead the way. Unlike the Landmines treaty, however, which it was thought could not meaningfully come into effect before forty countries ratified it, a relatively small number of countries, say twenty, could provide the founding basis to bring such an assembly into being. Though this number is but a fraction of what would eventually be needed if the assembly wished to have some claim to global democratic legitimacy, it is worth remembering that the European Coal and Steel Community, which evolved to become the European Union, started with only six countries. After all, once the assembly was established and functioning in an impressive way the task of gaining additional state members should become easier. There would then exist a concrete organization to which states could actually be urged to join by their own citizens. As more states joined, pressure on the remaining states to allow their citizens to vote and participate would likely grow, especially if the assembly built a positive reputation in its early years. Holdout states would increasingly find themselves in the embarrassing position of being in a dwindling minority of states denying their citizens the ability to participate along with persons from foreign countries in the world's only globally elected body. It would seem increasingly perverse to proclaim democratic values at home but resist democratic practices and possibilities abroad. The exact nature of the representative parliamentary structure that should or will be created remains to be determined, and should be resolved through vigorous discussion by many different actors drawn from all corners of the world. What is clear to us, however, is that the ongoing phenomena of global democratization are part of an evolutionary social process that will persist, and intensify. While it is still too early to determine the long-term implications of the events of September 11, the future will surely find many ways to remind the peoples of the world that a commitment to global democratic governance is a matter of urgency, and that a way to move forward is through the establishment of a GPA.

Until the onset of the global terror challenge, the two dominant themes of the post-Cold War years were globalization and democracy. Proclamations are now commonplace that the world is rapidly creating an integrated global political economy and that national governments that are not freely elected lack political legitimacy. In view of this, it is paradoxical that there has not yet been a serious global debate on concrete proposals to resolve the obvious contradiction between a professed commitment to democracy at the level of the sovereign state and a manifestly undemocratic global political-economic order. Perhaps this apparent tension can be explained as a form of political inertia, and possibly by the residual sense that such democratizing proposals are still *per se* utopian. Whatever the explanation, this contradiction will not be tolerated for long. Citizen groups and business and financial élites are not waiting around for governments to come up with solutions. They have taken direct and concrete action to realize their aspirations. These initiatives have created an autonomous dynamic resulting in spontaneous forms of global democratization. As this process continues in an attempt to keep pace with globalization, as it surely will, the movement for a coherent and legitimate system of global democracy will and should intensify. To political élites it will continue to become increasingly obvious that without legitimating institutions, governing the global order will be more difficult and contentious. They are likely to be plagued by the growing disinclination of citizens to accept the policy results of an ever-more encompassing system that is not based on a recognizable form of legitimate governance. To the organized networks of global civil society and business the inclination, reinforced by the practice of democratic societies, is to find direct accommodations and to work out differences. Such a process will naturally lead policy-makers to look toward familiar democratic structures to bridge present, widening cleavages. Finally, to all those who are seriously concerned about social justice, and the creation of a more peaceful global order, the democratic alternative to an inherently authoritarian global system will surely be ever more compelling.

## Notes

1. The authors would like to thank Erin Daly and Daniele Archibugi for their very helpful comments on early drafts of this chapter.

2. See Richard Falk and Andrew Strauss, 'Toward Global Parliament', *Foreign Affairs*, January–February 2001, p. 212; Richard Falk and Andrew Strauss, 'On the Creation of a Global Peoples' Assembly: Legitimacy and the Power of Popular Sovereignty', *Stanford Journal of International Law*, vol. 36, 2000; Andrew Strauss, 'Overcoming the Dysfunction of the Bifurcated Global System: The Promise of a Peoples' Assembly', *Transnational Journal of Law and Contemporary Problems*, vol. 9, 1999.

3. Jessica T. Mathews, 'Powershifts', *Foreign Affairs*, January–February 1997, p. 50.

4. These were: on sustainable development, the Rio Declaration and Agenda 21; to help safeguard the planet's biodiversity, the Biodiversity Convention; and perhaps most importantly, to combat the warming of the planet, the Climate Change Convention.

5. While still in their early stages, we believe various initiatives merit notice. An organization called the Assembly of the United Nations of Peoples has attempted to bring civil society organizations together into a quasi-representative assembly. In the fall of 2001 it included civil society organizations from the majority of the world's countries in its fourth assembly in Perugia, Italy. Also notable is the Global Peoples' Assembly Movement. This organization had its first major assembly in Samoa in April 2000. Like the Perugia initiative, its purpose is to model a globally democratic institutional structure that would enable the peoples of the world to have a meaningful voice in global governance. Also worthy of attention are efforts by an organization called Citizen Century to link the national parliamentarians of the world together through the Internet into what it calls a 'Global E-Parliament' and efforts by The World Citizen Foundation to promote the establishment of a globally elected parliament.

6. See Lori's War, *Foreign Policy*, March 2000, p. 28.

7. See http://europa.eu.int/comm/dg10/publications/brochures/docu/50ans/decl_en.html#declaratio

8. The Statute for the International Criminal Court was overwhelmingly adopted by a conference of states in Rome on 17 July 1998. The Statute received the necessary ratifications and came into force in 2002 despite obstruction from the United States.

9. See Richard Falk and Andrew Strauss, 'On the Creation of a Global Peoples' Assembly: Legitimacy and the Power of Popular Sovereignty', *Stanford Journal of International Law*.

# 12

# Democracy vs Globalization. The Growth of Parallel Summits and Global Movements

*Mario Pianta*

Political, economic, social and environmental problems of a global nature are all around us. The key decisions on such issues have been taken so far by governments (especially those of the most powerful states) and supranational institutions, as well as by a variety of large private bodies, such as financial and multinational corporations. What is the democratic foundation of such a system of global governance? Major problems of legitimacy, representativeness, accountability, participation and effectiveness are immediately evident in the present arrangements.

In this chapter, the emergence of summits as a way of assuring governance of global problems is the starting point for considering the extraordinary growth of parallel summits organized by an emerging global civil society. In the last decade, this challenge has opened the way to the growth of much broader global movements for international democracy and social and economic justice.

## The growth of summits

In the last decades the urgency of global issues has led to the creation of new or the strengthening of old inter-governmental organizations, and a proliferation of international government-level activities called to coordinate policy action.

The former process is associated with a *formal* transfer of power from states to supranational institutions, regulated by treaties or official agreements; as such, they are visible acts, which can be made the object of appropriate debate within countries through the usual procedures for deliberation on international issues. The creation of the World Trade Organization, the European Economic and Monetary Union, and the International Criminal Court are all examples of such developments, with widely differing degrees of popular participation in decision-making, public accountability, democratic structures and public support.

The latter process, on the other hand, leads to the emergence of *informal* supranational powers through inter-state agreements or cooperation; they still result from decisions of states – which have highly asymmetric resources, influence and force – and yet they reach well beyond the domestic sphere of state power. G8 meetings are examples of such events. Such inter-state activities tend to be much less visible and unaccountable to democratic processes, either at the domestic or at the international level.

In between these two patterns, a grey area has grown where inter-governmental organizations and powerful states have made increasingly important decisions in *informal* ways, either by stretching the official mandate of existing institutions (as in the case of the International Monetary Fund's Structural Adjustment Programmes), or by addressing, in an *ad hoc* way, emerging global problems for which no formal supranational transfer of power has yet been made (as in the case of several environmental problems).

While much of this expanding supranational decision power has remained hidden and unaccountable, largely in the hands of specialized government officials and international 'technocrats', in the last two decades a model of highly visible collective action on global issues by states and inter-governmental organizations has emerged: international summits. Summits represent an important institutional innovation in the world system, combining the legitimacy of supranational organizations, the flexibility of informal meetings of states, and the high-profile exhibition of concern and action on current global problems. Summits have become more frequent and influential, with far-reaching policy consequences at the national level. In a world dominated by media and instant communication, where global problems are immediately visible everywhere, summits are often the media-oriented events which 'show' that the powerful of the Earth are addressing them. Moreover, they are the visible part of the growing *informal* decision power on supranational issues.

Summits are now a key element of the emerging governance system of an increasingly globalized world; they have a widely differing nature, but their role and activities include the tasks of *framing the issue* (as in the case of environmental or human rights issues), *rule-making* (as in the WTO on trade rules), *providing policy guidelines* for national governments (as in the IMF structural adjustment programmes) and *enforcing decisions* on individual (usually not so powerful) countries, with diplomatic pressure, embargoes or military action.

It could be argued that this is what inter-governmental coop-eration has always been supposed to do. But what is new in the last decades is the extension in the range of issues addressed by summits; the greater policy impact of their decisions; their fre-quency which makes them part of institutionalized decision-making; the shift from bilateral to multilateral arrangements; the high media profile they have, in contrast to secretive diplomacy; in short, they are a crucial part of the shift in the balance of power from national to international decision-making. While there may be good reasons for transferring power at the suprana-tional level in order to address increasingly global problems, this shift is not unproblematic.

The range of activities carried out by summits spans the prerogatives of political power as it has historically emerged in states. But what is missing is the democratic process developed at the state level in order to extend participation and representation of citizens and social groups, and legitimize the decisions taken. In fact, the officials attending summits are either professional diplomats or – mainly unelected – government officials.

Moreover, the rules and nature of most summits – with the partial exception of the UN – reflect a strong unbalance of power among states, with a dominance of rich Western countries, and of the United States, in many decision-making processes. While summits' decisions always follow – at least indirectly – from actions of governments, who are supposed to be accountable to their countries, most summits fail the test of democratic legitimation both when we look at the distribution of power across players involved – the governments of countries included or excluded from decisions – and when we look at the relation between decision-makers, society and citizens, and more generally those affected by the decisions taken.[1]

## The three globalizations

Global powers make decisions that have consequences for a large number of world citizens, but those making decisions have almost never been elected, cannot be replaced through democratic processes, and do not respond in any way to those who are subject to the effects of their decisions. In short, all elements of democracy are missing, no possibility of change exists through the democratic processes consolidated at the national scale. *Democracy*, therefore, appears to have lost substantial ground to *globalization*, in terms of the political and economic power exercised beyond the level of states.

But globalization is a much more complex process, and three major strategies – shaping in a fundamental way the decisions of global powers – have to be identified.[2]

### Neo-liberal globalization

Neo-liberal globalization has emerged as the dominant force of the past two decades. Moving from economic processes, from the strategies of multinational corporations and financial institutions, it has affected the decisions of governments and international institutions. As Richard Falk points out, 'the characteristic policy vectors of neoliberalism involve such moves as liberalization, privatization, minimizing economic regulation, rolling back welfare, reducing expenditures on public goods, tightening fiscal discipline, favouring freer flows of capital, strict controls on organized labour, tax reductions and unrestricted currency repatriation,' essentially, a politics that could be described as 'predatory globalization'.[3]

Unregulated markets, dominated by multinational corporations and private financial institutions based mostly in rich countries, have been the driving force in economic growth and international integration, reducing the space for autonomous national politics in the fields of the public sphere. Neo-liberal globalization has institutionalized an overwhelming power of economic mechanisms – markets and firms – over human rights, political projects, social needs and environmental priorities. It is no surprise that over the last decades political activity has lost much of its relevance and appeal; social inequalities have become dramatic; and the environmental crisis has deepened.[4]

The political framework for neo-liberal globalization was prepared in the early 1980s by the policies of Margaret Thatcher in Britain and Ronald Reagan in the United States. In the aftermath of the collapse of the Soviet system in 1989–90, building on an unrivalled military supremacy, political power and cultural dominance, the neo-liberal project of globalization has become the new face of the hegemony of the United States.

## Globalization of rights and responsibilities

The emergence of global problems, and the necessity to confront them in a context that surpasses state dimensions, has led a second important project of globalization of rights and responsibilities. Some of the more 'enlightened' states and international institutions, social organizations, and labour and environmental groups have sustained a project of universalizing human, political and social rights, along with the recognition of the responsibility that countries, governments, and people have in facing these new global problems. This project has built on common values and has defined the understanding of major global problems, having a large influence on the agenda of the UN summits on human rights, women's rights, the environment, social development, food supply, and the creation of the International Criminal Court. Among the results are new norms for international rights, declarations of principles, a new space for democratic processes, greater attention by states to the respect of rights and some innovative policies, and a broader political cooperation on a regional or global level – the case of European integration being the most significant. Civil society has asked governments and international institutions to take initiatives in this direction. In many countries, policies that supported this project were developed in parallel to economic policies of neo-liberal orientation.

However, when a conflict emerged between these two projects, neo-liberal strategies have always prevailed; the project based on *rights* and *responsibilities*, therefore, has had a limited influence on the direction of the processes of globalization.

## Globalization from below

In addressing global issues, governments, inter-governmental organizations and large firms operating in world markets are not the only actors. An increasing visibility, voice and activism has come from a large number of civil society organizations operating across national borders; they have advocated change, opposed current processes or policies, and proposed alternative solutions to global issues.

This emerging *global civil society* can be defined as the sphere of cross-border relations and collective activities outside the international reach of states and markets. This concept identifies a sphere of international relationships among heterogeneous actors who share civil values and concern for global issues, communication and meanings, advocacy actions, and self-organization experiments. From global civil society a major challenge has emerged to the strategy of neo-liberal globalization and to the failures of globalization of rights and responsibilities.

Within global civil society, the most active players are the new social movements and the network of organizations working on international themes. Their origins are in the movements of past decades on the themes of peace, human rights, solidarity, development, the environment and women's issues. Starting with these specific themes, the new movements have developed the capacity to confront problems of a global nature, to construct networks of information, to prepare common actions, to find self-organized solutions beyond national borders, interacting also in an original way with the new sites of international power.[5]

All of this defines the emergence of an alternative project of *globalization from below* of global civil society. According to Richard Falk, who has introduced this concept, *globalization from below* has the potential to 'conceptualize widely shared world order values: minimizing violence, maximizing economic well-being, realizing social and political justice, and upholding environmental quality'.[6] Even if these values of global civil society remain far from representing a coherent alternative, they have inspired the actions of new global movements and are at the base of the resistance against the project of *neo-liberal globalization* and of the pressure for *global rights and responsibilities.*

In the last decade many cross-border campaigns and initiatives have shown how real and active global civil society can be, and have defined methods and contents of *globalization from below.* Such actions include: the campaigns for human rights, women's and children's rights; opposition to the death penalty; the peace movement; campaigns on environmental themes; the request for international labour rights; the initiatives of co-operation for development, fair trade, ethical finance and micro-credit; social self-organization; the campaigns on Third World debt, for the Tobin Tax on currency transactions, and against the international institutions – the IMF, the World Bank, the WTO. All such movements have come closer together in recent years, especially with events such as the World Social Forum of Porto Alegre in Brazil and the Assemblies of the United Nations of the People in Perugia, where their identity as global movements for international democracy and social and economic justice has become evident.[7]

## The invention of parallel summits

In order to confront the new power of summits of states and inter-governmental organizations, civil society organizations have invented *parallel summits*, events which could challenge the legitimacy of government summits, demand more democratic arrangements for decision-making, give visibility to the emerging global civil society, resist neo-liberal policies, and propose alternative solutions for global problems.[8]

Parallel summits can be defined as events:

- organized by national and international civil society groups with an international participation, independent of the activities of states and firms
- in coincidence or in relation to official summits of governments and international institutions (with few major exceptions)
- addressing the same fundamental problems of official sum-

mits, with a critical perspective on government and business policies

- using the means of public information and analysis, political mobilization and protest, proposal of alternative policies
- with or without formal contacts with the official summits.

## Some history

Government summits and civil society international meetings have a history as long as that of globalization itself. Charnovitz[9] has shown that, from the late nineteenth century to the 1920s, the establishment of supranational bodies such as the League of Nations and of scores of inter-governmental organizations, was accompanied by an equally strong flourishing of international non-governmental organizations and of civil society meetings. At several official summits and in the operation of the League of Nations, civil society groups were often able to articulate their proposals on a wide range of themes including peace, national liberation, economic, social and women's rights; in some cases they were even involved in official activities, opening the way to the formal recognition of NGOs in the Charter of the United Nations in 1945.

During most of the Cold War years the space for international activities of civil society was constrained and shaped by state power and policies. International mobilization of civil society had the task of putting pressure on state policies on the issues of decolonization, national self-determination, peace, human rights, development and the environment. The political movements of the 1960s and 1970s challenged the political and economic order at the national and international level with a transformative perspective still focused on state power. A major exception was the rise of the women's movement which opened the way to new forms of politics, social practices and culture based on identity politics.[10]

In the 1980s the new social movements on peace, ecology and women took up their heritage and concentrated on specific issues which had less to do with state power and more with global challenges, often marked by the lack of adequate supranational institutions. The rapid growth of NGOs turned the advocacy of movements into practical projects and proposals of alternative policies, demanding a voice in the existing global fora.

NGOs have found a substantial opening in the UN system, in ECOSOC and other activities; however, this official recognition of civil society work at the international level has led to very modest results in terms of visibility, relevance and impact on the operation of the international system.[11]

A new wave of state summits began in the mid-1970s spurred on by far-reaching political change – East-West détente, the completion of decolonization and a new attention to human rights – and by economic developments – the end of the Bretton Woods international monetary system, the oil shocks and the emergence of the North–South divide. Existing inter-governmental organizations, starting with the UN, played a renewed and broader role, and other fora were established (the first G5 meeting was in 1975).

As global issues and supranational decision-making became increasingly important, attention and action by civil society also increased. Moving on from the traditional efforts to put pressure on national states, attention started to focus on global problems, and on the failure of states to address them in events such as summits. Symbolic actions, at first small in scale and poorly organized, were followed by a more systematic international effort by civil society organizations, resulting in explicit challenges to the legitimation and policies of summits.

In the late 1970s the first summits of non-governmental organizations working alongside the United Nations summits on the environment and human rights were organized. The first Other Economic Summit, parallel to a G7 meeting, took place in London in 1984. A protest against the International Monetary Fund meeting brought 100,000 people to West Berlin in 1988, linking the German and European traditions of the new left, the peace movement and the solidarity activism with the Third World. In 1994, seven years before the Genoa G8 summit (again, shortly after an electoral victory by right-wing leader Silvio Berlusconi), an alternative summit to the G7 held in Naples was organised by a coalition of 30 organizations, with a conference on globalization, a convention of global movements and a march with 10,000 participants. While in Seattle, Prague, Genoa, Quebec City or Barcelona the scale and attention to the protest have been much larger, the same themes and forms of action can be found with few differences in the past twenty years.

## An analysis of parallel summits

The historical roots and the present diffusion of parallel summits make them an important object of analysis. A reconstruction of their development has shown the increasing importance they assume in terms of civil society activism on global issues and of demands for a more democratic world order. A specific survey was undertaken in order to investigate the nature of parallel summits, the events that occurred, their forms of organization, and their impact. A questionnaire was circulated to hundreds of civil society organizations, and dozens of newspapers, journals, NGO publications and websites were monitored in order to gather information systematically. From the findings, 89 cases of parallel summits have been selected, which are considered representative of the range of events, topics and locations, covering the period 1988–June 2002. The focus here is on the events of 2001 and of the first half of 2002, when 35 main events occurred. They will be compared with the evolution over the past 20 years presented in a previous work.[12]

### The activism of global civil society

The contemporary development of parallel summits began with the *pioneering years*, 1980–1987, when the first experiences in small events involving a limited number of NGOs were developed. The start of the recorded events was in the four years of *political transition*, 1988–1991, when seven per cent of all monitored parallel summits took place and the modes of operation, organization and action were established. In the next four years of *institutional expansion*, 1992–1995, the number of parallel summits more than doubled, to 15 per cent of all meetings, including a large number of events associated with the important UN conferences of that period. Close to 20 per cent of events marked the following years of *consolidation and diffusion*, 1996–1999, when a greater variety of issues was raised and more regional meetings took place, ending with the Seattle protest against the WTO. All this accounts for 40 per cent only of all events, and the year 2000 opened the current period of *frequency and radicalization*.

In the year 2000 the same number of parallel summits were recorded as in the four previous years, while in 2001 close to a quarter of all recorded events were concentrated, and the first semester of 2002 alone accounts for 15 per cent of all gatherings of global civil society. This exponential growth is the most effective indicator of the booming relevance of global civil society events.

In the period January 2001–June 2002, close to a third of parallel summits took place in Europe, a quarter in Latin America, a sixth both in North America and Africa, and the rest in Asia and Oceania. Data for the previous period (in *Global Civil Society 2001*) covering from 1988 to June 2001, reported much higher shares for Europe and North America (53 and 23 per cent); this shows the important diffusion of global civil society events in the South, and is particularly important as it suggests a shift also in the origin of participants, because the large majority of people involved tend to come from the country where the event is held or from neighbouring ones.

What are the types of summit civil society sets out to challenge? Since 2001, 40 per cent of events are meetings of global movements organized independently from official summits, while this was only about 10 per cent in the past 13 years. Close to 30 per cent of parallel summits deal with regional conferences (European Union, American or Asian government meetings), and less than one third shadows UN, G8, IMF or WTO meetings. In the past this group accounted for two thirds of all parallel summits.

The key actors in the organization of parallel summits have not changed; they generally are civil society groups of the hosting country, in 80 per cent of cases also involving international networks and NGOs. In a third of the cases local groups are also active, with lesser involvement of trade unions and local authorities.

Who are the organizers of parallel summits? Varying coalitions of civil society groups, which emerge with the following profile. In two-thirds of events – in recent months as well as in the whole period – they were active civil society organizations working on development and economic issues (trade, finance, debt and so on). Groups involved in democracy issues are active now in half of global events, as opposed to a quarter in the past. Human rights and peace organizations are present in 25–30 per cent of parallel summits, while environmental groups lose importance and are found only in one-fifth of events (almost half that in the past); a similar fall is found for the presence of trade unions. Groups active on gender, youth and other issues also appear to be less relevant than in the past.

This evidence may be associated with the two main challenges posed by parallel summits: on the one hand, resistance to neo-liberal globalization is likely to be the focus of events organized by groups active on economic, development and trade union issues; on the other hand, pressure for the globalization of rights and responsibilities may characterize those organized by human rights, environment, peace and democracy activists. The long-term trends appear to be confirmed by recent developments. The growth of mobilizations around economic globalization since the late 1990s has accelerated; they dominate the present activity of global civil society. Global rights issues were the most important theme in the 1992–95 period and have since remained more or less stable in terms of overall relevance up to the present, with a modest upward dynamic after 2000. Confronting neo-liberal glob-alization is at present the most important issue emerging from parallel summits, but it goes hand-in-hand with demands for global rights and responsibilities.

What type of event is a parallel summit? It is always a confer-ence, associated with street demonstrations in 80 per cent of the cases (in contrast to one-half of past parallel summits). In recent months media events and grassroots meetings have lost import-ance, while a broader range of fringe actions and initiatives occurred. Since January 2001, one-third of global civil society events has had more than 10,000 participants – in seven parallel summits the number of people involved was above 80,000. One-fifth of cases involved between 1000 and 10,000 people, and one-quarter between 200 and 500, suggesting that also global meetings with a more focused participation are on the rise. Relative to past trends, there is an increase of large demonstrations and of small events, while the smallest ones basically disappeared.

What are the objectives of the gatherings of global movements? Since 2001, in three-quarters of cases parallel summits have had three aims: networking among civil society organizations, dissem-inating public information and proposing alternative policies. The latter objective maintains the same relevance as in the past, while the other two aims have rapidly grown in importance. The development of stable networks of civil society organizations has emerged as a recent major priority for their action, as has happened similarly to the informing of public opinion.

The two parallel needs of building up the 'internal' strength of global civil society and making more effective its 'external' activity – based on alternative policy proposals and on the consensus of public opinion – are again confirmed.[13] Other objectives, including political confrontation and lobbying official summits, account for around 10 per cent of recent cases (while they accounted for up to one-third in the past). The relatively low priority given to lobbying official representatives may be due to the declining frequency of UN-type summits open to civil society lobbying.

Parallel summits now appear to have a substantial impact. A tentative evaluation can be provided, based on the judgement of organizers, participants or from media reports, and clearly these results have to be treated with great caution. From the evidence available, the strongest impact of parallel summits appears to be on global civil society itself, where three-quarters of events are judged to have a medium or strong effect, and this is no different from the past. In half of the cases there is a similarly medium or strong impact on public opinion, followed by the effect on international media. While the impact of parallel summits on specific national and international policies has remained very weak, official summits have started to feel the pressure of civil society. In the last year and a half, more than 60 per cent of parallel summits have had a medium or strong impact on official conferences – stopping their activity, influencing their location or agenda – an impact twice the one estimated in the past.

Strengths and weaknesses of parallel summits did not change much after 2001. In 60 per cent of cases the wide international network of organizations is the main factor of success, followed by the strong political alliance among them; this underlines again the importance of the 'internal' development of global movements. Mass participation is considered a success in one-third of parallel summits, while radical protest emerges as less important. The weaknesses of parallel summits are mainly due to the lack of attention of policy-makers (or to the failure to make them listen to civil society) and from the lack of 'external' visibility (or to the failure to make media and public opinion listen to the message of parallel summits), both relevant in more than 50 per cent of cases. A much lower number of cases point out 'internal' weaknesses, such as divisions among organizers (small, but on the increase), or poor participation.

With all the limitations that such data may have, there is little doubt that global civil society is coming of age. Global movements are active on all continents with a great variety of issues. Moving from protest against official summits, they have developed their own agenda, where the critique of neo-liberal globalization is joined by the proposal of alternatives and the exploration of new forms of political action. They have shown great organizational capacity in preparing global events and growing autonomy in charting their own course, independent of the pressure of the policy agenda of international institutions and from the short-term considerations of national politics. Even the surge of terrorism with the attacks of September 11 2001 against the United States, and the ensuing war in Afghanistan did not slow down global activism of civil society; rather, this has led to greater attention to the issues of peace, war and violence. The millions of people around the world mobilized in the last year and a half show that global civil society has now reached a role and relevance which should not be ignored either by national politics or by supranational institutions.

## The World Social Forum of Porto Alegre

For its size and importance, the second World Social Forum held in Porto Alegre, Brasil, on January 30–February 5, 2002, deserves a specific consideration. It has probably been the largest gathering of global civil society to date with 68,000 registered participants from 131 countries, representing 5,000 associations, NGOs and local authorities, 3,000 journalists and 800 members of parliament, meeting in 28 major plenaries, 100 seminars and 800 workshops. 40 per cent of the participants were women, 12,000 young people stayed in a city park, in a campsite named after Carlo Giuliani, the Italian youth killed by the police during the Genoa protests in July 2001. While Brasilians were by far the majority of people at the Forum, large contingencies came from Latin America (Argentina in particular) and Europe (1,000 Italians, 700 French) and smaller groups from the United States (140 delegates) and from Africa (200 participants).[14]

The Brasilian organizers had a strong institutional profile, with the systematic involvement of the President of the State of Rio Grande do Sul, of the Mayor of Porto Alegre, and of the leaders of the Workers' Party (PT) including Lula, who later won the 2002 presidential elections. The Porto Alegre experience of participatory democracy in the local budgeting process has been a key issue, receiving interest from all over the world, with hundreds of local authorities planning to replicate it. The Trade Union CUT was also active, with the coalition of civil society organizations responsible for the efficient organization of the event.

Participants included activists of social movements, political organizations, women's groups, representatives of all global campaigns, as well as environmentalists, peace activists, and smaller numbers of human rights campaigners, social economy organizations, development NGOs and Trade Unions.

The common analysis of global problems was the dominant theme of talks at the World Social Forum. The shared understanding of the roots of poverty, inequality, underdevelopment, hunger, environmental degradation, wars and human rights violations was remarkable, with activists of all continents sharing experiences, making links and learning the relevance of new issues, in events of great impact, such as the largest plenary of the Forum featuring Noam Chomsky.

Much less attention in Porto Alegre was devoted to the diversity of strategies to address global problems and to the priorities of campaigns. Different approaches were already visible, with the obvious division between North and South perspectives, but also with an emphasis on resistance from many North Americans and Asians, and greater attention to alternative projects from Europeans and Latin Americans.

The rejection of neo-liberalism and war have emerged as the two key elements of the global movements gathered in Porto Alegre. In a document agreed by hundreds of organizations (but which is not an official final document of the Forum), the 'Call of social movements. Resistance to neo-liberalism, war and militarism: for peace and social justice', activists define themselves as a 'global movement for social justice and solidarity'. The first in the list of its objectives is 'democracy: people have the right to know about and criticize the decisions of their own governments, especially with respect to dealings with international institutions.

Governments are ultimately accountable to their people. While we support the establishment of electoral and participative democracy across the world, we emphasize the need for the democratization of states and societies and the struggles against dictatorship.'

## Global movements in global civil society

In spite of the range and width of the global movements seen in Porto Alegre and in parallel summits all over the world, we should resist the identification of the new *global movements* with the action of *global civil society*.[15] The latter remains the sphere of cross-border relations and collective activities outside the international reach of states and markets. It contains a variety of collective agents, operating on the basis of diverse, often conflicting projects. What identifies *global movements* is that their cross-border actions move within global civil society with a broad common project demanding

- gobal democracy and peace to the *state* system,
- global economic justice to the *market* system, and
- global social justice and environmental sustainability to *both* systems.

The commonalities among the thousands of organizations and networks animating global movements largely stop here. In order to account for the heterogeneity of actors, of the fields of interest and of the political projects within global civil society, different typologies have been proposed, distinguishing for example, on the basis of the attitude towards economic globalization:

a) *reformists* with the aim to 'civilize' globalization
b) *radical critics* with a different project for global issues
c) *alternatives* who self-organize activities outside the mainstream of the state and market systems
d) *resisters* of neo-liberal globalization.

Outside this range of perspectives typical of global movements, we can find in global civil society two other perspectives:

e) *supporters* of the current order, stressing the benefits brought by globalization

f) *rejectionists* of global processes, favouring a return to a national dimension, often with a reactionary, nostalgic attitude.

Focusing on the strategies pursued by global movements, we can identify three major models: *resistance, lobbying,* and *production of policy alternatives.* These strategies shed new light on the vision and role of global civil society and its relationship to political and economic power.

## The politics of resistance

Resisting the decisions of illegitimate and arbitrary powers in the name of higher values or broader social interests has always been the point of departure of social mobilization and political change. The demonstrations in Seattle in November–December 1999 showed the importance of the *politics of resistance* of global movements, a strategy which has culminated in the protests against the G8 summit in Genoa in July 2001 and the EU Council in Barcelona in March 2002. In between we had had dozens of large-scale international demonstrations against the summits of the World Monetary Fund and the World Bank, in Washington in April 2000, Prague in September 2000, Washington again in April 2001; against the European Council meetings at Nice in December 2000 and at Gothenburg in June 2000; against the Summit of the Americas in Quebec City in April 2001; against the WTO meeting in Qatar in November 2001 when major protests were held in more than 50 cities all over the world.

The politics of resistance has been successful thanks to the convergence of four factors.

1. The large broadening of the *social base* involved: at Seattle there was an unprecedented alliance between environmentalists and US trade unions, local groups and global campaigns; at Genoa there was the Genoa Social Forum's capacity to open up to a new generation of activists and to bring together different forces, ranging from associations to radical 'social centres', from Left organizations and unions to many Catholic organizations.

2. A *simplification of the issues* at the centre of the protest with a strong element of political opposition: at Seattle the 'no' to

an unjust commercial system, at Genova the 'no' to a G8 without legitimacy.

3. The resort to a *form of radical struggle*, like civil disobedience, often successful in effectively obstructing the activities of summits.

4. A strong *resonance in the media* and vast attention from public opinion, thanks to a long effort at public information and, above all, to the visibility of the forms of action and of the repression taking place.

The success of this strategy of global movements is indisputable, measured not only by the growth from the 60,000 demonstrators at Seattle, to the 300,000 at Genoa and Barcelona. After Seattle, the next WTO summit was organized in Qatar, the location most protected from the requests of democratization and changes in policies coming from global civil society. After Genoa, the G8 summits of the past can no longer be repeated in the same way, and the 2002 meeting has been hidden in the Canadian mountains.

These successes, nevertheless, have had a high price. Genoa was the culmination of the resistance of global movements, but also the culmination of the arbitrariness of power with the savage police repression carried out by the Italian government and the killing of Carlo Giuliani. Violence in Genoa was used by a small minority of demonstrators who threw stones, broke glass, and set vehicles and offices on fire, but violence was used in a systematic way by the police – even after the arrest of demostrators – with the aim of making peaceful protest impossible.

Since Seattle, global powers and states have tried to portray global movements as violent extremists against which repression should be exercised. After Genoa, there was the risk of a spiral of violent protest and repression. In order to avoid this, movements in Italy after Genoa, like in Sweden after Gothenburg, have had to devote a large part of their energies to prevent this spiral and defend their democratic space.

In any case, after two years of rapid expansion, the politics of resistance seems to have initiated its point of descent. Every factor of success after Genoa could transform into an element of weakness. An excessive media orientation and simplification of issues may lead to an extreme fragility of movements, with a loss of substance and credibility for their proposals for change. The spiral of violence and repression may reduce the extension of the social base involved and lose public opinion consensus. The result might be a fall in participation and a radicalization of limited sectors of the movements, without significant results on the international issues on which they started out to act.


## Lobbying

At the opposite of resistance there is the lobbying model. The organizations of civil society try to influence the decisions of global powers by a systematic effort of documentation, contact with national decision-makers, and presence at international conferences. This work has led to important results in recent years, including treaties banning landmines, creating the International Criminal Court, the Kyoto protocol on the reduction of carbon emissions, and many other accords on environmental issues.

Success factors of this pressure are the following.

1. The existence of *legitimate international institutions* with the mission to address particular problems of global importance; they need to be recognized by civil society and need to recognize the role civil society may in turn play in these issues. Organizations of the United Nations family are the typical examples.
2. The concentration, on the part of non-governmental organizations and associations, on very *specific requests* to well-defined decision-makers, based on practical knowledge of the relevant problems and of the most effective potential solutions.
3. A *low intensity action*, in political terms, working in direct contact with those who make decisions, seeking the broadest possible agreements on the specific themes addressed, with a willingness to compromise.
4. The use of *public opinion campaigns*, the only form of mass participation envisaged, in order to build a consensus on the general objectives, and to put pressure on policy-makers.

This path of change of the global order relies on small improvements from inside the existing institutions, and it is possible only when there is a shared horizon of political action with existing supranational powers. It offers the opportunity to effectively implement necessary changes in global rules and issues, if only minor and partial ones. The risk is to keep civil society subordinate to the decisions of governments and supranational powers, removing the resources of protest and conflict.

The experiences of the most recent global summits (Johannesburg, Qatar and Monterrey) suggest that the space for a strategy of this type are increasingly limited.

### The production of alternative policies

The third path of change is the capacity of global movements to *produce alternative policies*, autonomous from the actions of governments and traditional politics. Examples include the campaign for a Tobin Tax,[16] and the rapid growth of Attac as a global movement demanding its introduction; the mobilization around the Jubilee 2000 campaign to cancel the debt of Southern countries; the campaigns to reform the IMF and the World Bank; the request for access to drugs by poorer countries, in particular those for the AIDS epidemic; the rejection of genetically modified organisms in Europe; the efforts on energy issues and for developing renewable energy sources; the solidarity actions, initiatives for conflict resolution and constructions of peace in the Balkans.

Ideas for alternative policies are generally present, to some extent, also in the initiatives of resistance, and in lobbying efforts. However, specific initiatives for developing alternatives have increasingly characterized the action of global movements and parallel summits since 2001, as seen above, with major international meetings such as the World Social Forum of Port Alegre held in January–February 2001, 2002 and 2003 and the four Assemblies of the People's United Nations in Perugia.[17]

A strategy focusing on alternative policies combines in an interesting way some features of the politics of resistance and of lobbying.

1. The alternative policies proposed by global movements target the *weak points of international institutions*, asking for radical reforms (for example of the International Monetary Fund) or for the creation of new organizations (for example

to administer the Tobin Tax) able to deal with global problems. They confront well-defined international institutions, pointing out their limits and proposing ways to move beyond existing arrangements; in this way such a strategy avoids the risk of subordination, typical of lobbying, and the limits of a resistance without proposal.

2. Policies of global movements combine *a broad political vision with specific demands*; moving from a concrete knowledge in the relevant fields (for example the effects of the lack of access to AIDS drugs in Africa), the appropriate proposals for solving them are advanced, changing existing power relations and institutional arrangements (e.g. modifying the norms on patents and on the prices of drugs set by companies).

3. The campaigns present a *high politicization* and a *high participation* because they must build a broad social base supporting their alternative project. For example, the opposition to genetically modified organisms has been transformed from an issue for biotechnology specialists to a problem for all citizens, constructing alliances among scientists, environmentalists, farmers and consumers, and raising fundamental questions to society and politics on what should be produced and consumed.

4. The construction of the *consensus of public opinion* is essential to these campaigns in order to mobilize a diversity of social forces, and to create pressure, as lobbying does, on decision-makers in national governments and supranational organisms. For example, the success of the Jubilee 2000 debt campaign is associated first with the huge involvement of the media, the churches, all sorts of civil society organizations; second to its presence in dozens of parallel summits – G8, IMF–World Bank, European Council, etc. – and third to its influence on political forces and governments which has led to positive steps and legislation in several countries.

Such developments have taken place entirely *outside* the mechanisms of institutional politics, which continues to ignore the elaboration of global movements. This confirms the *autonomy* of global movements, but at the same time reveals a major weakness in this route to change: the lack of an *effective, contractual power* of civil society, of social movements, for change 'from below' – against existing global powers. In all sorts of fields – the requests to reform and democratize the UN, for non-military solutions to conflicts, for protection of workers and immigrants in the global economy, for the Tobin Tax, etc. – global powers have always responded in the same manner: 'It is not possible.' Hence the immediate popularity of the radical statement that *another world is possible*, used as a common banner by global movements.

In contrast to this stalemate, the modest ambitions of *lobbying* show that small changes are in fact feasible, and the protests of *the politics of resistance* show that global powers cannot escape radical criticism. The proposals for alternative policies coming from global movements – important as they are – risk being *innocuous* to global powers, as long as they can afford to ignore the role, ideas and influence coming from civil society.

This stalemate concerns not only global movements, but the question of global democracy itself and has important consequences for the prospects of effective governance of global problems. The ways out are three. On the one hand, states and supranational institutions have to formally recognize the role of civil society on global issues, granting rights to its organizations and movements to have a *voice* (not necessarily a *vote*) on global issues, as members, for example, of the delegations of national representatives to UN bodies, regional organizations (such as the EU) and international conferences; some very initial steps in this direction have already been taken in the case of the UN. It should be reminded that one century ago the same route was taken by the labour unions when they obtained formal recognition for the representation of workers before the government and the employers.

The second way out requires the reactivation of the mechanisms of democracy in national politics; the proposals of the movements should systematically influence the positions of national governments, and in doing so, change the balance of power in international bodies. There are many examples of success using this method: France's decision to block the negotiations for the Multilateral Agreement on Investment (MAI) at the OECD; Malaysia's decision to control the movements of capital after the Asian financial crisis; South Africa's and Brazil's decision to challenge multinational pharmaceutical companies

for anti-AIDS drugs; the European decisions on genetically modified organisms; even the UK decision to arrest General Pinochet.
This is the concrete ground where national politics can meet civil
society anew.

The third road passes through the strengthening of the global
organization of civil society and movements. Stable arrangements,
systematic coordination and regular meetings are important first
steps, such as the ones developed after the second World Social
Forum of Porto Alegre, with the Continental Social Fora and the
greater, permanent role taken up by the International Council of
its organizers. The search for more democratic forms of deliberation and participation of civil society also from poorer countries
is a continuing challenge for the legitimacy and representativeness of global movements. The definition of a common agenda
and the development of common identities, visions and policy
proposals are the more difficult, but necessary steps.

The variety of strategies being pursued by social movements in
confronting global powers should not be seen as a factor of
division and weakness. Rather, a perspective of *globalization from
below* requires a combination of capacity of resistance, radical
visions, political alternatives, and instruments that introduce
specific reforms. A weakness would emerge if sections of global
movements confine themselves to a politics of resistance alone,
seen as the way for affirming an antagonistic identity, independent of the objectives of change. Or if other sections are co-opted
and integrated into a strategy of global governance, legitimating
particular international institutions.

The future of global movements is tied to their roots in society
and to the capacity to affirm an alternative vision for global
problems. However, much will also depend on the ability of
politics to pay attention to civil society, on the response of
governments, and on the effective possibilities of reform of
supranational organizations.

The question of the international order, of *democracy vs globalization*, remains too important to be left to a handful of ministers,
diplomats, technocrats and military leaders. A major hope for the
future has come from the global movements for democracy and
justice, which have asked for (and have practised) a more democratic order, more equal international relations, and a more just
economy and society.

# Notes

1. See Susan Strange, *The Retreat of the State*, Cambridge 1996; Daniele Archibugi, David Held and Martin Köhler, eds, *Re-imagining Political Community. Studies in Cosmopolitan Democracy*, Cambridge 1999.

2. Mario Pianta, *Globalizzazione dal basso. Economia mondiale e movimenti sociali*, Rome 2001.

3. Richard Falk, *Predatory Globalization: A Critique*, Cambridge 1999, p. 2.

4. See, among a large literature, United Nations Development Programme, *Human Development Report 1999 – Globalization*, Oxford 1999; Noam Chomsky, *Profits over People: Neoliberalism and Global Order*, New York 1999.

5. See Giovanni Arrighi, Terence Hopkins and Immanuel Wallerstein, *Antisystemic Movements*, London 1989; R.D. Lipschutz, 'Reconstructing World Politics: The Emergence of Global Civil Society', *Millennium: Journal of International Studies*, vol. 21, 1992, pp. 389–420; M.E. Keck and K. Sikkink, *Activists Beyond Borders: Advocacy Networks in International Politics*, Ithaca and London 1998; Donatella Della Porta, Hans Kriesi and Dieter Rucht, eds, *Social Movements in a Globalizing World*, London 1999; Ann Florini, ed., *The Third Force: The Rise of Transnational Civil Society*, Tokyo and Washington 2000; R. O'Brien, A.M. Goetz, J.A. Scholte and M. Williams, *Contesting Global Governance: Multilateral Economic Institutions and Global Social Movements*, Cambridge 2000; R. Cohen and Shirin Rai, eds, *Global Social Movements*, London 2000; Naomi Klein, *No Logo*, London 2000; Helmut Anheier, Marlies Glasius and Mary Kaldor, eds, *Global Civil Society 2001*, Oxford 2001, in particular the chapters 'Introducing Global Civil Society', pp. 3–22, by the editors, and the chapter by Mario Pianta, 'Parallel Summits of Global Civil Society', pp. 169–94.

6. Cit. in note 3, p. 130. See also Jeremy Brecher and Tim Costello, *Global Village, Global Pillage*, Cambridge 1998; Jeremy Brecher, Tim Costello and Brendan Smith, *Globalization from Below. The Power of Solidarity*, Cambridge 2000; and Pianta, cit. in note 2.

7. See, among others, Ann Pettifor, 'The Economic Bondage of Debt – And the Birth of a New Movement', *New Left Review*, no. 230, 1998, pp. 115–22; Flavio Lotti and Nicola Giandomenico, eds, *L'Onu dei popoli*, Turin 1996; Flavio Lotti, Nicola Giandomenico and Rosario Lembo, eds, *Per un'economia di giustizia*, Perugia 1999; Francois Houtart and Francois Polet, eds, *L'autre Davos. Mondialisation des résistances et des luttes*, Paris and Montréal 1999; Giulio Marcon and Mario Pianta, 'New Wars and New Peace Movements'. *Soundings: A Journal of Politics and Culture*, no. 17, 2001, pp. 11–24; Lunaria, ed., *Mappe di movimenti. Da Porto Alegre al Forum Sociale Europeo*, Trieste 2002.

8. For a detailed analysis of parallel summits see Mario Pianta, cit. in note 5.

9. Steve Charnovitz, 'Two Centuries of Participation: NGOs and International Governance', *Michigan Journal of International Law*, vol. 18, no. 2, 1997, pp. 183–286.

10. See Giovanni Arrighi, Terence Hopkins and Immanuel Wallerstein, cit. in note 5.

11. See Leon Gordenker and Thomas Weiss, 'Pluralising Global Governance: Analytical Approaches and Dimensions', *Third World Quarterly*, vol. 16, 1995, pp. 357–87, and the contributions in the same special issue.

12. The background to this analysis is in the chapter of *Global Civil Society 2001* by Mario Pianta, cit. in note 5, where a periodization and a typology of parallel summits is presented. The data referring to the 2001–2002 period are in Mario Pianta, 'Parallel Summits and Global Civil Society Events: An Update', *Global Civil Society 2002*, Oxford 2002.

13. On this, see also the evidence from Benchmark Environmental Consulting, *Democratic Global Civil Governance. Report of the 1995 Benchmark Survey of NGOs*, Oslo 1996.

14. *Correio do povo*, 6 February 2002. See also Lunaria, ed., cit. in note 7.

15. See the debate in the literature cited in note 5.

16. The Nobel Prize winner James Tobin suggested introducing a small tax on international capital flows to stabilize the international financial system.

17. The Assemblies were held in the fall of 1995 on the reform of the UN, in 1997 on a just economy, in 1999 on global civil society, in 2001 on globalization from below. See Flavio Lotti, Nicola Giandomenico and Rosario Lembo, eds, cit. in note 7.

# 13

# Demos and Cosmopolis

*Daniele Archibugi*

In the light of the political philosophy of the last two millennia, it may seem odd to find the terms 'democracy' and 'cosmopolis' paired together.[1] Democracy is the power of the many and, internally, the rule of the majority. It came into being not as an abstract concept but as a means for taking the most concrete decisions: what government to appoint; what taxes to collect, and from whom; how public money should be spent, or schools and hospitals organized. Another defining feature: for the power of the demos to work, all those who constitute it must belong to the same community. Until a few centuries ago, the members of the few existing democracies – some Greek *polis*, the Swiss Cantons, a few Italian republican cities – would know each other by sight. The term 'cosmopolis' is no less ancient than that of 'democracy', but from its very origin it has referred to an ideal condition. The notion that the individual is a citizen of the world and, indeed, that the world might become his or her *polis*, was an individual aspiration rather than a mass reality. Only merchants, soldiers, the odd intellectual and a few potentates were acquainted with lands, cities and people outside their own native communities. All the rest, the majority – in other words, the demos – could only imagine what the other parts of the planet were like from legends and travellers' tales.

The ideas of democracy and cosmopolis have passed through many stages, being progressively modified down the centuries, and there is no shortage of learned treatises charting their semantic, cultural, historical and even anthropological evolution.

The first, groundbreaking transformation of democracy was the result of the American Revolution, when the idea was asserted on a hitherto unthinkable geographical scale. The Founding Fathers, however – understanding the term as 'direct' democracy – thought it inappropriate for the system they were designing; they preferred to christen their creature a 'republican' system. In his celebrated philosophical project *Towards Perpetual Peace* Kant, too, favours the term 'republic'.[2] Only in the nineteenth century was the modern system of electoral proxy by citizens deemed a form of 'democracy' – of representative democracy, that is.

The changing fortunes of 'cosmopolitanism' have been no less dramatic. Over the millennia it has shed its original, ideal dimensions and materialized into reality. The number of people – merchants, explorers, writers, intellectuals and, ultimately, tourists – able to travel and find out about the world has grown hand-in-hand with the economic expansion and the assertiveness of mass society. These cosmopolitans, as they became acquainted with 'the other', developed two attitudes towards it: the first was curiosity – which, as Giambattista Vico reminds us, is the child of ignorance and mother of science – about the habits and customs of non-Western societies; the second, parallel to the first, was the idea that different civilizations should ultimately converge towards the best of these. Cosmopolitanism meant not just discovering but also assessing, comparing, selecting and, finally, wherever possible, applying the ways of life deemed most valid. If cosmopolitans have – too often, alas – fallen prey to the conviction that, by coincidence, the best customs are their own, they have never claimed the use of violence to impose their ideals.[3]

Yet not even in today's mass society – not even within the narrow confines of the Western world – can the epithet 'cosmopolitan' be applied to the demos, the majority. In the era of the computer, a third of the inhabitants of our planet have never even used a telephone; cosmopolitanism remains the prerogative of an élite.[4] It is certainly curious that the two terms – virtually the product of a twin birth in the Greek cradle of the West – have stayed so resolutely apart from one another over the centuries. Perhaps the cause lay in this intrinsic difference between their social reference points: while one spoke of the many, the people, the other implicitly evoked the privilege of a few. But when, about a decade ago, we began to work on cosmopolitan democracy, new conditions had arisen which arguably justified the conjunction of two such apparent antitheses.[5]

## Apotheosis of globalization

The first of these conditions was the forceful advent of what has been called globalization – a neologism without a precise date of birth, but already, at such a tender age, invoked even more frequently than Rossini's Figaro. Under this capacious term are classified events that charge into daily life without even knocking at the door. Jobs, mortgage payments, contagious diseases and the style of the shoes sold in the local shops may now depend on decisions taken in remote places: a Japanese manager's bid to buy a European firm, the Federal Reserve's decision to increase the interest rate, an African government's desire to cover up an epidemic, or the creative flair of a handful of designers in Milan.

We tend to find globalization disarming. All we can do is resign ourselves and think of Nietzsche: 'The world is independent from my will.' But it is not only individuals who feel helpless. Equally unprepared seem the institutions – families, parties, trade unions, associations, churches and, above all, the state – from which he or she might demand protection. States increasingly fail to control their borders, fall victim to the blitzkriegs of financial speculators, or find their political autonomy strictly restrained. Even the United States, the new hegemon, realized on the morning of September 11 that its soil was not a safe haven. The nation-state – the institution that once imposed itself as the oligarch of the planet – is progressively losing its power.

Globalization is far from being a headless monster, and much has been written in recent years to identify the forces which regulate its dynamics. Some have coined new terms – 'international regimes', 'control mechanisms', 'governance' and so on – to describe how decisions are taken even where there is no explicit chain of command. David Chandler has pointed out the ways in which a political and military hegemony is being recreated; Peter Gowan has shown that economic interests have been the fastest to reorganize in the new international climate. In both cases, only one country, the United States, has the political, economic and military power to assert its interests. But no country today can escape interactions with other parts of the globe. We are not, of course, living in a situation of international anarchy; nevertheless, many of the decisions that affect our lives are taken behind the scenes, by shadowy figures – people over whom neither we nor, it seems, our governments exercise any control. The state may pose itself as a protective womb, assuaging the anxieties of its population, but it has too often failed to deliver what it has guaranteed. Globalization makes it all the harder for it to fulfil its contract with its citizens.

The disorientation caused by the lack of a visible and recognized political authority should not make us overlook the fact that, at the same time, democracy has asserted itself as the sole legitimate form of government within states. Quantitative data show that 120 sovereign states out of 192 are democratic, embracing 58 per cent of the world's population. Not all these states achieve the level of democracy we are accustomed to in the West; political scientists have coined the oxymoron *democradura* to define the mixture of formal democracy and *de facto* dictatorship in force in many countries of the world.[6] The new regimes experience difficulties in keeping their promises: democracy does not automatically generate wealth, reduce infant mortality or eliminate hunger. Nor should we assume that Western democracies are secure: they are always in danger of sliding over the precipices of oligarchy, demagogy and populism. After more than a decade of the new wave of democracy, many problems remain unresolved and new ones have sprung into life.

But although celebrations of democracy's triumph have been premature, we should recognize that, for the first time in the history of the planet, a single, albeit variegated, form of power management – whereby government is the expression of the majority – has asserted itself as globally legitimate; in theory if not in practice. The cosmopolitans of the Enlightenment might see here a confirmation of their prophecy, that when peoples are placed in contact with one another they 'naturally' select the most progressive, advantageous form of government for themselves. For Franklin, Condorcet and Kant, the success of today's democracy could be considered a fruit of cosmopolitanism.

Yet while globalization has helped to impose democracy inside more states, it has also rendered them less autonomous. Is it possible to reconcile this paradox? Of the many problems of democratic systems still waiting to be solved, one has been stubbornly ignored for decades: why must the principles and rules of democracy stop at the borders of a political community? If the communities on this planet lived in conditions of splendid isolation, we might suppose that each of them would pursue its internal happiness in its own way. But this is far from the case, and the incessant dynamic of globalization will make it even less so. Must we then resign ourselves to a schizophrenic situation in which we make our democracies increasingly sophisticated internally, while refusing to enter into democratic relations with communities external to our own? In the long run, this is unsustainable. The waters in which democracy sails are progressively sinking and, if we fail to replenish them from suitable tributaries, they will dry up altogether. Today new sources can only be found at the level between countries. But when we speak about extending democracy beyond our privileged domestic pond, eyebrows are raised and scepticism reigns.

The political project of cosmopolitan democracy can thus be expressed very simply: it is the attempt to reconcile the phenomenon of globalization with the successes of democracy. It sets out from an acknowledgement of the fact that state-based democracy, the only form we know today, risks being hollowed out by the processes of globalization. At the same time, the dynamics of globalization have to be regulated, and carrying this out exclusively at state level is difficult, sometimes impossible.

Timothy Brennan has argued that, while state communities are known to be manageable units, there is no guarantee that the globe is, too.[7] Yet cosmopolitan democracy does not mean replicating, *sic et simpliciter*, the model we are acquainted with across a broader sphere. Passing from national to planetary democracy is not a mere question of expansion, still less a matter of replacing state by global government. To respond to the challenges facing us today we have to reconstruct democracy, with an effort of the imagination analogous to that of the eighteenth-century passage from direct to representative forms.

Many believe it is too ambitious to expect democracy to embrace the global dimension. Yet the transformations that have taken place in the world over the last few decades are just as vast: the population of the planet has doubled; technological transformations now make it possible to create connexions that were once unthinkable, in both quantity and quality; financial resources – and terror and risk – travel at unprecedented speeds. Political institutions, too, have changed, not only because the democratic model has asserted itself internally, but also because national governments have had to extend their degree of policy coordination on questions such as air travel, health, immigration, finance and even public order. But as Marx grasped very clearly, transformations in institutional arrangements are slower than those in the economic and social structure. If we still want our society to be managed in response to the will of citizens, we will have to adjust our institutions to meet socio-economic change.

## Vernacular democracy?

Will Kymlicka has gone so far as to propose that a political system must be either democratic or cosmopolitan.[8] He has argued that cosmopolitan democracy exaggerates the political consequences of globalization; that public policies should be made more incisive, to ensure that each community remains effectively 'autonomous'. He exhorts the democratic state to assume additional responsibilities in addressing such issues as migration, capital flow, multiethnic communities and minority rights; and, at the same time, to make a positive contribution to global society by strengthening international human rights and development aid. To exempt existing states from these responsibilities in the name of a non-specific global order, still in the process of being constituted, risks creating a power vacuum.

Kymlicka's concerns may certainly be shared. This is precisely why, unlike the many world-federalist projects to which it is indebted, cosmopolitan democracy aims to boost the management of human affairs at a planetary level not so much by replacing existing states as by granting more powers to existing institutions, and creating new ones. Democracy, recalls Kymlicka, works much better on the small scale that Pericles and Rousseau had in mind; but when he argues that 'democratic politics is politics in the vernacular', he ignores the many aspects of our daily lives that already elude this dimension, at the state level as well as globally. What does vernacular politics mean in India or China – not to mention Rousseau's native Switzerland? What proportion of the population would be excluded from it in Canada or the United States?

On closer inspection, then, the question of the vernacular is already a problem for state democracy. Hence, we either reduce democratic politics to an exclusively tribal level – leaving the other aspects of collective life to be addressed in non-democratic ways – or we have to invent democratic dimensions that are also meta-vernacular. In their first years, many national parliaments suffered from the lack of a common language. The problem recurs in the UN General Assembly and the European Parliament, and is sure to reappear if a world parliament is set up.[9] But to date democracy has been versatile enough to find ways around it, and I am confident that the same will be true in the century ahead. However pertinent, Kymlicka's point applies to any form of democracy in a multilingual community.

Some believe that we have made improper use of the term 'cosmopolitan': Brennan deems 'internationalism' more appropriate.[10] Concepts count more than words, but I feel I must defend the former epithet as a qualifier of democracy. The word 'international', introduced by Jeremy Bentham just prior to the French Revolution, evokes two stages of representation: first, the definition of government inside states; second, the formation of an 'international society' based on those governments. Bentham and many others after him felt it was sufficient for nation-state governments to be fully democratic to ensure that the global level would be so too. A similar position is argued today by John Rawls.[11]

The reason I have preferred to speak of cosmopolitan, as opposed to international, democracy is that I do not believe that the democratization of world affairs can be achieved solely by proxy, through single state governments, however democratic they may be. A set of democratic states does not generate a democratic globe, any more than a set of democratically elected town councils generates a democratic nation-state. National governments have proved too weak – or even too conniving – to forestall imperial dominance of world politics. Existing international organizations, the United Nations first and foremost, still fail to possess the legitimacy needed to oppose the hegemonic states. Just as state-level democracy is based on rules and procedures that differ from those of local authorities, and does not boil down to the sum of their various parts, so global democracy cannot be founded exclusively on democracy within states. It is necessary to add a level of political representation to those that already exist. Citizens will need to play a more active role, with a dual function – within the state they belong to, and the world in which they live.

## After the proletariat

Brennan evokes the internationalism of another glorious tradition of which I am very fond, that of the working-class movement and the various international workers' associations of the nineteenth and early twentieth centuries, their emblem anticipated in the celebrated call, 'Workers of the world, unite!' If still an inspiring beacon in the fight for a just global society, the slogan nevertheless needs to be reviewed. Proletarian internationalism presumed that a classless world would be one without organized group conflict, and that no community, dominated by workers, would feel the urge to subjugate another. As a consequence, there was no need to envision international political forms through which conflicts might be mediated and resolved. The sovereignty appealed to by Brennan, Chandler and Gowan would evaporate, it was held, together with its bearer, the bourgeois state. We need to rethink the political programme but not the spirit of proletarian internationalism. Cosmopolitan democracy suggests the creation of institutions and channels of representation for all individuals, not just for a single class. The objective is not the abolition of classes, but the more modest one of ensuring that the demands of citizens, irrespective of their class, are directly represented in global affairs. It means resolutions being taken by the majority, rather than by a single class. Paraphrasing the *Communist Manifesto*, Ulrich Beck has issued a new call: 'Cosmopolitans of the world, unite!' To be a cosmopolitan now is no longer simply to feel oneself a citizen *of* the world but also, and above all, a citizen *for* the world.

The programme of cosmopolitan democracy is not politically neutral. Substantial disparities exist in access to global resources: some already have global fora at their command. The big multinational companies, defence apparatuses and state administrations coordinate their policies across the world. While there can be an element of transparency, in practice decisions are usually only taken by a handful of oligarchs (e.g. the UN Security

Council), while elsewhere (the G8 or NATO spring to mind) there is a higher degree of secrecy than at national level. Then there are those – effectively defined by Brennan as 'unofficial party organizations across national frontiers' – that operate without any form of control: we have no idea what decisions are taken, or when, or where.

These hidden centres of power are nothing new. They operate within all states, including the most refined democracies. But the goal of state-democratic procedures has been to limit their range of action; it is the absence of accountable institutions at the global level that allows these shadowy practices to prevail – a democratic vacuum that needs to be filled. Today cosmopolitan democracy would largely benefit those excluded from decision-making processes – the majority of the planet. Chandler, Brennan and Gowan rightly point to the dangers inherent in a new hegemony founded on the predominance of the United States, for whom institutions such as NATO, the IMF and WTO provide effective instruments. Disagreement here is not over the analysis of this new world order but over the political project needed to counter it. One cannot help remarking that these authors devote far more space to critical analysis of the present situation than to concrete proposals for a way out of it. Rashly, the supporters of cosmopolitan democracy think it more effective to counter this hegemonic design by imposing a global network of democratic control, rather than by shutting themselves inside existing state communities.

## Politics and power

Another line of criticism – more directly realist – accuses cosmopolitan democracy of ignoring the fact that political authority is generated only by the use of force. Any more intensified form of centralization cannot but translate into a totalitarian world government – an opinion that Geoffrey Hawthorn has voiced in these pages. His line of attack, however, staggers precariously between two views: one which sees the democratization of global society as impossible and another which sees it as dangerous. I agree with Hawthorn when he points out that 'parties are organizations for power', but he fails to add that political systems would work better without parties. Would he call for the winding up of the British Labour and Conservative Parties? It seems unlikely. So why be so scandalized at the thought of transnational parties? This seems typical of a form of schizophrenia often found in political thinking: what is taken for granted at home is deemed impracticable or even dangerous abroad.

Students of international politics should be aware of the fact that one of the reasons why political authority was founded on force was the perception of continuous menace, real or presumed, from outside. The existence of democratic global institutions would undermine states' principal pretext for the misuse of their own coercive power – that of external threat. The strengthening of international organizations and the formation of a world order founded on legality would therefore not only lessen tensions between states, but would favour democratization inside them. As Erasmus and Rousseau grasped, this is precisely the reason why state apparatuses are opposed to more effective international organization. After the Soviet menace, other threats have periodically appeared. Devoid of warriors, the battlefield is now populated by puppets in terrorist masks.

It is not enough to repeat, as Hawthorn does, that force is the principal source of political legitimacy; it is also necessary to ask whether force can be domesticated. The populations of the majority of nation-states have now constituted themselves as citizens of democratic communities. Ballot papers and judicial systems have replaced the cannon fire of the battlefield: antagonistic systems have turned into competitive ones. Why should global society not undergo a similar metamorphosis? Only prophets and astrologers can claim the mission is impossible. Everyone else, sooner or later, will have to take sides. This is not a theoretical question but a political choice. Cosmopolitan dreams are a programmatic counter to the horrors of the modern world.

Some, however, have argued that such dreams have served to ease the passage from Cold War bipolarism to the new American hegemony. Chandler has effectively, if somewhat speciously, described how the old world order, founded on the formal sovereign equality of states, is being replaced by one that sanctifies a one-sided military interventionism, albeit gilded with 'humanitarian' motives. Eluding the self-defence limits set by the UN Charter, the United States and its allies have carved out for themselves a new right to the use of force. Although Chandler admits that the practical application of 'sovereignty' has been, to say the least, dubious, he believes that, in the face of a full-blooded drive towards a new US hegemony, it is still a concept that can be used in the defence of Third World countries against the predations of the wealthiest, most powerful states. Chandler argues that notions of 'global democratic governance' have weakened the principle of sovereignty and thus indirectly favoured the increased use of military force. But why then was the US still so ready to go to war before this – not least in Vietnam? Similarly, the overblown military reaction to the terrorist attacks of September 2001 has been justified primarily on traditional self-defence grounds, not in terms of promoting democracy or defending human rights.

Any uncritical re-proposition of the now baroque category of sovereignty as bulwark of autonomy is ineffective both in theory and in practice. When has the sovereignty principle ever guaranteed non-interference? How many times, instead, has it permitted state governments to perpetrate massacres with absolute impunity? Sovereignty has allowed dictators to 'use' their subjects at their leisure far more often than it has helped weak states to defend themselves against stronger ones. Of the 200 million people killed in political conflicts in the course of the twentieth century, two-thirds were the victims of internal state violence.[12] The protection of human life is rightly seen as one of the mainstays of the architecture of a global political system; to assert the principle of sovereignty and non-interference does nothing to protect the victims of violence inside states.

The real problem, as Chandler correctly points out, is that the humanitarian interventions of the last ten years have been a string of incredible failures. At the start of the war in Kosovo, some appeared to be hoping that NATO had turned into the armed branch of Amnesty International. Alas, the outcome of the intervention proved as catastrophic as those in Iraq, Somalia and elsewhere. NATO's preferred mode of conflict – obsessive aerial bombardment from an altitude of 10,000 metres – is designed to minimize its own losses, with pitiless disregard for those of its presumed 'enemies'. If there were no victims among NATO's forces, the human rights of those who were supposed to benefit from the bombing were systematically trodden down. On what grounds is it possible to describe such a process as 'humanitarian'? More than illegitimate, the interventions of the 1990s were ineffective. Here lies their real failure – not in the violation of the now moribund concept of sovereignty.

The guidelines for genuine humanitarian interventions have yet to be written. For cosmopolitan democracy, these could only be carried out by the institutions and organizations that have the vocation and competence to do so. In the face of ethnic cleansing, we have left the most powerful states free to programme 'humanitarian' interventions as they see fit, leaving out the individuals and organizations of civil societies. The principle of non-interference is no solution for the victims of genocide. Rather, the category of sovereignty should be replaced by that of global constitutionalism, in which the use of international force – especially when geared to internal problems – is not only decided upon but actively managed by global institutions who would also be responsible for the recreation of the social fabric after the conflict.

The experience of the 1990s would seem to indicate that, in the absence of institutions and procedures designed to guarantee truly humanitarian interventions, it is better if (Western) states abstain from the use of force. But this obliges us to find non-violent instruments of intervention to prevent genocide, to defend human rights and the freedom of peoples to choose their own governments. Chandler keeps silent precisely when he should speak up: how should we react to daily violations of human rights?

Both Chandler and Gowan are highly sceptical about the possibility of creating a genuine international system of justice, citing the example of the War Crimes Tribunal for the former Yugoslavia – instrumentalized for US political ends on more than one occasion. I share many of their reservations about these new institutions, but not the idea that there would be greater international justice without them. For all their flaws, existing bodies are the embryos of the more robust ones that will be needed to guarantee global legality. Like the Nuremberg Trials, the Yugoslav War Crimes Tribunal is based on the recognition that statesmen have to answer for their actions before the law – a principle now being asserted at national levels, as the Pinochet affair demonstrates. A fully-fledged International Criminal Court is on its way; in the autumn of 2001 it could have been used to try terrorists, providing a genuine alternative to the bombardment of Afghanistan. The strongest have no need for legality; all they need is force. It is the weakest who need to seek protection under the wing of law.

## Knowing the enemy

Before they took up arms to claim their independence from the British crown, American settlers had demanded the right to participate in the political decisions of their community with the slogan: 'No Taxation without Representation.' 'No Globalization without Representation' must be the rallying cry of today.[13] The meaning is analogous; but present difficulties are greater. In George III, the Americans had a visible polemical interlocutor. They knew which door to knock on, and who to fight against. Our opponent is more chameleon-like. Who should we protest against, if we are to achieve greater accountability in global choices? The governments of the strongest countries? The most important multinational companies? Powers so strong that they are invisible?

In Seattle, Prague, Gothenburg, Genoa, recent intergovernmental summits have been met by lively counter-demonstrations – in fact, the most conspicuous effect of these meetings of the powerful seems to have been to reawaken the spirit of opposition. But protest prevails over proposal. One marked feature of these confrontations has been the extreme use of violence by the state apparatuses – not just in Italy, where Berlusconi's police felt the need to teach the 'law of the truncheon' to the Genoa demonstrators, but also in civilized Sweden. The hysterical reaction against anti-globalization protesters reflects the paranoia of governments fearful that their most recondite secret – that not even they have control over globalization – is about to be revealed.

American settlers learnt first-hand that their political battle could not only be won by revolt. To free themselves from the British crown, they had to draw up a charter of rights and a constitution. Today the motley movement that is fighting the hegemonic project of capitalism has to pass from revolt to project. It is not enough to be against what is happening; it is also necessary to propose workable solutions. The cosmopolitan project intends to follow the long and winding road to global society, founded on the values of legality and democracy. But the fact that we are still a long way from our destination does not mean that there are no concrete objectives to deal with here and now; it is on the basis of these that we need to select our allies and adversaries.

After the welter of commentary that followed September 11, it hardly needs to be restated here that globalization encompasses not only finance and fashion but also terror. No corner of the world is safe any more. Cosmopolis is not only a utopia but a nightmare, too. Yet the terrorist attacks and the US military reaction both serve to confirm that what we need is democratic management of global events, not high-tech reprisals. The fall of the Berlin Wall raised expectations that world politics might be moving from the rule of force towards a global society founded on legality. The last decade has fallen short of these in many respects. Nonetheless, September 11 should not be allowed to erase the hopes of the last ten years forever. In the face of both that day's terrorist attack and the months-long bombardment of Afghanistan, the cosmopolitan perspective remains what it was during the Gulf War and the crisis in the former Yugoslavia: a criminal act is not enough to justify the unleashing of brute force.

Terrorists cannot be fought with their own arms; the democratic states must target only those directly responsible for criminal acts. The terrorists and their accomplices will be best equipped to escape bombardment, whereas ordinary Afghanis, already worn out by a seemingly interminable civil war and a hysterical, bloody regime, are certainly the ones to suffer most from Western military intervention. If and when the casualties are ever totalled, it will surely emerge that the vast majority are civilian 'collateral' (to use the sinister euphemism), with perhaps a few hundred armed and illiterate fanatics, and only a tiny handful of terrorists connected with the events of September 11.[14] Democratic cosmopolitanism would propose exactly the opposite course to that which the US government has taken: the use of police, international tribunals and the UN to punish criminal terrorists. *Pace* sceptics such as Chandler, these institutions are the best tools we have to defend civilians from the indiscriminate use of force.

The United States has obtained virtual unanimity among governments, not only on the condemnation of terrorism but also on the reprisals: Saudi Arabia, Pakistan, Libya, the Palestinian authorities have all come out in favour of military intervention.

Yet at the same time, numerous masses of the world's outcasts are singing the praises of a petty paranoid criminal, Osama bin Laden; the danger is that the ranks of potential terrorists will be swollen with new recruits. In fighting one monster you risk generating others. Saddam Hussein was armed to contain Iran, bin Laden and the Taliban to counter the Soviet invasion. After September 11 it was the new nuclear power, Pakistan, that enjoyed the indiscriminate support of the West. Golems turn against their masters sooner or later, and sometimes become fiercer than the enemies they were created to annihilate. Cosmopolitan democracy has been called ingenuous and ineffective; but after years of *Realpolitik*, what is the result? A new conflict has moved onto history's stage, one that the political and military supremacy of the United States and the West has proved incapable of preventing. There could not be a clearer argument for turning to the politics of cosmopolitan dreams.

## Notes

1. My article 'Cosmopolitical Democracy', *New Left Review*, no. 4, received the critical comments of Geoffrey Hawthorn, 'Running the World through Windows', *New Left Review*, no. 5; David Chandler, 'International Justice', *New Left Review*, no. 6; Timothy Brennan, 'Cosmopolitanism and Internationalism', *New Left Review*, no. 7; and Peter Gowan, 'Neoliberal Cosmopolitanism', *New Left Review*, no. 11. These contributions are now included in this volume as, respectively, chapters 1, 2, 3, 4 and 5.

2. Hawthorn, *New Left Review*, no. 5, p. 103, fails to grasp the philological question: for Kant, what we call direct democracy can become a form of despotism. Hawthorn also accuses me of 'misdescribing' Kant's position, but the view he ascribes to me does not correspond to my interpretation of Kant's texts. I believe, in fact, that Kant suggests an international system midway between a confederation of states and a federal state. See my 'Models of International Organizations in Perpetual Peace Projects', *Review of International Studies*, vol. 18, 1992, pp. 295–317, and 'Immanuel Kant, Peace and Cosmopolitan Law', *European Journal of International Relations*, vol. 1, 1995, pp. 429–56.

3. Gowan (*New Left Review*, no. 11) describes the international hegemonic design of the last decade very well. But I believe he is over-gracious to call it 'the new liberal cosmopolitanism' rather than, more crudely, 'the new imperialism'.

4. United Nations Development Report, *Making New Technologies Work for Human Development*, New York 2001.

5. Cosmopolitan democracy has been a collective political project, jointly conceived by David Held, Mary Kaldor, Richard Falk and myself. See Daniele Archibugi and David Held, eds, *Cosmopolitan Democracy*, Cambridge 1995.

6. Guillermo O'Donnell, Philippe Schmitter and Laurence Whitehead, eds, *Transitions from Authoritarian Rule*, vol. 1, Baltimore 1986, p. 17.

7. 'Cosmopolitanism and Internationalism', *New Left Review*, no. 7.

8. Will Kymlicka, 'Citizenship in an Era of Globalization: Commentary on Held', in Ian Shapiro and Casiano Hacker-Cordón, eds, *Democracy's Edges*, New York 1999.

9. This ancient and utopian ideal is reproposed by Richard Falk and Andrew Strauss in 'Toward Global Parliament', *Foreign Affairs*, Jan–Feb 2001. See also their chapter in this volume.

10. In a similar vein, Alan Gilbert puts forward the idea of 'international democracy from below'. See his thoughtful book *Must Global Politics Constrain Democracy?*, Princeton 1999.

11. *The Law of Peoples*, Cambridge, MA 1999.

12. Rudolph Rummel, 'Power, Genocide and Mass Murder', *Journal of Peace Research*, vol. 31, no. 1, 1994, pp. 1–10. Although these data are controversial – Michael Mann, for example, has pointed out that a majority of internal state massacres have occurred in times of war – it remains the case that sovereign state borders have been no bulwark against political violence. See 'The Dark Side of Democracy: The Modern Tradition of Ethnic and Political Cleansing', *New Left Review*, I/235, May–June 1999, pp. 18–45.

13. I plagiarize Ian Clark, *Globalization and Fragmentation*, Oxford 1997.

14. Contrary to Richard Falk, I do not see how this war could ever have been turned into a just one. See his 'In Defence of "Just War" Thinking', *The Nation*, 24 December 2001.

# 14

# Globalization, Democracy and Cosmopolis: A Bibliographical Essay

*Daniele Archibugi and Mathias Koenig-Archibugi*

In the last decade, the hope of an international system based on the rule of law and democracy has revived. It is certainly not the first time in history that these expectations have emerged and it is easy to see why they had a comeback at the end of the twentieth century. The conclusion of the Cold War and the extension of democracy to many countries of the East and of the South have created new hopes that democratic principles could be applied also in the realm of international relations. Although the wars in the Persian Gulf, in Kosovo, in Afghanistan and in many other places have made people less optimistic, they have not demolished those aspirations.

These political developments have generated a growing number of studies on questions of world order, which are often connected to policy proposals. The aim of this bibliographical essay is to point to the most significant studies related to the idea that democracy – qualified as international, supranational, transnational, global, cosmopolitan or cosmopolitical – could be extended beyond the state.

## A long genealogy

The idea that the rule of law, justice and democratic participation – the core issues of the project of cosmopolitan democracy – could be applied also across and among states is certainly not new. The emergence of modern states in European history created the need for an orderly regulation of their relationship. In seventeenth- and eighteenth-century Europe two powerful intellectual traditions dealt with these issues: the *ius gentium* and the perpetual peace projects.

### *Ius gentium*

Since the early seventeenth century this tradition was developed by Alberico Gentili, Hugo Grotius, Samuel Puefendorf, Emmerich de Vattel and many others. In English, the expression *ius gentium* was pragmatically translated as 'Law of Nations' and today its exponents are considered, and with full merit, the founding fathers of international law. They gave to sovereigns codes of conduct to be followed when dealing with each other, in particular regarding the crucial aspect of inter-state relations, i.e. war and peace. It is highly significant that none of these authors envisioned the foundation of 'inter-' or 'supra-'state institutions. Since the principal aim of this tradition was to affirm sovereignty, these authors were reluctant to suggest any institutional device that could interfere with or limit state autonomy.

According to this tradition, states certainly must respect a number of prescriptions, and the legal thinkers declared that they were deriving these principles from natural law. But legal theorists left to state sovereigns the responsibility to decide unilaterally how to behave in international affairs, although they were keen to offer their services in interpreting the principles of natural law.

Among the recent analyses devoted to *ius gentium*, we recommend the study by Richard Tuck, *The Rights of War and Peace: Political Thought and the International Order from Grotius to Kant*, Oxford 1999. This tradition has certainly not disappeared, and the idea that states can decide unilaterally on resorting to force is discussed in Michael Walzer, *Just and Unjust Wars: A Moral Argument with Historical Illustrations*, New York 1977.

The recent book by John Rawls, *The Law of Peoples*, Cambridge,

MA 1999 (already the title recalls the old term and debate) suggests many deontological norms that states, and liberal states especially, should follow in the international sphere, but it never discusses the need to defer the resolution of disputes to a third party. Rawls' theses have been widely debated. Authors such as Charles Beitz, *Political Theory and International Relations*, Princeton 1979, and Thomas Pogge, 'An Egalitarian Law of Peoples', *Philosophy and Public Affairs*, vol. 23, no. 3, 1994, applied the ideas presented in Rawls' *Theory of Justice* to international affairs. See also the analyses by Andrew Kuper, 'Rawlsian Global Justice: Beyond the Law of Peoples to a Cosmopolitan Law of Persons', *Political Theory*, vol. 28, no. 5, 2000; Jean-François Thibault, 'L'interprétation limitée du politique dans le droit des gens de John Rawls', *Politique et Sociétés*, vol. 20, no. 2–3, 2001; Chris Brown, 'The Construction of a Realistic Utopia: John Rawls and International Political Theory', *Review of International Studies*, vol. 28, no. 1, 2002. A symposium on Rawls has appeared on *Ethics*, vol. 110, no. 4, 2000, with contributions from Charles Beitz and Allen Buchanan. The debate generated by Rawls' recent volume is reviewed in Simon Caney, 'Cosmopolitanism and the Law of People', *Journal of Political Philosophy*, vol. 10, no. 1, 2002.

## Perpetual peace projects

Rather than regulate and classify wars as 'just' or 'unjust', the authors working in the second tradition aimed at finding ways to eliminate them. In this perspective, the authorization to use force should not be left to state sovereigns, but rather transferred to international institutions that these authors, often with ingenuity, sought to generate. These authors were not always clear in specifying the nature of these international institutions: some were conceived with coercive powers, others had the function to mediate or arbitrate only. The distinction between judicial, legislative and executive powers was often vague.

It is very significant that, in spite of the fact that the *ius gentium* and the perpetual peace projects marched through the same centuries, were nurtured by the same historical circumstances, and were addressing the same issues, the two traditions interacted under no circumstances: almost never the authors of the first referred to the second and vice versa. Peace projects have always been less realistic than the treaties of the law of nations. Peace thinkers have been considered naïve, utopian and bizarre. Still, all contemporary international organizations have been anticipated in some often forgotten peace project of the past: the General Assembly of the United Nations in the writings of the Parisian Monk Emeric Crucé (1623), the European Parliament in the project of the English Quaker William Penn (1693), the Universal Declaration of Human Rights in the booklet by Immanuel Kant (1795), the International Court of Justice in the project of the American thinker William Ladd (1844), the recently constituted International Criminal Court in the ungrammatical writings of the galley slave Pierre-André Gragaz (1796).

Jacob ter Meulen has compiled the most complete bibliography of perpetual peace projects, and Peter van den Dungen, ed., *From Erasmus to Tolstoy, The Peace Literature of Four Centuries; Jacob ter Meulen's Bibliographies of the Peace Movement before 1899*, New York 1990, has recently republished it. The classics of pacifist thinking are now available in *The Garland Library of War and Peace*, edited by Blanche Wiesen Cook, Charles Chatfield and Sandi Cooper, New York 1971–76. Among the readers, see Elisabeth York, ed., *Leagues of Nations: Ancient, Mediaeval, and Modern*, London 1919; Kurt von Raumer, ed., *Ewiger Friede. Friedensrufe und Friedenspläne seit der Renaissance*, Freiburg 1953; Zwi Batscha and Richard Saage, eds, *Friedensutopien. Kant, Fichte, Schlegel, Görres*, Frankfurt a. M. 1979; Anita and Walter Dietze, eds, *Ewiger Friede? Dokumente einer deutschen Diskussion um 1800*, Leipzig 1989; Daniele Archibugi and Franco Voltaggio, eds, *Filosofi per la pace*, Roma 1999.

Among the critical analyses of peace projects, the most complete work is still Jacob ter Meulen, *Der Gedanke der Internationalen Organisation in seiner Entwicklung*, 3 vols, The Hague 1917, 1929, 1938. Cf. also Christian Lange and August Schou, *Histoire de l'internationalisme*, 3 vols, Kristiana and Oslo, 1919, 1944, 1954; Jacques Hodé, *L'idée de féderation international. Les précurseurs de la Societé des Nations*, Paris 1921; Sylvester John Hemleben, *Plans for World Peace through Six Centuries*, Chicago 1942; Francis Harry Hinsley, *Power and the Pursuit of Peace*, Cambridge 1963; Murray Forsyth, *Unions of States. The Theory and Practice of Confederation*, Leicester 1981; Hidemi Suganami, *The Domestic Analogy and World Order Proposals*, Cambridge 1989; Daniele Archibugi, 'Models of International Organizations in Perpetual Peace Projects', *Review of International Studies*, vol. 18, no. 3, 1992; Derek Heater, *World Citizenship and Government. Cosmopolitan Ideas in the History of Western Political Thought*, Macmillan 1996; Cornelius Murphy, *Theories of World Governance: A Study in the History of Ideas*, Washington, D.C. 1999.

## The Kantian legacy

The 200th anniversary of Immanuel Kant's project for perpetual peace has provided the occasion for a new flourishing of initiatives, conferences and studies. Among the most significant recent studies, see Andrew Hurrell, 'Kant and the Kantian Paradigm in International Relations', *Review of International Studies*, vol. 16, no. 3, 1990; Otfried Höffe, ed., *Immanuel Kant: Zum ewigen Frieden*, Berlin 1995; Daniele Archibugi, 'Immanuel Kant, Peace, and Cosmopolitan Law', *European Journal of International Relations*, vol. 1, no. 4, 1995; David Held, 'Democracy and the Global Order: Reflections on the 200th Anniversary of Kant's "Perpetual Peace"', *Alternatives*, vol. 20, no. 4, 1995; Various Authors, *La paix perpétuelle. Le bicentenaire d'une idée kantienne*, Paris 1996; Reinhard Merkel and Roland Wittman, eds, *Zum ewigen Frieden: Grundlagen, Aktualität und Aussichten einer Idee von Immanuel Kant*, Frankfurt a. M. 1996; James Bohman and Matthias Lutz-Bachmann, eds, *Frieden durch Recht*, Frankfurt a. M. 1996 (many of the chapters of this book are also available in English in a volume edited by the same editors: *Perpetual Peace. Essays on Kant's Cosmopolitan Ideal*, Cambridge, MA 1997); Pierre Laberge, Guy Lafrance and Denis Sumas, eds, *L'année 1795. Kant. Essai sur la paix*, Paris 1997; Vincent Martínez Guzmán, ed., *Kant: La paz perpetua, doscientos años después*, Valencia 1997; Giuliano Marini, *Tre studi sul cosmopolitismo kantiano*, Pisa 1998; Charles Covell, *Kant and the Law of Peace. A Study in the Philosophy of International Law and International Relations*, Houndsmill 1998; George Cavallar, *Kant and the Theory and Practice of International Right*, Cardiff 1999.

## Modern judicial peace thinking

Hans Kelsen resumed the themes of judicial peace thinking and gave to them a full development in international legal theory. Among the many works of this author, see *Das Problem der Souver-*

*nität und die Theorie des Völkerrechts; Beitrag zu einer reinen Rechtslehre,* Tübingen 1920; the first exposition of the thesis about the unity of internal and international law; *Peace through Law,* Chapel Hill 1944, which includes a proposal for a League for Peace that influenced the drafting of the UN Charter; *The Law of United Nations. A Critical Analysis of Its Fundamental Problems,* London 1950; a very detailed interpretation and comment of the UN Charter: *Principles of International Law,* New York 1967; which describes systematically Kelsen's vision of international law after the United Nations. On Kelsen's international legal thought, see the symposium 'The European Tradition in International Law: Hans Kelsen', *European Journal of International Law,* vol. 9, no. 2, 1998; with contributions by Charles Leben, Danilo Zolo, François Rigaux, Anthony Carty, Norberto Bobbio, Clemens Jabloner and Nicoletta Bersier Ladavac.

Norberto Bobbio has further developed legal thinking on peace. His essays on the subject are collected in *Il problema della guerra e le vie della pace,* Bologna 1984; and *Il terzo assente. Saggi e discorsi sulla pace e la guerra,* Torino 1988. Most of these essays are not yet translated into English.

## Cosmopolitan democracy

The idea of cosmopolitan democracy can be considered a reaffirmation and a development of perpetual peace projects in the historical conditions of our age, which is marked by the end of the Cold War, a growing number of democratic states, and an increasing interdependence among countries. Cf. Daniele Archibugi and David Held, eds, *Cosmopolitan Democracy. An Agenda for a New World Order,* Cambridge 1995; David Held, *Democracy and the Global Order: From the Modern State to Cosmopolitan Governance,* Cambridge 1995; Richard Falk, *On Humane Governance: Towards a New Global Politics,* University Park, PA 1995; Daniele Archibugi and Martin Köhler, eds, 'Global Democracy', Special Issue of *Peace Review,* vol. 9, no. 3, 1997; Daniele Archibugi, David Held and Martin Köhler, eds, *Re-imagining Political Community. Studies in Cosmopolitan Democracy,* Cambridge 1998; Andrew Linklater, *The Transformation of Political Community,* Cambridge 1998; Mary Kaldor, *New and Old Wars. Organized Violence in a Global Era,* Cambridge 1999; Barry Holden, ed., *Global Democracy,* London 2000;

David Held, 'Law of States, Law of Peoples: Three Models of Sovereignty', *Legal Theory*, vol. 8, no. 2, 2002; David Held, *Cosmopolitanism: Globalization Tamed*, Cambridge, forthcoming; Teresa Chataway, 'Why Cosmopolitical?', *Indiana Journal of Global Legal Studies*, 2003, forthcoming.

Jürgen Habermas, in his writings collected in the volumes *The Inclusion of the Other*, Cambridge 1998, and *The Post-National Constellation*, Cambridge 2001, has linked the issue of democracy beyond states to theories of deliberative democracy and the universality of human rights. His theses are discussed by Craig Calhoun 'Constitutional Patriotism and the Public Sphere: Interests, Identity and Solidarity in the Integration of Europe', in Pablo De Greiff and Ciaran Cronin, eds, *Global Ethics and Transnational Politics*, Cambridge, MA 2002.

John Dryzek, 'Transnational Democracy', *Journal of Political Philosophy*, vol. 7, no. 1, 1999, and Dennis F. Thompson, 'Democratic Theory and Global Society', *Journal of Political Philosophy*, vol. 7, no. 2, 1999, explore the application of concepts of deliberative democracy to global society. More generally on deliberative democracy, see James Bohman, 'The Coming Age of Deliberative Democracy', *Journal of Political Philosophy*, vol. 6, no. 4, 1998, and John Dryzek, *Deliberative Democracy and Beyond: Liberals, Critics, Contestations*, New York 2000.

In his recent writings, Ulrich Beck has also discussed the urgent need for cosmopolitan political organization: see *World Risk Society*, Cambridge 1999, especially chaps 1 and 2; 'The Cosmopolitan Society and its Enemies', in Luigi Tomasi, ed., *New Horizons in Sociological Theory and Research*, Aldershot 2001; *Cosmopolitan Social Science: Reading Power in a Global Age*, paper presented at the New School University, New York April 2001.

Discussions of cosmopolitan democracy can be found also in: April Carter, *The Political Theory of Global Citizenship*, London 2001; Wolfgang Kersting, 'Philosophische Friedenstheorie und internationale Friedensordnung', in Wolfgang Kersting and Christine Chwaszcza, eds, *Politische Philosophie der internationalen Beziehungen*, Frankfurt a. M. 1998; Otfried Höffe, *Demokratie im Zeitalter der Globalisierung*, München 1999; Antonio Franceschet, 'Popular Sovereignty or Cosmopolitan Democracy? Liberalism, Kant and International Reform', *European Journal of International Relations*, vol. 6, no. 2, 2000; Klaus Dieter Wolf, *Die Neue Staatsräson – Zwischenstaat-*

*liche Kooperation als Demokratieproblem in der Weltgesellschaft*, Baden-Baden 2000; Anthony McGrew, 'Transnational Democracy: Theories and Prospects' in April Carter and Geoffrey Stokes, eds, *Democratic Theory Today*, Cambridge 2002. On the democratization of the global system see also Fred Dallmayr, *Achieving Our World. Toward a Global and Plural Democracy*, Lanham 2001, and Bruce Morrison, 'Transnational Democracy: The Pursuit of a Usable Past', paper presented at the Conference *Transnational Democracy: Lessons from the Nation-State?*, University of Western Ontario, March 15–17 2002.

For a comparison of the norms of cosmopolitan democracy with the international regimes of finance and agriculture, see William Coleman and Tony Porter, 'International Institutions, Globalization and Democracy: Assessing the Challenges', *Global Society*, vol. 14, no. 3, 2000.

David Beetham *et al.*, *The State of Democracy*, The Hague 2002, and David Beetham, 'Assessing Democracy at the National and International Levels', paper presented at the Conference *Transnational Democracy: Lessons from the Nation-State?*, University of Western Ontario, March 15–17 2002, propose a set of criteria for assessing national and international dimensions of democracy.

The relationship between democracy and international law, already discussed by James Crawford, 'Democracy in International Law', *British Yearbook of International Law*, vol. 64, 1993, is further explored by James Crawford and Susan Marks, 'The Global Democratic Deficit: An Essay in International Law and its Limits', in Archibugi, Held and Köhler, eds, cit.; Susan Marks, *The Riddle of All Constitutions: International Law, Democracy and the Critique of Ideology*, Oxford 2000; and Eric Stein, 'International Integration and Democracy: No Love at First Sight', *American Journal of International Law*, vol. 95, 2001.

## The critics of cosmopolitan democracy

A critique to the idea of world government and to any concentration of power above the state is provided by Danilo Zolo, *Cosmopolis. Prospects for World Government*, Cambridge 1997. Others have argued that a democracy above the state is not possible: see Christoph Görg and Joachim Hirsch, 'Is International Democracy Possible?', *Review of International Political Economy*, vol. 5, no. 4, 1998.

Another type of criticism comes from those democratic theorists that argue that the world is too vast for democracy to work. This criticism is inspired by the classic work by Robert Dahl and Edward Tuftle, *Size and Democracy*, Stanford 1973. A similar argument is presented by Philippe Schmitter, 'The Future of Democracy: Could It Be a Matter of Scale?', *Social Research*, vol. 66, no. 3, 1999. Cf. also Ekkehart Krippendorff, 'Against a Politics of Scale', in *Peace Review*, vol. 9 no. 3, 1997. Dahl himself has discussed the issue further in 'Can International Organizations be Democratic? A Skeptical View', in Ian Shapiro and Casiano Hacker-Cordón, eds, *Democracy's Edges*, Cambridge 1999. A thoughtful critical analysis can be found in Nadia Urbinati's chapter in this volume and in James Bohman, 'International Regimes and Democratic Governance: Political Equality and Influence in Global Institutions', *International Affairs*, vol. 75, no, 3, 1999.

Winfried Thaa, 'Lean Citizenship: The Fading Away of the Political in Transnational Democracy', *European Journal of International Relations*, vol. 7, n. 4, 2001, and Glyn Morgan, 'Democracy, Transnational Institutions, and the Circumstances of Politics', paper presented at the Conference *Transnational Democracy: Lessons from the Nation-State?*, University of Western Ontario, March 15–17 2002, argue that the lack of a proper 'demos' makes the development of transnational democratic society impossible. Similar concerns are voiced by Alexander Wendt, 'A Comment on Held's Cosmopolitanism', in Ian Shapiro and Casiano Hacker-Córdon, *Democracy's Edges*, cit.

The perspective of multiculturalism seems also to be in tension with the cosmopolitan approach because of the high value it gives to group identity; see Will Kymlicka, ed., *The Rights of Minority Cultures*, Oxford 1995, and the papers in Will Kymlicka, *Politics in the Vernacular: Nationalism, Multiculturalism and Citizenship*, Oxford 2001. The suggestions to satisfy ethnic and cultural minorities within the state, however, are not very different from the suggestions provided by the cosmopolitan democracy approach in order to deal with diversity at the global level. These issues are discussed in Craig Calhoun's chapter in this volume and in the follwing publications: James Tully, *Strange Multiplicity. Constitutionalism in an Age of Diversity*, New York 1995; Jeremy Waldron, 'Minority Cultures and the Cosmopolitan Alternative', in Will Kymlicka, ed.,

*The Rights of Minority Cultures*, cit.; Iris Marion Young, 'Self-Determination and Global Democracy: A Critique of Liberal Nationalism', in Ian Shapiro and Stephen Macedo, eds, *Designing Democratic Institutions*, New York 2000; and Alain-G. Gagnon and James Tully, eds, *Multinational Democracies*, Cambridge 2001.

## Cosmopolitan citizenship

A parallel and partially overlapping research programme inspired by the cosmopolitan ideal focuses on citizenship. Among the contributions in this field, see Richard Falk, 'The Making of Global Citizenship', in Bart van Steenbergen, ed., *The Condition of Citizenship*, London 1994; Joseph Rotblat, ed., *World Citizenship*, Houndmills 1995; Ulrich Preuss, 'Citizenship in the European Union: A Paradigm for Transnational Democracy?' and Janna Thompson, 'Community Identity and World Citizenship', both in Archibugi, Held and Koehler, eds, cit.; Andrew Linklater, 'Cosmopolitan Citizenship', *Citizenship Studies*, vol. 2, no. 1, 1998; Kimberly Hutchings and Roland Dannreuther, eds, *Cosmopolitan Citizenship*, Houndmills 1999; Chris Brown, 'Cosmopolitanism, World Citizenship and Global Civil Society', *Critical Review of International Social and Political Philosophy*, vol. 3, no. 1, 2000; Nigel Dower, 'The Idea of Global Citizenship – A Sympathetic Assessment', *Global Society*, vol. 14, no. 4, 2000; Janna Thompson, 'Planetary Citizenship: The Definition and Defence of an Ideal', in Brendan Gleeson and Nicholas Low, eds, *Governing for the Environment. Global Problems, Ethics and Democracy*, Houndmills 2001. Some of the most significant texts are collected in Nigel Dower and John Williams, eds, *Global Citizenship: A Reader*, Edinburgh 2002.

Among the critics of cosmopolitan citizenship see, among others, Iris Marion Young, 'Polity and Group Difference: A Critique of the Ideal of Universal Citizenship', *Ethics*, vol. 99, January 1989; and David Miller, 'Bounded Citizenship', in Kimberly Hutchings and Roland Dannreuther, eds, *Cosmopolitan Citizenship*, cit.

## Cosmopolitism as cultural aspiration

Cosmopolitanism was a cultural aspiration even before it became a political project. The rediscovery of cosmopolitanism in the seventeenth and eighteenth centuries is explored in Stephen Toulmin, *Cosmopolis: The Hidden Agenda of Modernity*, New York 1990, and Thomas Schlereth, *The Cosmopolitan Ideal in Enlightment Thought*, Notre Dame 1977.

The cosmopolitan ideal in our age is discussed in Timothy Brennan, *At Home in the World. Cosmopolitanism Now*, Cambridge, MA 1997; Martha Nussbaum, *Cultivating Humanity*, Cambridge, MA 1998. Other relevant studies in the field include Phen Cheah and Bruce Robbins, eds, *Cosmopolitics: Thinking and Feeling Beyond the Nation*, Minnesota 1998; Derek Heater, 'Does Cosmopolitan Thinking Have a Future?', *Review of International Studies*, vol. 26, 2000; Jeremy Waldron, 'What is Cosmopolitan?', *Journal of Political Philosophy*, vol. 8, no. 2, 2000; and Vinay Dharwadker, ed., *Cosmopolitan Geographies: New Locations in Literature and Culture*, London 2001.

Pippa Norris, 'Global Governance and Cosmoplitan Citizens', in Joseph S. Nye and John D. Donahue, eds, *Governance in a Globalizing World*, Washington, DC 2002, presents empirical research on personal identities, which indicates that younger people and those with a higher education are more likely to feel members not only of their nations, but also of the cosmopolitan polity.

## The reform of the United Nations system

The most obvious political outcome of the cosmopolitan democracy project is related to the reform of existing international institutions and notably of the United Nations system, the protection of human rights and the conditions of humanitarian intervention, the effect of domestic democracy on international peace, the domestic impact of international law, and the possibility of global justice. Scholars on European and global governance, furthermore, have contributed important insights on the possibilities of governance beyond the state. In the remaining part of this bibliographical essay we suggest some readings on these issues.

The richest source for those interested in the various proposals to reform the United Nations system is: *Reforming the United Nations: New Initiatives and Past Efforts*, The Hague 1997, a three-volume set edited by Joachim Müller, which contains 50 key

reform proposals originating inside and outside the United
Nations. Another volume edited by Joachim Müller, *Reforming the
United Nations: The Quiet Revolution*, The Hague 2001, reviews the
reform proposals presented in the period 1996–2000. Among the
most important proposals of the past: Grenville Clark and Louis
Sohn, *World Peace through World Law*, Cambridge, MA 1966; William O. Douglas, *Towards a Global Federalism*, New York 1968; and
Richard Falk and C.E. Black, eds, *The Future of the International
Legal Order*, Princeton 1969.

The drive to reform the UN has resumed after 1989 and many
hoped that, given the new international environment, the organization could be democratized, notably by limiting the veto power
of the permanent members of the Security Council, increasing
the involvement of non-governmental organizations, and
strengthening the judicial mechanisms. See Richard Falk, Samuel
S. Kim and Saul H. Mendlovitz, eds, *The United Nations and a Just
World Order*, Boulder, CO 1991; Frank Barnaby, ed., *Building a
More Democratic United Nations*, London, Frank Cass, 1991; Richard
Falk, Robert C. Johansen and Samuel S. Kim, eds, *The Constitutional Foundations of World Peace*, New York 1993; Erskine Childers
and Brian Urquhart, *Renewing the United Nations System*, Uppsala
1994; Commission on Global Governance, *Our Common Neighbourhood*, Oxford 1995; Independent Working Group on the Future
of the United Nations, *The United Nations in Its Second Half-Century*,
New Haven 1995; Eric Fawcett and Hanna Newcombe, eds, *United
Nations Reform: Looking Ahead after Fifty Years*, Toronto 1995;
Daniele Archibugi, *Il futuro delle Nazioni Unite*, Roma 1995; Flavio
Lotti and Nicola Giandomenico, eds, *L'Onu dei popoli*, Torino
1996; Chadwick F. Alger, ed., *The Future of the United Nations
System*, Tokyo 1998.

The idea of a world peoples' assembly advocated by Richard
Falk and Andrew Strauss in this volume is also discussed in
Andrew Strauss, 'Overcoming the Dysfunction of the Bifurcated
Global System: The Promise of a Peoples' Assembly', *Transnational
Law & Contemporary Problems*, vol. 9, no. 2, 1999; and in Richard
Falk and Andrew Strauss, 'On the Creation of a Global Peoples'
Assembly: Legitimacy and the Power of Popular Sovereignty',
*Stanford Journal of International Law*, vol. 36, no. 191, 2000.

## Human rights and armed humanitarian intervention

A central concern and goal of cosmopolitan democracy is the worldwide protection of human rights. The literature on international human rights protection is extensive. A good overview of the debates is provided by Jack Donnelly, *International Human Rights*, Boulder, CO 1998. The judicial protection of human rights is the topic of A.H. Robertson and J.G. Merrills, *Human Rights in the World*, Manchester 1996 and Steven R. Ratner and Jason S. Abrams, *Accountability for Human Rights Atrocities in International Law: Beyond the Nuremberg Legacy*, Oxford 2001. Other useful books are: Philip Alston and James Crawford, eds, *The Future of UN Human Rights Treaty Monitoring*, Cambridge 2000; Thomas Risse, Stephen C. Ropp and Kathryn Sikkink, eds, *The Power of Human Rights: International Norms and Domestic Change*, Cambridge 1999; Richard Falk, *Human Rights Horizons: The Pursuit of Justice in a Globalizing World*, New York 2000, and The Belgrade Circle, ed., *The Politics of Human Rights*, London 2000. On the debates about the universal nature of human rights: James T.H. Tang, ed., *Human Rights and International Relations in the Asia-Pacific Region*, London 1994.

As discussed in David Chandler's chapter in this volume, in the 1990s, governments have increasingly justified military interventions by referring to the need to protect civilians and prevent human rights abuses. The legitimacy and effectiveness of humanitarian intervention is discussed by: Richard Falk, *Law in an Emerging Global Village. A Post-Westphalian Perspective*, Ardsley 1998; Mona Fixdal and Dan Smith, 'Humanitarian Intervention and Just War', *Mershon International Studies Review*, vol. 42, 1998; Mary Kaldor, *New and Old Wars*, cit.; Nicholas Wheeler, *Saving Strangers: Humanitarian Intervention in International Society*, Oxford 2000; Thomas Pogge, 'Preempting Humanitarian Interventions', in Ian Carter and Mario Ricciardi, eds, *Freedom, Power and Political Morality. Essays for Felix Oppenheim*, London 2001; David Chandler, 'The Road to Military Humanitarianism: How the Human Rights NGOs Shaped a New Humanitarian Agenda', *Human Rights Quarterly*, vol. 23, no. 3, 2001; David Chandler, *From Kosovo to Kabul: Human Rights and International Intervention*, London 2002; Adam Roberts, 'The Role of Humanitarian Issues in International Politics in the 1990s', *International Review of the Red Cross*, vol. 81, 1999. A wide-ranging critique of Western policies can be found in Noam Chomsky, *A New Generation Draw the Line. Kosovo, East Timor and the Standards of the West*, London 2002.

## Domestic democracy and international relations

The relationship between democracy within states and the international environment is generally considered from one of two different perspectives: some observers focus on the impact of external factors on domestic democracy and democratization, while others focus on the effect of domestic democracy on the foreign policy of states.

Concerning the first perspective, the implications of international law for domestic democracy are discussed in Gregory H. Fox and Brad R. Roth, eds, *Democratic Governance and International Law*, Cambridge 2000. The influence of the external political environment on democracy and democratization is explored by: Alan Gilbert, *Must Global Politics Constrain Democracy? Great-Power Realism, Democratic Peace, and Democratic Internationalism*, Princeton 1999; Thomas Pogge, 'Achieving Democracy', *Ethics and International Affairs*, vol. 15, no. 1, 2001; Laurence Whitehead, ed., *The International Dimensions of Democratization: Europe and the Americas*, Oxford 1996; and Mathias Koenig-Archibugi, 'International Electoral Assistance', *Peace Review*, vol. 9, no. 3, 1997. In his 'The New Raison d'État as a Problem for Democracy in World Society', *European Journal of International Relations*, vol. 5, no. 3, 1999, Klaus Dieter Wolf argues that governments often choose to cooperate with one another in the context of international institutions in order to escape from domestic political constraints; and therefore international cooperation, as it is currently practised, represents a threat to democracy.

The second perspective focuses on the effect of political regime types on external behaviour, and specifically it is concerned with the thesis that democratic states almost never wage war against each other. A corollary of this 'democratic peace' thesis is that, if all countries of the world became democracies, war would disappear. Prominent supporters of the thesis are Michael Doyle, 'Kant, Liberal Legacies, and Foreign Affairs', *Philosophy and Public Affairs*, vol. 12, nos 3 and 4, 1983, and Bruce M. Russett and John Oneal, *Triangulating Peace: Democracy, Interdependence, and International*

*Organizations,* New York 2001. Among the critics of this thesis are Joanne Gowa, *Ballots and Bullets: The Elusive Democratic Peace,* Princeton 1999, and Jack Snyder, *From Voting to Violence: Democratization and Nationalist Conflict,* New York 2000. Several important contributions to the debate are reprinted in Michael E. Brown, Sean M. Lynn-Jones and Steven E. Miller, eds, *Debating the Democratic Peace,* Cambridge, MA 1996.

Italian authors have offered valuable contributions on the relationship between democracy and peace, notably Norberto Bobbio, 'Democracy and the International System', and Luigi Bonanate, 'Peace or Democracy?', both in Daniele Archibugi and David Held, eds, *Cosmopolitan Democracy,* cit. See also Luigi Cortesi, *Storia e catastrofe,* Napoli 1984; Angelo Panebianco, *Guerrieri democratici. Le democrazie e la politica di potenza,* Bologna 1997; and Luigi Bonanate, *Democrazia tra le nazioni,* Milano 2001.

## Ethics and norms in international affairs

If the goal of cosmopolitan democracy has to be realized, it must certainly appeal to the interests of large sectors of the world's population. It requires also that interests are not static, but can be redefined on the basis of evolving norms and ideas. The literature on norms in world politics generally belongs to one of two categories. Some authors ask which norms are valid from an ethical-philosophical point of view. Others want to show that the behaviour of the actors in international politics is actually influenced by norms and does not follow only the logic of power and self-interest.

The following books belong to the first category: Charles R. Beitz, *Political Theory and International Relations,* cit.; Stanley Hoffmann, *Duties beyond Borders. On the Limits and Possibilities of Ethical International Politics,* Syracuse 1981; Terry Nardin, *Law, Morality and the Relations of States,* Princeton 1983; Janna Thompson, *Justice and World Order: A Philosophical Inquiry,* London 1992; Joel H. Rosenthal, ed., *Ethics and International Affairs: A Reader,* second edition, Washington, DC 1999; Terry Nardin and David R. Mapel, eds, *Traditions of International Ethics,* Cambridge 1992; David R. Mapel and Terry Nardin, eds, *International Society: Diverse Ethical Perspectives,* Princeton 1998; Ian Shapiro e Lea Brilmayer, eds, *Global Justice,* New York 1999; Luigi Bonanate, *Ethics and Inter-*

*national Politics*, Cambridge 1995; Thomas Pogge, ed., *Global Justice*, Oxford 2001; Pablo De Greiff and Ciaran Cronin, eds, *Global Ethics and Transnational Politics*, Cambridge, MA 2002; Paul K. Wapner and Lester Edwin Ruiz, eds, *Principled World Politics: The Challenge of Normative International Relations*, Lanham 2000; Robert E. Goodin, 'Globalizing Justice' in David Held, Mathias Koenig-Archibugi, eds, *Taming Globalization: Frontiers of Governance*, Cambridge 2003.

The following books, on the other hand, aim at showing that ideas about morality and legitimate authority can have an important role in world politics: David Lumsdaine, *Moral Vision in International Politics: The Foreign Aid Regime, 1949–1989*, Princeton 1993; Daniel Philpott, *Revolutions in Sovereignty: How Ideas Shaped Modern International Relations*, Princeton 2001; Margaret E. Keck and Kathryn Sikkink, *Activists Beyond Borders: Advocacy Networks in International Politics*, Ithaca 1998; Christian Reus-Smit, *The Moral Purpose of the State: Culture, Social Identity, and Institutional Rationality in International Relations*, Princeton 1999; Audie Klotz, *Norms in International Relations: The Struggle Against Apartheid*, Ithaca 1995.

## European governance

Two crucial developments of the past decades might indicate that the transition to cosmopolitan democracy is a real possibility. The first is the development of the European Union, a new kind of polity that includes states and peoples with a long history of rivalry and war. The second is the emergence of a system of global governance.

The complex institutional structure of the European Union is analysed by Simon Hix, *The Political System of the European Union*, Basingstoke 1999. Important contributions to the debate about the EU are collected in Peter Gowan and Perry Anderson, eds, *The Question of Europe*, London 1997. The importance of EU policies for the daily lives of its citizens has fostered a lively debate about the 'democratic deficit' of its institutions. According to some, the EU urgently needs to be democratized, or it will lose its legitimacy: see Philippe C. Schmitter, *How to Democratize the European Union . . . And Why Bother?*, Lanham 2000, and Jürgen Habermas, 'Why Europe Needs a Constitution', *New Left Review*, second series, no. 11, 2001. According to others, the EU is sufficiently legitimized by its current institutions, since its functional scope is narrow and a number of checks and balances ensure that its power is limited. Indirect democratic legitimization is sufficient, as the EU is not a 'superstate' in the making. For this position, see Andrew Moravcsik, 'Federalism in the European Union: Rhetoric and Reality', in *The Federal Vision: Legitimacy and Levels of Governance in the United States and the European Union*, edited by Kalypso Nicolaidis and Robert Howse, Oxford 2001.

Other contributions to the debate on democracy in the European Union include: Richard Bellamy, Vittorio Bufacchi and Dario Castiglione, eds, *Democracy and Constitutional Culture in the Union of Europe*, London 1995; Mario Telò, ed., *Democratie et construction européenne*, Bruxelles 1995; Thomas Pogge, 'Creating Supra-National Institutions Democratically: Reflections on the European Union's Democratic Deficit', *Journal of Political Philosophy*, vol. 5, no. 2, 1997; David Beetham and Christopher Lord, *Legitimacy and the European Union*, London 1998; Joseph Weiler, *The Constitution of Europe*, Cambridge 1999; Fritz W. Scharpf, *Governing in Europe: Effective and Democratic?*, Oxford 1999; Michael Th. Greven and Louis W. Pauly, eds, *Democracy beyond the State? The European Dilemma and the Emerging Global Order*, Lanham 2000; and Richard Bellamy and Dario Castiglione, 'Legitimising the Euro-polity and its Regime', in Lars Tragardh, ed., *After National Democracy: Rights, Law and Power in America and the New Europe*, Hart 2002.

## Global governance

The second major development is the emergence of a complex system of governance at the global level, composed of intergovernmental regimes, supranational agencies, various non-governmental organizations, transnational advocacy networks, transnational corporations, and private regimes set up by business actors. The idea that states are the only important actors in world politics, defended by authors such as Kenneth Waltz, seems no longer plausible to a growing number of scholars and observers. See, for instance, Kenneth N. Waltz, 'Structural Realism after the Cold War', *International Security*, vol. 25, no. 1, 2000; and the criticisms voiced by Justin Rosenberg, *The Empire of Civil Society: A Critique of the Realist Theory of International Relations*, London 1994.

Among the works that explore the different facets of contemporary global governance are: James N. Rosenau and Ernst-Otto Czempiel, eds, *Governance Without Government: Order and Change in World Politics*, Cambridge 1992; Robert W. Cox with Timothy J. Sinclair, *Approaches to World Order*, Cambridge 1996; James N. Rosenau, *Along the Domestic-Foreign Frontier: Exploring Governance in a Turbulent World*, Cambridge 1997; Wolfgang H. Reinicke, *Global Public Policy: Governing Without Government?* Washington, DC 1998; Peter Gowan, *The Global Gamble: Washington's Faustian Bid for World Dominance*, London 1999; Ian Clark, *Globalisation and Fragmentation*, Oxford 1997; Ian Clark, *Globalisation and International Relations Theory*, Oxford 1999; John Braithwaite and Peter Drahos, *Global Business Regulation*, Cambridge 2000; Joseph S. Nye, Jr, and John D. Donahue, eds. *Governance in a Globalizing World*, Washington, DC 2000; David Held and Mathias Koenig-Archibugi, *Taming Globalization: Frontiers of Governance*, cit; Antonio Franceschet, 'Justice and International Organization: Two Models of Global Governance', *Global Governance*, vol. 8, no. 1, 2002; Robert O. Keohane and Joseph S. Nye, Jr, *Power and Interdependence: World Politics in Transition*, third edition, New York 2000. Books that survey the current state of governance in various global issue areas are: P.J. Simmons and Chantal de Jonge Oudraat, eds. *Managing Global Issues: Lessons Learned*, Washington, DC 2001; Volker Rittberger, ed., *Global Governance and the United Nations System*, Tokyo 2001; David Held and Anthony McGrew, eds, *Governing Globalization*, Cambridge 2002. In the latter volume, the chapter by Mathias Koenig-Archibugi, *Mapping Global Governance*, explores the variety of forms that governance can take in the contemporary global system.

The issue of global governance is intimately linked, on the one hand, to patterns of economic, environmental, cultural and military globalization and, on the other hand, with what many consider an emerging transnational civil society. On globalization: David Held, Anthony McGrew, David Goldblatt and Jonathan Perraton, *Global Transformations: Politics, Economics and Culture*, Cambridge 1999; Paul Hirst and Grahame Thompson, *Globalization in Question*, second edn, Cambridge 1999; Justin Rosenberg, *The Follies of Globalization Theory*, London 2001.

## Transnational civil society and social movements

In the burgeoning literature on transnational civil society and social movements especially notable are the following: Giovanni Arrighi, Terence H. Hopkins and Immanuel Wallerstein, *Antisystemic Movements*, London 1989; Paul Wapner, *Environmental Activism and World Civic Politics*, Albany 1996; Margaret E. Keck and Kathryn Sikkink, *Activists Beyond Borders: Advocacy Networks in International Politics*, cit.; Robert O'Brien, Anne Marie Goetz, Jan Aart Scholte and Marc Williams, *Contesting Global Governance: Multilateral Economic Institutions and Global Social Movements*, Cambridge 2000; Helmut Anheier, Marlies Glasius and Mary Kaldor, eds, *Global Civil Society 2001 and 2002*, Oxford 2001 and 2002; and Mario Pianta, *Globalizzazione dal basso*, Roma 2001. On the post-Seattle movements see Mike Prokosch and Laura Raymond, eds, *The Global Activists' Manual*, New York 2002 and Alexander Cockburn and Jeffrey St. Clair, *Five Days that Shook the World: The Battle of Seattle and Beyond*, London 2002.

# Notes on Contributors

**Daniele Archibugi**
Technological Director at the Italian National Research Council.
He has worked at the Universities of Sussex, Cambridge, Naples
and Rome. He has been one of the promoters of the cosmopolitan democracy approach. He will be Leverhulme Visiting Professor at the London School of Economics and Political Science in
2003–4. Among his publications, he has co-edited *Cosmopolitan
Democracy. An Agenda for a New World Order* (1995), *Global Democracy*
(special issue of *Peace Review*, 1997), *Re-imagining Political Community. Studies in Cosmopolitan Democracy* (1998), *Innovation Policy
in a Global Economy* (1999) and *The Globalizing Learning Economy*
(2001).

Contact details: Daniele Archibugi, National Research Council,
Via dei Taurini, 19, 00185 Rome, Italy.
Email: archibu@isrds.rm.cnr.it

**Robin Blackburn**
Professor of Sociology at the University of Essex and Visiting
Professor in the Graduate Faculty of the New School University,
New York. He is the author of *The Overthrow of Colonial Slavery, The
Making of New World Slavery*, and *Banking on Death: the History and
Future of Pensions*.

Contact details: Robin Blackburn, Department of Sociology,
University of Essex, Wivenhoe Park, Colchester, CO4 3SQ.
Email: roblack@essex.ac.uk

**Timothy Brennan**
Professor of Cultural Studies and Comparative Literature at the

University of Minnesota. His essays on cultural theory, media politics, American intellectuals, and race and imperialism have appeared in *South Atlantic Quarterly, Transition, Critical Inquiry, The Nation, TLS, The London Review of Books,* and other places. He is the author of *Salman Rushdie and the Third World: Myths of the Nation* (1989) and *At Home in the World: Cosmopolitanism Now* (1997). He recently introduced, co-translated, and edited *Music in Cuba* by Alejo Carpentier (2001), and has just completed a book of essays titled *Cultures of Belief.*

Contact details: Timothy Brennan, Department of Cultural Studies, 350 Folwell Hall, 9 Pleasant Street, University of Minnesota, Minneapolis, MN 55455, USA.

Email: brenn032@umn.edu

### Craig Calhoun

President of the Social Science Research Council and Professor of Sociology and History at New York University. Among his books are *Neither Gods Nor Emperors: Students and the Struggle for Democracy in China* (1994), *Critical Social Theory: Culture, History, and the Challenge of Difference* (1995), and *Nationalism* (1997). He also served as editor-in-chief of the *Oxford Dictionary of the Social Sciences* (2002), and co-editor for international and area studies in the *International Encyclopedia of Social and Behavioral Sciences* (2001).

Contact details: Craig Calhoun, Social Science Research Council, 810 Seventh Avenue, New York, NY 10019, USA.

Email: calhoun@ssrc.org

### David Chandler

Senior Lecturer in International Relations, Centre for the Study of Democracy, University of Westminster. He has written widely on democracy, human rights and international relations, including *Bosnia: Faking Democracy After Dayton* (1999, 2000) and *From Kosovo to Kabul: Human Rights and International Intervention* (2002).

Contact details: David Chandler, Centre for the Study of Democracy, University of Westminster, 100 Park Village East, London, NW1 3SR.

Email: d.chandler@wmin.ac.uk

### Richard Falk

Albert G. Milbank Professor of International Law and Practice

Emeritus at the Woodrow Wilson School of Public and International Affairs at Princeton University. He has been a major contributor to world order literature for four decades. His most recent books include *On Humane Governance: Towards a New Global Politics* (1995), *Law in an Emerging Global Village. A Post-Westphalian Perspective* (1998), *Predatory Globalization. A Critique* (1999), *Human Rights Horizons: The Pursuit of Justice in a Globalizing World* (2000).

Contact details: Richard Falk, Center of International Studies, Princeton University, Bendheim Hall, Princeton, NJ 08544, USA.

Email: rfalk@princeton.edu

**Peter Gowan**

Principal Lecturer in International Politics and Director of International Relations at the University of North London. He is a member of the Editorial Boards of *New Left Review, Labour Focus on Eastern Europe* and *Europe politique*. His recent books include (with Perry Anderson) *The Question of Europe* (1997) and *The Global Gamble* (1999), which won the Isaac Deutscher Memorial Prize in 2000. He is currently completing a book on European transformations in the 1990s.

Contact details: Peter Gowan, SALS, London Metropolitan University, 166–220, Holloway Road, London N7 8DB, UK.

Email: p.gowan@unl.ac.uk

**Geoffrey Hawthorn**

Professor of International Politics, University of Cambridge, UK. His books include *Plausible Worlds* (1991) and *The Future of the Asia Pacific* (1998). He is presently writing about Thucydides, and thinking about global 'governance'.

Contact details: Geoffrey Hawthorn, Faculty of Social and Political Sciences, University of Cambridge, 8–9 Jesus Lane, Cambridge CB5 8BA, UK.

Email: gph21@cus.cam.ac.uk

**David Held**

Graham Wallas Professor of Political Science at the London School of Economics and Political Science. He is the author of many works including *Democracy and the Global Order* (1995), *Models of Democracy* (second edn, 1996), and, as co-author, *Global Transfor-*

*mations* (1999). He is currently working on a volume entitled *Cosmopolitanism: Globalization Tamed.*

Contact details: David Held, Department of Government, London School of Economics and Political Science, Houghton Street, London WC2A 2AE.

Email: held.polity@dial.pipex.com

**Mathias Koenig-Archibugi**

Marie Curie Postdoctoral Fellow at the London School of Economics and Political Science. Currently he is studying the institutional structure of global governance, which is the topic of his 'Mapping Global Governance', in David Held and Anthony McGrew, eds, *Governing Globalization*, Cambridge 2002.

Contact details: Mathias Koenig-Archibugi, Department of Government, London School of Economics and Political Science, Houghton Street, London WC2A 2AE.

Email: m.koenig-archibugi@lse.ac.uk

**Mario Pianta**

Professor of Economic Policy at the University of Urbino and associate researcher at ISPRI-CNR in Rome. He is the author of the chapter on 'Parallel Summits of Global Civil Society' in the *Global Civil Society* 2001 (2001); his latest book is *Globalizzazione dal basso. Economia mondiale e movimenti sociali* (2001). He works on international economic policy, global civil society, technological change and employment.

Contact details: Mario Pianta, ISPRI-CNR, Via dei Taurini, 19, 00185 Roma, Italy.

Email: pianta@isrds.rm.cnr.it

**Thomas Pogge**

Associate Professor at the Department of Philosophy, Columbia University. He has worked extensively on global justice, human rights, poverty and development. He has recently edited a collection of essays on *Global Justice* for Blackwell (2001). His latest book is *World Poverty and Human Rights* (2002).

Contact details: Thomas Pogge, 410 Riverside Drive (143), New York, NY 10025, USA.

Email: tp6@columbia.edu

**Andrew Strauss**
Professor of International Law at the School of Law, Widener University, in the United States. He has published widely in the field of international law and global governance with articles appearing in the *Harvard Journal of International Law* and *Foreign Affairs Magazine* among others. He has taught on the law faculty at the National University of Singapore, has been a Fulbright Scholar in Ecuador and has been a director of the Geneva and Nairobi international law institutes.

Contact details: Andrew Strauss, Widener University School of Law, 4601 Concord Pike, PO Box 7474, Wilmington, DE 19803, USA.

Email: andrew.l.strauss@law.widener.edu

**Nadia Urbinati**
Associate Professor of Political Theory at Columbia University. Her most recent books are *Individualismo democratico* (1997) and *Mill on Democracy: From the Athenian Polis to Representative Government* (2002). She is presently working on a new project on democratic representation.

Contact details: Nadia Urbinati, 410 Riverside Drive, Apt. 132, New York, NY 10025, USA.

Email: nu15@columbia.edu

# Acknowledgements

'Cosmopolitical Democracy' by Daniele Archibugi was first published with the same title in the *New Left Review*, second series, no. 4, July–Aug 2000.

'Running the World through Windows' by Geoffrey Hawthorn was first published with the same title in the *New Left Review*, second series, no. 5, Sept–Oct 2000.

' "International Justice" ' by David Chandler was first published with the same title in the *New Left Review*, second series, no. 6, Nov–Dec 2000.

'Cosmopolitanism and Internationalism' by Timothy Brennan was first published with the same title in the *New Left Review*, second series, no. 7, Jan–Feb 2001.

'The New Liberal Cosmopolitanism' by Peter Gowan was first published with the same title in the *New Left Review*, second series, no. 11, Sept–Oct 2001.

'The Influence of the Global Order on the Prospects for Genuine Democracy in Developing Countries' by Thomas Pogge was first published in *Ratio Juris*, vol. 14, no. 3, 2001, published here with permission from Blackwell Publishers, Oxford.

'The Imperial Presidency and the Revolutions of Modernity', by Robin Blackburn, was first published in a slightly different form in *Constellations*, no. 1, vol. 9, March 2002.

'Demos and Cosmopolis' by Daniele Archibugi was first published in the *New Left Review*, second series, no. 13, Jan–Feb 2002.

Special thanks are due to Marcela Bulcu for the preparation of the typescript, to Liz Rawlings for copy-editing and to Jane Hindle for producing the volume. Susan Watkins has not only co-ordinated the contributions that appeared in the *New Left Review*, but also provided on more than one occasion sound political advice.

# Index